THE BETTER HOMES AND GARDENS®
NEW BABY BOOK
BECAUSE . . .

It's the baby care book parents have trusted most for three generations. Since it first appeared in 1943, there have been many new
ideas about child raising and many medical advances. The hundreds
of professionals behind the *New Baby Book* made sure you knew
about them by carefully revising and updating each new edition. But
the wonderful features that made it the one baby care book mothers
and fathers prefer have remained the same. And today's parents will
find it the most helpful and informative guide they can buy. Including:

*Your part before and after delivery
*Setting a new routine at home
*Father as care giver
*When mother returns to work
*Feeding, toilet-training, and sleep problems
*Common complaints and diseases
*A fill-in baby record book
*First aid for children
And much, much more.

Better Homes and Gardens®

NEW
BABY
BOOK

by **Edwin Kiester, Jr.**
and Sally Valente Kiester
and the Editors of
Better Homes & Gardens Books

Photography by
Kathryn Abbe and Frances McLaughlin-Gill
Medical Illustrations by
Elton Hoff

BANTAM BOOKS
NEW YORK · TORONTO · LONDON · SYDNEY · AUCKLAND

*This edition contains the complete text
of the original hardcover edition.*
NOT ONE WORD HAS BEEN OMITTED.

BETTER HOMES AND GARDENS® NEW BABY BOOK

*A Bantam Book / published by arrangement
with Meredith Corporation*

PRINTING HISTORY

*Meredith edition published March 1979
Bantam edition / October 1980
Revised Meredith edition published August 1985
Revised Bantam edition / October 1986
Meredith Copy and Production Editor: Carl Voss
Graphic Designer: Naomi Alt West
Photograph on page 2 by Robert L. Wolfe
Food, Equipment, and Clothing Illustrations
by Hellman Design Associates
Back cover photo by Pamela Villy / Image Bank*

ISBN 0-553-26114-2

Published simultaneously in the United States and Canada

Bantam Books are published by Bantam Books, a division of Bantam Doubleday
Dell Publishing Group Inc. Its trademark, consisting of the words "Bantam Books"
and the portrayal of a rooster, is Registered in U.S. Patent and Trademark Office
and in other countries. Marca Registrada. Bantam Books, 666 Fifth Avenue, New
York, New York 10103.

PRINTED IN THE UNITED STATES OF AMERICA

OPM   15 14 13 12 11

Acknowledgments

Frederick H. Berman, M.D., M.P.H., F.A.C.O.G., Attending Physician, Mount Zion Hospital, San Francisco, California.

Mary Ward Brady, B.S., R.N., Childbirth Instructor, Marin General Hospital, San Rafael, California.

C. Walter Brown, M.D., F.A.A.P., Attending Physician, Santa Teresa Community Hospital, San Jose, California.

David E. Carter, Director Audiovisual Services, Mercy Hospital, Cedar Rapids, Iowa.

Robert Creasy, M.D., F.A.C.O.G., Professor of Obstetrics and Gynecology, University of California, San Francisco.

Michael Eliastam, M.D., M.P.P., Associate Professor of Surgery and Medicine and Director of Emergency Services, Stanford University Medical Center, Stanford, California.

Carolyn Ferris, R.N., Nursing Care Coordinator, Obstetrical Complex, Mount Zion Hospital, San Francisco, California.

Oscar Frick, M.D. Professor of Pediatrics, University of California, San Francisco.

Alvin Jacobs, M.D., Professor of Dermatology and Pediatrics, Stanford University, Stanford, California.

Michael M. Kaback, M.D., Professor, Departments of Pediatrics and Medicine; Associate Chief, Division of Medical Genetics, Harbor General Hospital, UCLA School of Medicine, Torrance, California.

Todd Kiskaddon, Coordinator, Life Support Training Center, Stanford University Medical Center, Stanford, California.

Jack E. Obedzinski, M.D., Assistant Clinical Professor of Pediatrics, Child Study Unit, University of California, San Francisco; Center for Families and Children, Corte Madera, California.

Peggy Pipes, Assistant Chief, Nutrition Section, Child Development and Mental Retardation Center, University of Washington, Seattle.

Diana Pulsipher, R.N., Supervisor, Labor and Delivery Unit, Santa Teresa Community Hospital, San Jose, California.

Robert S. Roth, M.D., Coordinator, Newborn Services, Mount Zion Hospital, San Francisco, California.

D. Stewart Rowe, M.D., Associate Clinical Professor of Pediatrics, University of California, San Francisco.

Eugene C. Sandberg, M.D., Associate Professor of Gynecology and Obstetrics, Stanford University Medical Center, Stanford, California.

Pamela Schrock, R.P.T., M.P.H., Childbirth Educator, American Society for Psychoprophylaxis in Obstetrics, Evanston, Illinois.

Helen D. Ullrich, M.A., R.D., Executive Director, Society of Nutrition Education, Berkeley, California.

Lenox Hill Hospital, New York, New York.

Maternity Center Association, New York, New York.

New Baby Book

Bringing up Baby is an art that is steadily changing, steadily evolving. That is as true in the 1980s as it was in the 1940s, when the first edition of the *Better Homes and Gardens Baby Book* was published. Today, mothers and fathers who both may work outside the home are likely to share child-care duties equally. But in the 1940s, mothers cared for babies alone, far from fathers who were off on military service and far from the reassuring counsel and experience of their parents.

It was this need that led to the *Better Homes and Gardens Baby Book*. In 1942 while the country was mobilizing for war, the late Gladys Denny Schultz, a long-time child-care columnist, proposed that Better Homes and Gardens assist young mothers with a new, basic, illustrated manual of child care. The editors agreed, and the book first appeared in 1943. It was an instant success, and in four decades has sold nearly four million hardcover copies and more than 2½ million paperbacks.

With war's end, needs changed—and so did the *Baby Book*. Returning servicemen married and began long-delayed families— 34 million births in the immediate postwar years alone. The *Baby Book* was reprinted five times in five years just to keep up with the baby boom. So many parents relied on it that one consultant to the present edition, whose children are now grown, recalls, "For ten years, every time I went to a baby shower, someone got a copy of the *Better Homes and Gardens Baby Book*."

The *Baby Book* has been revised several times since to encompass new ideas in child-raising, as well as changes in society. And, in recent years, changes have been frequent. Today, mothers give birth "naturally without anesthesia" and often in the presence of the father and other children. Women who were fed by the bottle prefer to nourish their own babies at the breast. More women today expect to work outside the home, so the lines between fathers' and mothers' duties and responsibilities have become blurred. Even childhood health problems have changed. Many of the old scourges are nearly extinct, thanks to immunizations—although runny noses and earaches still persist.

This edition of the *Better Homes and Gardens New Baby Book* thus is aimed at both parents, not simply at mothers as in the World War II and the baby-boom years. At heart, though, it differs little from the first edition published in 1943. Although the third generation of "*Baby Book* children" will be raised quite differently from their parents and grandparents, the theme of the *Better Homes and Gardens New Baby Book* is the same.

The most important ingredient in raising a child isn't knowledge, but love. There is no single, right way to raise a child—or, indeed, several children in the same family. Parents know more than they think they do, and, at the same time, are helped along by their own compassion and concern.

Literally hundreds of physicians, nurses, child-development specialists, psychologists—and parents—have contributed to the *Baby Book* throughout its history—so many that it is no longer possible to list them all individually. Those who contributed to and guided the *New Baby Book* are listed and, like their predecessors, their contributions—and their common sense—have been invaluable.

Contents

III. TWO TO SIX YEARS

IV. ADVICE FOR EVERY DAY

New Baby Book

SECTION
1

Before the Birth

Your baby is a miracle—
there simply is no other word.
Millions of babies are born
every year, some in riches, some
in poverty, some in cities,
some in jungles, some unwanted,
some devoutly wished for and
jubilantly welcomed. The
birth of a baby is the most
everyday event of all. Yet each
birth is an occasion of mystery,
marvel, and wonder.

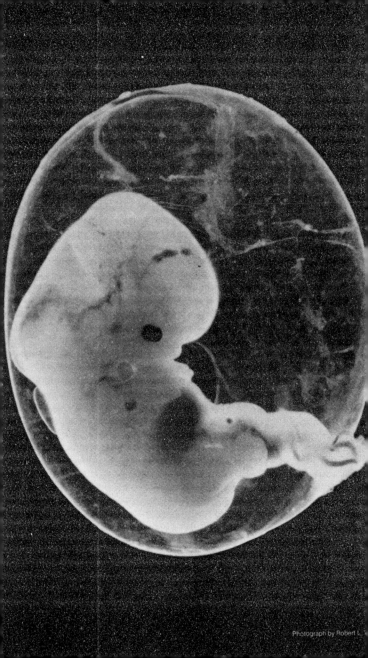

1

The Miracle of Birth

Think of your pregnancy. You certainly weren't aware of the precise moment it began. Two tiny cells, each barely distinguishable under a microscope, united into one, unnoticed even by the donors, and began the inexorable process of multiplication. Nine months later, they have produced a fantastic spectrum of specialized cells for skin, hair, fingernails, teeth, internal organs, bones—all arranged into a new seven-pound being resembling his or her parents, yet carrying a distinctive identity.

The journey from conception to birth encompasses three-fourths of a year, more or less. That period is a mysterious sequence of exquisitely orchestrated, carefully followed steps, each of which must occur precisely on schedule in order to bring on the next. Just as a symphony conductor cues first the brass, then the percussion, and finally the strings, the body signals biological and chemical changes to advance the performance. Each part of the body has a score to follow; each bodily function, a part to play.

Fifty years ago, little was known about the conception and development of human life beyond the crudest outlines. Modern research and technology have since supplied many important details. Doctors can peer into the womb itself and even take photographs; they can measure heartbeats, count breaths, even observe thumb sucking. They can observe and chart fetal development and extract samples of a baby's blood. Yet great gaps remain in the knowledge of reproduction and the fascinating first nine months of life.

Opposite: Photograph by Robert L. Wolfe

TWO TO MAKE ONE

The woman's role in procreation is most familiar, centering on the ovaries, two walnut-size glands on either side of the pelvis, and the uterus or womb, an organ about the size and shape of a small pear. The ovaries and uterus are connected by the fallopian tubes, two tiny canals about the diameter of a soda straw (see diagram, right).

Each month, the lining of the uterus, or endometrium, prepares for the possibility of conception. Tissues thicken and enrich, nutrients accumulate, blood vessels proliferate. Midway in the month, the ovaries release an egg to be fertilized by a male sperm. If fertilization takes place, the egg embeds itself in the rich uterine wall and grows there. If it does not, the uterine bed breaks down and is flushed away in the process called menstruation.

A little girl is born with several million eggs in her ovaries. The number dwindles to a half million by puberty, still more than adequate for a lifetime of ovulation. Each month, 500 to 1,000 eggs begin a maturation process, but gradually, like runners in a marathon, eggs drop out. Eventually, only one (usually) remains. Cells surrounding the chosen egg nourish it, ripen it, and form a protective covering for it. When ready, the egg erupts from this follicle and travels down the fallopian tube toward the uterus.

Before fertilization, the egg is one of the largest cells in the human body but is still barely visible to the naked eye. The egg has no power to move on its own. Cilia, the threadlike fibers in the funnel-shaped opening of the fallopian tube, wave like blades of grass in the wind and lure the egg inside after it is ejected from the ovary. From there, currents of fluid and muscular contractions carry it toward the uterus. The egg completes the first third of the tubal journey rapidly, within a few hours. Then it halts, as if awaiting the arrival of its "date."

A sperm is one-thousandth of the egg's size, too small to be seen with unaided sight. It would take hundreds of billions to fill a thimble. A sperm resembles a tadpole, with an oval-shaped head and long, whiplike tail. Unlike the egg, the sperm can move under its own power; vigorous kicks of the tail propel it forward at a rate of six inches an hour. Beginning in adolescence and continuing until old age, millions of sperm are manufactured each day by the testicles in the male scrotum, each theoretically capable of fathering a child.

Sperm age, ripen, and then are stored until needed. At the climax of intercourse, they come tumbling from storage, are mixed with other substances to form semen, and are ejaculated by the

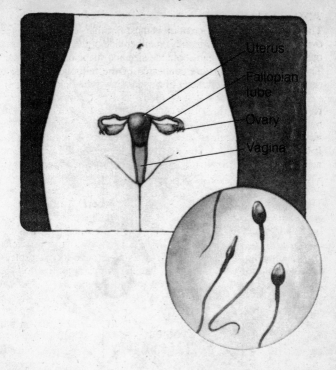

millions. Because only one sperm will eventually combine with the egg, the reasons for this profligacy are among reproduction's chief unknowns.

An official of the Population Council once calculated the odds of pregnancy from a given act of unprotected intercourse at 50 to one, because optimum conditions cover only a brief period each month. The egg is fertilizable—ready for fertilization—for about 12 to 24 hours, and sperm normally can survive within the female body for only 24 to 48 hours. Against these odds, conception truly approaches the miraculous.

THE BABY'S HEREDITY

Sperm and egg approach each other carrying parts of a blueprint that will shape the new child's life. The cell nucleus of each contains an arrangement of dark-colored, rod-shaped bodies called

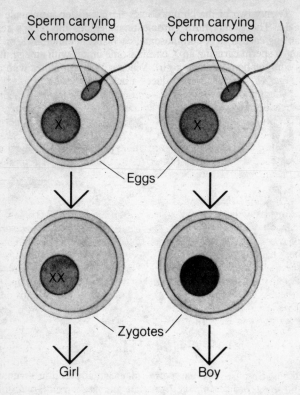

chromosomes, composed of deoxyribonucleic acid (DNA) and protein. Within the chromosomes are genes, the basic units of heredity.

These submicroscopic genes incorporate characteristics handed down from previous generations. They determine whether your baby will be blond or brunette, blue- or brown-eyed, tall or short, fat or lean, even how long he or she will live. They also influence the child's personality and shape the intelligence.

There are 23 pairs of chromosomes (46) in every human cell—except in the egg and sperm. The chromosomes in the sex cells are not paired; each of the sex cells contains a single strand of 23 chromosomes. When the cells combine, the strands match up to form a new cell consisting of 23 chromosomal pairs.

Twenty-two of the chromosomes do not differ from male to female. The twenty-third chromosome decides the baby's sex. Each egg carries an X chromosome; each sperm either an X or Y. When a sperm carrying an X chromosome unites with an egg, the XX combination produces a girl. When a Y sperm unites with an egg, the XY combination produces a boy.

Thus, it is the father who determines—involuntarily—whether a baby will be a boy or a girl. The odds are nearly equal because X and Y chromosomes are about evenly distributed among the sperm. About 106 boys are born for every 100 girls. Your baby's sex is determined at the moment of conception, and not much can be done to influence it. Like many of the fascinating aspects of reproduction, it seems to be a matter of pure chance.

THE BEGINNING OF LIFE

Appropriately, perhaps, life starts with a race. At the moment of ejaculation, millions of sperm spurt into the female body, zeroing in on the awaiting egg. Some are old and tired; they drop out early. Others head in the wrong direction or become lost in the folds of tissue. A hardy 10 percent swim to the top of the uterus, where the fallopian tubes branch. Half head into the empty tube containing no fertilizable cell that month. Of the remaining sperm, perhaps only 4,000 move into the proper fallopian tube to approach the egg waiting for fertilization.

Why so many sperm when only one is needed to fertilize an egg? One reason may be that they must work together to break down the defenses of the well-protected egg. The egg's nucleus, containing the chromosomal arrangement, is housed in a central core, along with necessary nourishment for the embryonic life. This mass is enclosed by a thick, transparent coating covered by a halo of follicle cells embedded in a gelatinous structure.

The sperm must make its way to the nucleus. An enzyme secreted from the cap of the sperm—or perhaps from the caps of many sperm—seems to open the way. It apparently dissolves part of the egg's outer layer, opening a pathway through the follicle cells and the outer covering of the egg. Only one sperm will pass through the opening. The egg then closes itself to all other intruders.

Now, gradually, the two cells move toward union. Following an arclike path, the sperm penetrates into the central core of the egg. Soon both bodies are enclosed within the same envelope. They begin to combine, the two sets of chromosomes arranging themselves into a new 46-chromosome cell called a zygote. At this moment, a new individual has started. The whole process from intercourse to union of the two cells only takes about 12 hours.

When the two cells are one, a message goes out to the rest of the woman's bodily systems. Carrying the message is a hormone called human chorionic gonadotropin (hCG). The hCG is issued in minute, but unmistakable, quantities to signal that procreation has succeeded. The signal stimulates increased flows of the female hormones estrogen and progesterone, needed to support the pregnancy; the husk of the follicle left behind by the egg converts to a corpus luteum, or "yellow body," that produces more hormones; and the uterus lining continues to grow instead of beginning the degenerative process of menstruation. All the preparations made for a possible pregnancy are told to continue.

The new being develops quickly. Within hours, the single cell divides and redivides, producing first two cells, then four, then eight, and so on until it has become an entire mass of cells, more compact, but not much larger than the original. This cluster of cells is called a morula, or "mulberry," because it resembles that fruit.

The zygote has taken shape this way in the upper half of the fallopian tube. Now it begins a slow, week-long descent toward an eventual nesting place in the wall of the uterus. Once more, it is carried along by currents of fluid and the muscular contractions of the tube.

Why does it take so many days for such a short trip? What is happening during the journey from tube to uterus? These are among the important unanswered questions about the beginning of a new life. It appears the morula requires three days to complete its voyage to the uterus. Then it apparently floats free within the uterus, for perhaps an additional four days.

At about the seventh day after fertilization, the endometrium has reached its greatest thickness and lushness. Simultaneously, the new organism has consumed most of the nourishment it started with. Now it embeds in the succulent uterine wall to absorb nourishment from the mother. The usual place is near the top of the uterus, although implantation may occur nearly anywhere on the uterine wall. At this point, the mother may notice a small spot of vaginal bleeding—so-called implantation bleeding.

The implanted organism looks quite different from the one that began the journey. Now called a blastocyst, it is a hollow, fluid-filled sphere. Its cells have been rearranged and have begun to specialize. One clump holds those that will grow into the embryo. Around the periphery, other cells take on the mission of implanting and nourishing the embryo. These are the trophoblastic cells, or "feeding layer."

The trophoblastic cells have the ability to digest or liquefy other tissues they contact. The trophoblasts break down the cells of the endometrium and the walls of its tiny blood vessels. The cellular contents and blood nourish the blastocyst, which settles deeply into the lining. The trophoblastic cells multiply and form fingerlike projections called villi. Some wave freely in the maternal blood supply, others tap new vessels, and still others form anchors to maternal tissue to strengthen the link between the blastocyst and its nest.

These free-floating villi now begin to serve as lungs and digestive organs. From the mother, they take on oxygen, air, and simple foodstuffs, like sugar and calcium; in the opposite direction, they pass off fetal wastes. The barrier between mother and embryo is permeable, but the circulations of the two never mix.

At this point, the blastocyst resembles a tiny blister surrounded by a slight pool of the mother's blood caused by the process of embedding. Soon a membrane develops around the cells that will become the embryo. Fluid collects within this membrane and forms the so-called "bag of waters." This is the amniotic fluid in which the embryo-fetus will float and move about throughout pregnancy. The portion of the blastocyst wall closest to the uterine wall becomes a second, reinforcing membrane.

Meanwhile, the trophoblast and the maternal cells of the uterine lining combine to form the placenta, or "afterbirth," which will nourish the fetus through the umbilical cord, a long, coiled structure that passes through the amniotic membrane, carrying fetal blood containing oxygen and food from the placenta to the fetus and fetal waste products out through the mother's excretory system.

THE FETUS GROWS

Doctors usually calculate fetal development in lunar months, or four-week periods—ten lunar months, also stated as 40 weeks or 280 days, is the term of pregnancy. But most of us think in terms of nine calendar months. Here is how the baby develops in those nine months.

If you could peer inside the uterus a month after conception, you would hardly believe the tiny bit of tissue before your eyes could grow into a breathing, squalling baby. The diminutive being measures only a quarter of an inch long—less than the length of a newborn's fingernail—and weighs perhaps one-hundredth of an

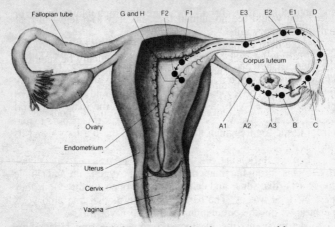

(*The drawings, A to H below, correspond to the numbers and letters above.*) *Eggs are stored in the ovaries—more than enough for a lifetime of ovulation. Before the eggs are released and fertilized, they undergo a selective maturation process (A1, 2, 3). Each month, numerous eggs ripen (B), although normally only one egg does so completely. The ripened egg (C) is expelled from the ovary and is picked up by the fallopian tube. At the same time, the ruptured follicle begins its conversion into the corpus luteum. Although many sperm work to penetrate the egg (D), only one realizes that goal. After fertilization, cell division begins (E1, 2). A cluster of cells called a morula, or mulberry (E3), is formed. Next, cells rearrange to form a blastocyst (F1). A specialized layer of cells (trophoblastic cells, F2) will eventually become the placenta and unite with the mother's uterine lining. Once the blastocyst is embedded (G), the initial stages of the development of the placenta (H) take place.*

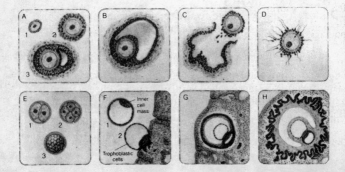

ounce. You would see no human face, no arms, no legs—just a small rudimentary tail.

Yet the most complex and vital organs already have begun to form. Five weeks after fertilization, they can actually be seen by ultrasonography. A U-shaped tube two millimeters long forms the heart and will be pumping blood within a week thereafter. The fetus has a microscopic brain, a threadlike spinal cord, and a spiderlike nervous system. A tube leading from the mouth is a rudimentary digestive tract.

A month later, there is no mistaking the human qualities. Eyes, a nose, mouth, and ears give it a decidedly human countenance. Arms and legs have developed, complete with fingers, toes, elbows, and knees. Sex organs have become apparent, though it is still difficult to distinguish male from female. And the fetus has grown. It now measures a full inch from head to heel and weighs one-thirtieth of an ounce.

At the end of the third month, the baby is three inches long and weighs a full ounce. Fingernails and toenails show; tooth buds appear in the jawbone. The presence or absence of a uterus can be detected. A rudimentary kidney excretes waste into the amniotic fluid. The fetus moves, but too slightly for the mother to feel.

At four months, all vital organs have formed and many are functioning. The fetus is now about six and one-half inches long and weighs about four ounces. Fine hair covers the body, and a few hairs appear on the head. More active now, the baby waggles tiny arms and legs. Using an amplified stethoscope, the doctor can hear the fetal heartbeat—a rapid 140 beats per minute, faster than that of the mother.

By five months, the fetus has developed hair, eyebrows and lashes, and even facial expressions. The father can hear the fetal heartbeat by placing an ear against the mother's abdomen. And the fetus now moves vigorously and frequently; the mother can "feel life." The baby is now nearly a foot long and weighs almost a pound and a half.

At six months, the fetus is 15 inches long, weighs two and a half pounds, and is growing rapidly. For the first time the fetus looks like a miniature human being. The skin is covered with fuzz and a creamy substance called vernix caseosa ("cheesy varnish"), a one-eighth-inch-thick layer that protects the fetus's skin from the fluid environment.

At seven months, the fetus is 16½ inches long and weighs four pounds. Development now is mainly a process of fine-tuning, the organs getting ready for independent existence. The intricate biochemistry governing many bodily functions is maturing in its production of the body's 20,000 enzymes. The nerve cells mature. And the fetus fattens.

During the last two months, the fetus gains a half-pound per week, accumulating layers of fat to increase its ability to survive in the outside world. At eight months, the fetus weighs six pounds and at full term, seven and one-half.

The last organs to be fine-tuned are the lungs. Even though the child appears fully mature, the respiratory system may not be ready; the lungs cannot function until acted upon by chemicals that are among the last to be produced. Labor begins only after the fetal respiratory system has completed this maturation.

Each additional day or week spent in the womb increases the odds that the baby will be born robustly healthy. But thanks to obstetrical advances and intensive-care nurseries, babies born prematurely in hospitals specializing in high-risk deliveries, even those as small as three pounds and as early as six and one-half months, have nearly a 99 percent chance of survival. Even a $1\frac{1}{2}$ pound, 25-week infant has an 82 percent chance of being born healthy.

LIFE BEFORE BIRTH

What is life like within the womb? Scientists have been able to observe and photograph it. These amazing records show that life before birth is more eventful than commonly supposed. To some extent, the bag of waters insulates the floating fetus from the outside world. Suspended in the buoyant fluid, the fetus is cushioned against sudden impacts, sharp blows, or other potential injuries. The fluid is at a constant temperature, providing additional protection against extreme heat and cold. The placental "barrier" separating maternal and fetal circulations protects against some (but by no means all) harmful foreign substances.

The fetus sleeps and wakes at irregular intervals, probably sleeping more than waking. Babies seem to have a favorite position, called a "lie." Typically, they coil with knees drawn up and chin on chest. The fetus can move about in the amniotic fluid, shifting from side to side or occasionally changing its lie. The mother at first feels these movements as tiny flutters, but soon they are pronounced kicks and pokes. Occasionally, the baby will hiccup, and the mother's abdomen will twitch in a series of rhythmic jolts. Activity slows a little in the final month of pregnancy, when the fetus occupies so much space in the sac that such movements are greatly inhibited.

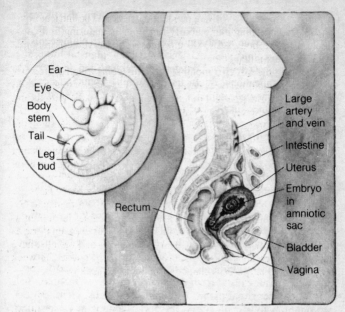

Eight weeks after fertilization, there is a noticeable human shape. Many times as large as a month ago, the fetus is an inch from head to heel and weighs 1/30 of an ounce.

Tests indicate that a fetus may be able to see and almost certainly hear. Touch and the ability to distinguish changes in temperature are sensations developed with the first few months after conception. Sensitivity begins in the face and then spreads over the entire body.

The fetus both swallows and breathes the amniotic fluid; the breathing can be seen readily with ultrasonography. The fluid changes completely three to four times a day, for reasons not fully understood.

An old wives' tale says a baby can be marked or affected by a mother's experiences during pregnancy. There is probably no truth to this belief; the nerves of mother and child are not connected in any way. Even so, a fetus may respond to a mother's emotional patterns. Fetal movements increase when the mother undergoes emotional stress. Apparently, these changes result from an increased secretion of maternal hormones during stress that cross the placental barrier and stimulate the fetus. (Movements also increase after she eats, especially if she consumes sugar.)

Is life inside the womb enjoyable? The unborn child seems to lead a placid, comfortable existence; certainly prenatal life is serene as long as nutrition and oxygen are adequate and there are no maternal complications. But by the end of nine months, the baby's quarters are cramped, with a reduced supply of oxygen and food, and an exit to the outside world may be welcome.

THE MOTHER CHANGES, TOO

As the fetus grows, the mother changes, too. The greatest changes are in the reproductive system, especially the uterus. This small, muscular organ is described as having—in its nonpregnant state—a potential, rather than an actual, cavity; the front and back walls touch at the center of the organ, with only a narrow passage between. The accompanying drawings show how the uterus changes over nine months. The uterine walls thin and stretch; the cavity enlarges until, by the time of birth, it encloses 500 times its original volume.

Changes in the uterus also affect nearby organs. Some discomforts of pregnancy result from the uterus pressing on the intestinal tract, the bladder, and the major arteries and veins. Uterine pressure on the body's main artery, the aorta, and the main vein, the vena cava, restrict circulation in the lower extremities and may lead to such complaints as varicose veins and hemorrhoids.

The breasts also are changing. Almost from the beginning of pregnancy, they increase in size (most women find they need a brassiere at least one size larger). The nipples darken and increase in circumference, and tiny "blisters" develop in the areola, the dark area around each nipple. Inside the breasts, the treelike structure of milk ducts proliferates—more branches develop and existing ones enlarge.

The volume of blood increases by one-third to nourish the organs and to help carry off the wastes of pregnancy. The heart works harder to pump the increased supply through the system.

The most noticeable change is in the posture. As the uterus distends, the abdomen expands, and the expectant mother carries a 15- to 20-pound load in front of her. To compensate, she leans backward to balance the burden.

THE ROLE OF THE HORMONES

Most of the physical changes during pregnancy result from increased amounts of the female hormones, estrogen and progester-

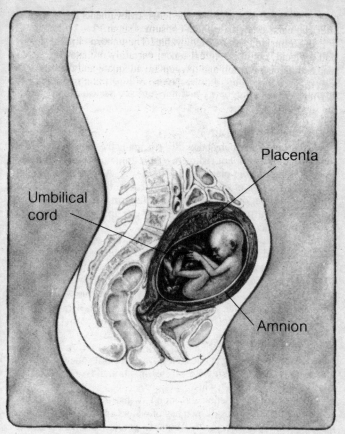

Placenta

Umbilical cord

Amnion

At six months, the fetus truly resembles a miniature human being. The uterine walls thin and stretch, and the abdomen expands as the baby demands more room.

one. Progesterone is produced by the corpus luteum, the yellow body produced from the husk left behind by the matured egg. Progesterone helps soften and thicken the endometrium to prepare for the implantation of the fertilized egg. Later, the placenta manufactures progesterone to maintain the pregnancy, prevent premature labor, and keep all systems functioning properly.

The increase of estrogen produced by the placenta also causes many changes within the mother's body. It acts on the involuntary muscles, slowing the actions of the gastrointestinal and urinary systems, and is responsible for the swelling of the breasts.

Prolactin is a hormone that appears involved with the production of milk in the breast. It is produced in progressively greater quantities during pregnancy and may prepare the breasts for feeding the infant.

BABY THE DEPENDENT

The old saying that "baby takes all" (meaning the fetus depletes the mother's supply of nourishment) isn't quite accurate. But the mother's system *does* place fetal welfare first. After all, the mother has many sources of sustenance available to her, but the fetus is totally dependent on the nourishment she provides. The fetus is— and must be—a parasite, if you define one in the strictest, most limited biological sense.

Thus, a baby feeds on the mother's store of iron to build a personal blood supply—the reason a pregnant woman must have iron in her diet plus supplementary iron medication as well. The fetus also takes calcium to build bones and teeth. (However, it is not true that the fetus destroys the mother's teeth in the process.) In addition, the baby has first call on glycogen, the substance that provides energy.

WILL YOU HAVE TWINS?

Normally, only one egg is released per month. But sometimes there are two (rarely even more). Result: fertilization of two eggs and the conception of fraternal twins.

Fraternal twins technically aren't twins, just siblings born at the same time. Each has its own bag of waters and placenta; there is no connection between them. About 70 percent of twin births are fraternal. Identical twins develop from one egg that has split apart during early stages of pregnancy. They usually share a placenta, although each may have an individual sac.

Your chance of having twins is about one in 80. The odds of twinning increase somewhat with the mother's age, and there seems to be a tendency for fraternal twins to run in families. The doctor may detect two heartbeats as early as the fifth month and may then confirm the finding by ultrasonography or X ray (see Chapter 3). Twins are usually born several weeks early, with each about a pound lighter than a single baby. Otherwise, twins are equally healthy, if their lungs have matured.

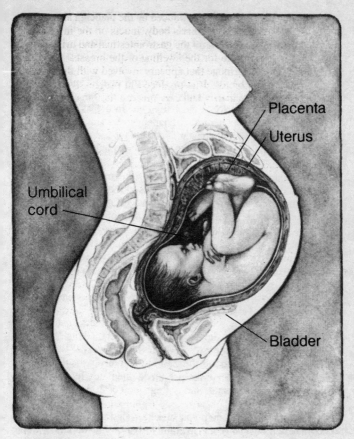

At nine months, the uterus has 500 times its original volume. The baby weighs more than seven pounds, and because this weight is carried in front, the mother leans backward to balance it.

PREPARING FOR BIRTH

Both fetus and mother normally begin preparation for birth at about the beginning of the ninth month. The baby gains weight; the lungs, nerves, and biochemical systems mature. The baby's customary "lie," at this point, is head downward.

Meanwhile, the mother's cervix softens and thins in a process called effacement, which continues through labor itself. Tissues at the mouth of the cervix are gradually drawn up into the sides of that organ; the remaining ones become more elastic. The pelvic joints continue to loosen.

What signals the moment for labor to begin? That question is still a mystery. All that is truly known is that the uterus begins contractions that will force the baby out through the neck of the uterus. Even this explanation is challenged by some doctors who say the uterus contracts constantly—whether the woman is pregnant or not—and the contractions merely heighten with the onset of labor.

An endocrine secretion may start the process. Substances called the prostaglandins may be responsible, because they seem to trigger many bodily processes. Another explanation indicates that the placenta can no longer function at its previous level. This theory is partly confirmed by the discovery of a sharp drop in hormonal secretions in the final weeks of pregnancy. Or the baby simply grows too large and too demanding for the placenta to support further. In any case, whatever the signal, mother and child receive it unmistakably.

WHEN WILL THE BABY BE BORN?

For all its precision in cuing each step of pregnancy, nature is remarkably lenient about signaling the moment of birth itself. Technically, pregnancy encompasses 280 days, or 40 weeks. But only 10 percent of births occur on the 280th day. Only half of all births occur within two weeks of the presumed due date. Ten percent are more than two weeks late, and a pregnancy of 300 days is not unheard of.

Two methods can help you make a rough guess of when your baby will arrive. The first is to count *forward* nine months from the first day of your last menstrual period, then add seven days. If your last period started on January 2, for example, nine months would bring you to October 2; an additional seven days would make the presumed date of delivery October 9. The second method is to count *backward* three months from the beginning of the last period, then forward seven days. Starting from January 2 and counting back three months would be October 2; counting forward seven days would make the due date October 9.

Your doctor will probably estimate your delivery date on one of your early visits, then try to pinpoint it more exactly as time passes. The prediction may be in error partly because you have miscalculated the starting date of your previous period. Or it may just be nature's way of taking her time.

CHAPTER
2

Nine Months of Pregnancy

Pregnancy is normal. And healthy—a fact both parents and doctors sometimes forget. You *will* be a patient, you *will* have medical care, and you'll probably deliver your baby in a hospital. But that doesn't mean you're sick or need to sharply restrict your way of living.

Of course, not all pregnancies are equally easy. Nor are they all the same. Your own second pregnancy may differ greatly from your first. There are certain general rules for taking care of yourself during pregnancy, and the best judges of what you should and shouldn't do are mother, father, and doctor. Don't be guided by what other women remember about their pregnancies, or what your mother says about how it was when she was having children. *You're* having this baby.

Most doctors are more liberal than they used to be about the maternity regimen and acknowledge that they don't have all the answers. Bringing a healthy child into the world is not their responsibility alone, but yours and theirs together. A mother-to-be isn't expected to be passive, quiet, and obedient. Today, she's expected to be as independent in pregnancy as in other matters, to be responsible for herself and her decisions.

Of course, giving birth to a healthy baby means being healthy yourself. Good health is a lifelong process. Habits of nutrition, physical development, freedom from disease, amount of exercise, and rest should have been established before you became pregnant. Many rules for a healthy pregnancy are merely extensions of rules for good health outside of pregnancy.

HOW DO YOU KNOW WHEN YOU'RE PREGNANT?

Usually, the first clue to a pregnancy is a missed menstrual period. If your menstrual cycle is fairly regular and ten days pass after your period is normally due, you can suspect you're pregnant. If a month passes and you miss a second period, pregnancy is practically assured—especially if you occasionally feel nauseated, visit the bathroom often, and have tender breasts.

Don't immediately rush to the doctor if your period is a few days late. Two of three women miss a period at some time in their life, for reasons other than pregnancy. A bad cold, anemia, certain chronic conditions, even fatigue or emotional stress can disrupt a woman's menstrual cycle. The condition usually rights itself. Women runners may stop menstruating while in serious training.

TEST FOR PREGNANCY

Sometimes, of course, it's important to know quickly if you're pregnant. Having a baby may mean a change in plans. If you can't wait a month or more to decide your future, pregnancy tests can give you a quick and usually accurate answer before you have even missed a period—within a week after conception with certain tests.

There are several types of pregnancy tests, all designed to detect human chorionic gonadotropin (hCG), a hormonal signal of pregnancy. The woman furnishes a urine sample, collected just after arising when the hormone is most heavily concentrated. The sample is then analyzed by a laboratory or perhaps by the doctor's staff technicians.

Immunologic tests (immunoassays) have for several years been the most commonly used tests for pregnancy. There are several types, all quick, convenient, and highly accurate. Performed in a doctor's office, an immunoassay can give results in two minutes to two hours, depending on the test. Each test uses antibodies produced in laboratory animals.

In one type of test, antibodies are mixed with the woman's urine in a test tube or on a slide, then latex particles coated with hCG are added. If the donor *is* pregnant, there will be no reaction, because all antibodies have previously united with the hCG in the urine sample. If the donor is *not* pregnant, the hCG-coated particles and antibodies will agglutinate, or cling together.

The second test is more sensitive to small amounts of hCG. This test measures direct agglutination. The hCG antibodies and the woman's urine are placed together on a slide. Bonding of the two substances means pregnancy.

These forms of immunologic tests are designed to detect for the entire hCG molecule. But a far more sensitive and rapid form of immunoassay, which concentrates only on one unique portion of the molecule, is rapidly replacing the whole-molecule version in laboratory tests. The beta-subunit test reacts to very scanty amounts of hCG, and is nearly 100 percent accurate only a few days after conception. The test is inexpensive, and can be performed as easily as other immunoassays.

A radioimmunoassay, like a beta-subunit test, can detect pregnancy early, before a missed period. In a radioimmunoassay the antibodies are "tagged" with radioactivity, making them easier to measure. The test is thus sensitive to the very small amounts of hCG present just after implantation. Radioimmunoassay usually is performed on a sample of blood rather than urine. The test takes slightly longer to complete.

A monoclonal-antibody test uses the methods of biotechnology to produce antibodies that are purer and more sensitive than those produced in animals. The tests then use agglutination methods. Pregnancy can be detected with almost 100 percent accuracy within eight days of fertilization. There are five tests of increasing sensitivity, the least sensitive requiring two minutes for results, the most sensitive an hour and 20 minutes.

There also are tests you can buy over the counter and administer yourself. Most of these are of the whole-molecule immunoassay variety, but a monoclonal-antibody test using a chemical-impregnated dipstick to detect hCG is being introduced. It is said to be accurate two weeks after fertilization. However, unless you have reasons to conduct the test privately, a laboratory test is generally considered the most reliable.

THE SECONDARY SIGNS OF PREGNANCY
Besides a missed menstrual period, other bodily changes may lead you to think you're pregnant.

For many women, the first hint of pregnancy is their changing breasts. The breasts often feel full just prior to the beginning of menstruation, and the alterations in early pregnancy merely exaggerate this feeling. The breasts enlarge; they become firmer and seem tender. Sometimes they tingle, as if the skin were being stretched. The nipples and surrounding brown areas, the areolae, increase in diameter. The areolae puff, and the network of small milk glands proliferates.

Frequent urination is another indication of possible pregnancy.

You may find yourself hurrying to the bathroom two or three times an hour. The reasons why this occurs aren't known but seem to have a hormonal basis. Higher levels of estrogen may stimulate the pituitary gland to release additional quantities of a diuretic hormone that triggers urination. Or the estrogen may act on the smooth muscles of the ureters, the tubes carrying urine from the kidneys to the bladder. The need to urinate often decreases after the first three months but may recur later.

Morning sickness—which actually can occur at any time of day—affects two of three women in the first two to six weeks of pregnancy. It may even occur before the first missed period. It's a feeling of mild nausea, combined with lack of energy and loss of appetite. Sometimes it's worsened by nervousness and anxiety about the pregnancy. Fortunately, only one woman in three is sick enough to vomit.

Fainting is an infrequent sign that you're pregnant, although you may feel lightheaded and dizzy during the early part of the pregnancy. It can be relieved by sitting for a while with the head lower than the heart.

CHOOSING A DOCTOR

Once you're convinced you're pregnant, the next step is to plan your care. Although "alternative birth methods" described in Chapter 4 have increased in popularity, 98 of 100 women still have their babies in hospitals, under the care of a physician. So the first step in your care is choosing a doctor.

Technically, any licensed physician is qualified to provide obstetrical care and preside at the birth of a baby. But, in practice, the task usually falls to an obstetrician-gynecologist—a doctor who specializes in maternity care and in problems of the female reproductive system. You may have already consulted one for contraceptive or other advice. If so, you'll probably want to continue seeing that doctor.

If you don't have a doctor, choose carefully, because he or she is important to you and your baby. Seek someone in whom you'll have confidence and with whom you'll have rapport. If you have a family doctor, ask him or her to recommend a specialist. Or consult friends about doctors with whom they've been pleased.

You might also call a local medical school or large hospital. A community hospital usually will provide the names of members of its obstetrics staff. Or consult the local medical society.

THE FIRST VISIT

The best time for a first appointment is about the time of a second missed menstrual period. Most doctors like to begin care when a woman is about eight weeks pregnant. By then the signs of pregnancy are unmistakable, but it is still early enough to outline a full program of care.

You can expect this first visit to last a half hour or more, although some of the time may be spent with a nurse or other members of the medical team. The examination should be thorough, yet comfortable. It's nothing to dread.

You'll be asked to provide a full medical history, including a record of all previous illnesses and any inherited conditions. In particular, you'll be asked about any previous pregnancies or miscarriages and about menstrual regularity. Your doctor will also want to know if you've been inoculated against rubella, or German measles, a mild disease that can cause serious complications for the baby if contracted in early pregnancy.

You'll also be weighed and measured. Your heart and pulse rate will be recorded and a blood and urine sample taken or you'll visit a lab to have this done.

The doctor will want to accurately record your blood pressure, because a sharp rise later may be the first indication of serious maternal complications.

You will have a "Pap smear" test. Named for the scientist who devised it, Dr. George Papanicolaou, this is a routine test in which cells are taken from the cervix with a tiny utensil, similar to a long-handled spoon or cotton-tipped applicator. The cells are then microscopically examined for changes that could be early evidence of uterine cancer. This test is important because the rate of cure is 80 to 100 percent in cases where the cancer is detected early.

A pelvic examination will be performed while you're lying undressed, but draped by a sheet, on an examining table. This painless internal checkup will show whether the common changes of pregnancy have yet appeared. Vaginal tissues, normally pink in color, assume a bluish tinge in the early stages of pregnancy. The normally stiff cervix, or mouth of the uterus, assumes a softer feel. The uterus changes in size, shape, and consistency, too. The bony structure of your pelvis will be measured to assess the potential difficulty or ease of a vaginal birth and to help the doctor decide whether a cesarean section may be necessary.

The doctor will ask about your family's medical history and may recommend that you visit a genetics counselor. This type of counseling is designed to identify inherited conditions that might be caused by a union of your family and the father's family. Such genetic problems are seldom a cause for concern, but both you and the doctor should be aware of them during, or after, the pregnancy.

You and the doctor also will establish a schedule for future visits. How often you see each other will depend on your condition and your doctor's routine. A common schedule calls for the second visit two weeks after the initial examination, when you should ask questions that have occurred to you in the meantime. Visits usually are scheduled three weeks to a month apart until you're 32 weeks pregnant. Then you'll see the doctor twice at two-week intervals, after which you'll visit the office every week until delivery.

Don't hesitate to speak frankly with your doctor during any of your visits. There's no longer one standard, unvarying way to manage a pregnancy; as we shall see in Chapter 4, prospective parents must make many decisions about prenatal care, hospitalization, and delivery. You'll want to know the doctor's philosophy about medication during labor, childbirth classes, and the father's presence in the labor and delivery rooms, and the doctor's recommendation on breast-feeding. Discuss finances, too. Usually the doctor sets a flat fee, covering prenatal and postnatal visits, as well as the delivery. In most cases, the doctor's fee and the hospital charges will be at least partially covered by prepaid insurance, but the benefits vary from policy to policy—and they may not cover the entire bill. If you don't see eye to eye, or the fees don't fit your budget, discuss your feelings and problems. If you still aren't satisfied, feel free to seek medical care elsewhere.

Future visits to the doctor are likely to be shorter and somewhat routine. Usually, they are checks to confirm that the pregnancy is progressing normally. At each visit, you'll be asked to provide a urine sample collected on arising which will be tested for chemical evidence that things are going well. Your blood pressure will be taken regularly and your weight recorded. The doctor will listen to the baby's heartbeat and check the baby's position. You'll probably have an abdominal examination at each visit, although some doctors confine them to the last few months. You may have other tests, too. These are described in Chapter 3.

HOW LONG CAN YOU WORK?
Pregnancy and childbirth are going to cause changes in your life, no question about that. But these changes need not be so drastic as they were in the past. Given an uneventful pregnancy, a woman can

continue living normally within the limits of her energy and endurance.

You may want to keep your job during pregnancy, perhaps until the very day of delivery. Medically, there seems to be little reason not to do so. The belief that a woman should stop work six weeks before her due date for the sake of her baby is a thing of the past. Studies have shown that babies born to mothers who worked throughout pregnancy are just as healthy as those born to mothers who remained at home. Whether to quit and when to quit are, therefore, matters to be decided by you, your mate, and your physician. As your pregnancy advances, you may feel too awkward and tire too easily to continue working. Or, you may feel you need the stimulation of a daily job. Many doctors think the longer you work the better it is for you emotionally, as long as the job is pleasing and rewarding.

After an extensive study, the American College of Obstetricians and Gynecologists (ACOG) concluded that women whose jobs involve sitting most of the time or resting frequently should be permitted to continue working so long as they feel able. Women who are on their feet a great deal or whose work is more strenuous should be permitted to transfer to lighter duties during pregnancy. In particular, women performing physically demanding jobs should be allowed to accept other employment during that time.

Of course, certain jobs may be riskier than others. Although evidence isn't yet clear, working in certain manufacturing plants, for instance, may be hazardous to both mother and baby. Discuss your job and its environment with a doctor.

Your employer cannot legally dismiss you nor require you to stop working because you are pregnant, nor can you be transferred to other duties, However, you may be requested to produce a letter from your physician certifying that it is safe for you to continue in your job. Most employers now provide maternity leave, guaranteeing your job when you return; some provide leave for the father, too.

THE NEED FOR EXERCISE
Whether or not you continue working, regular exercise is important for you and the baby. Although pregnancy isn't the time to climb ladders and wash windows, even routine household chores can be handled readily and beneficially. Lifting, once considered taboo for pregnant women, isn't harmful if done properly. Gardening is an especially good way to get exercise and can be enjoyable as well.

At the very least, you should schedule a morning and evening walk of about 20 minutes' duration or a mile in length. Walking helps tone the muscles, boost circulation, and maintain good breathing habits that will be beneficial during labor. In addition, it's exercise you and your husband can enjoy together.

WHAT ABOUT SPORTS

The general rule about recreation is: continue any sport in which you have participated regularly and proficiently prior to pregnancy. That includes swimming, dancing, bowling, golf, jogging, or tennis. Most doctors will advise you to discontinue any sports involving violent motion, no matter how accomplished you are. You probably should eliminate such sports as skiing, skating, motorcycle riding, water-skiing, surfing, and judo, especially in the later months of pregnancy when your expanding abdomen may cause you to lose your balance or make you unsteady on your feet. Although the baby is well-cushioned by the fluid environment against bumps and jolts, such restrictions are designed to protect you and the baby from a hard fall.

TRAVELING AND DRIVING

Until the eighth month, there's little need to restrict travel by car. The old taboo that kept expectant mothers close to home probably dated from the days when long-distance travel meant an arduous ride over bad roads. A long car trip can still be tiring, of course, so stop to rest and walk around every hour or two.

Some doctors still warn against air travel, mainly because of possible motion sickness. This view is considered exceptionally cautious. The medical committee of the International Air Travel Association (IATA) has said flying causes no harmful effects in a normal pregnancy. IATA says expectant mothers may be accepted for flights up to the 35th week of pregnancy, and later than that for short trips with a certificate from the physician stating it's okay to travel. The certificate must be dated not earlier than 72 hours before departure. Reassuringly, IATA says, cabin attendants have been instructed on handling a premature birth.

The limitation on travel after seven months is chiefly for convenience. You may unexpectedly enter labor far from home and from the physician familiar with your case. A good rule for the last two months is not to travel more than an hour from home. If you're planning to give birth in another city, move there at the end of the seventh month and remain until the baby comes.

As for driving a car, you can continue so as long as you feel comfortable behind the wheel. There are no legal restrictions, and some women in the early stages of labor have actually driven themselves to the hospital. Throughout pregnancy, however, you should wear a safety restraint. A shoulder harness is preferable, because it reduces possible impact. If only a lap belt is available, wear it low on the abdomen to prevent pressure on the fetus.

SMOKING AND DRINKING

Women who smoke cigarettes during pregnancy run an increased risk of delivering undersized babies. A government study has shown that babies born to smokers weigh an average of 6.1 ounces less than those born to nonsmokers. The difference in weight is directly related to the number of cigarettes smoked. Women who smoke two or more packs a day during pregnancy also have an increased risk of stillbirth.

It was once believed that the placenta was a magic barrier to harmful substances, but it is known now that most drugs (including alcohol) used by the mother reach the baby. Children born to alcoholic mothers commonly suffer from what is called the fetal-alcohol syndrome. Such a child is undersized, had a characteristic facial appearance and a low IQ. Moderate drinking also may have slight effects on the baby. Several studies have shown that even when women consumed only one or two drinks a day, their babies were below average in size and growth.

Another reason to limit drinking during pregnancy is that alcohol provides empty calories. It adds weight without providing nourishment and saps the appetite for more nutritious foods. In addition, a few drinks may make you feel unsteady on your feet, increasing the unbalanced posture and heightening the danger of falling.

DRUGS AND MEDICINES

You should not use any drugs or medications during pregnancy without first consulting your doctor. These include over-the-counter preparations as well as prescription drugs. Aspirin, laxatives, sleeping tablets, and other medications may be prescribed by your doctor but should not be used without the physician's knowledge. If you are visiting another doctor for a condition unrelated to your pregnancy, ask him or her to check with and inform your obstetrician before prescribing any medicine and to discuss the effects of medicine already prescribed.

The so-called hard drugs are definitely taboo during pregnancy. These include not only illegal drugs, but prescription barbiturates, amphetamines (pep pills), and sleeping pills.

BATHING

During pregnancy, you'll probably prefer a shower to a bath, although either is acceptable. Many persons used to believe that pregnant women should neither bathe in a tub nor swim, but there is no evidence that immersing the body in water is harmful to the fetus in any way. If you do bathe, however, be careful while entering and leaving the bath, because of the danger of falling on the slippery surfaces. This is a particular danger in late pregnancy when movements tend to be awkward. A long soak in a tub of hot water may sap your energy and tire you unnecessarily.

Studies show that women who use hot tubs and spas during the first month of pregnancy have two to three times the risk of bearing a child with certain birth defects. Although this is still a small risk, doctors advise against exposure to excessive heat during this critical month. A warm bath is fine, but if you normally soak in a scalding tub, avoid it during early pregnancy.

CARE OF THE TEETH

"For every child, a tooth is lost," the saying used to go. Many persons thought the growing baby built teeth and bones by robbing the mother's system of calcium, causing her teeth to decay. The American Dental Association (ADA) says there is no evidence that pregnancy advances tooth decay in any way. The idea may have arisen because pregnancy usually occurs during that time of life when cavities are also frequent. And women may neglect their teeth during pregnancy. The ADA advises women to have dental work performed early in pregnancy or postpone it until after delivery. If X rays are needed, be sure your abdomen is covered by a lead shield. If dental work will require an anesthetic, it may be wise to postpone it until after delivery.

INTERCOURSE

How long you continue to have intercourse is strictly up to you. The only dangerous times are when vaginal bleeding occurs, when you have pain, or when the amniotic sac surrounding the baby ruptures, increasing the possibility of infection.

Your attitude toward sex may change during pregnancy. Some women report a decrease in sexual desire, while others say they enjoy sex more than ever. Your feelings may be different, too, at different times during the nine months. During the last few months of pregnancy, you may need to experiment to find the most comfortable position.

THE IMPORTANCE OF DIET

What you eat during pregnancy is important to both you and the baby. A successful pregnancy depends on the proper nutrients to assist the baby's development and to help you remain healthy. In fact, what you've eaten all your life will, in part, determine the baby's development. Women whose diet is poor have a higher percentage of stillbirths, growth-retarded babies, and babies with brain damage.

Fortunately, you needn't worry quite so much about gaining weight as women did in the past. The ACOG's Committee on Nutrition has revised standards for weight gain during pregnancy.

Instead of limiting women to a gain of 20 pounds over the nine-month period, the committee now says a women should *gain at least* 25 pounds during pregnancy, with gains up to 35 pounds considered normal. Of this amount, the baby accounts for seven pounds; the placenta, one pound; increased weight of the breasts, two pounds; increase in blood, three pounds; amniotic fluid, two

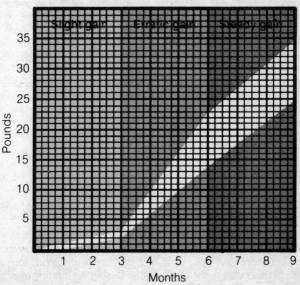

MOTHERS' WEIGHT GAIN

pounds; and increased size of the uterus, two pounds. The balance of the weight represents accumulated fats and fluids retained by the body during pregnancy; most will be lost spontaneously after pregnancy.

Weight gain was once severely restricted during pregnancy because it was believed to be a forerunner of certain birth complications. But more recent evidence disputes this association. In fact, sharply restricting weight gain may result in low-birthweight babies, who are themselves at greater risk of complication. And other studies have shown that malnourished women generally have a higher percentage of birth complications.

Thus, if you are now underweight, your doctor probably will encourage you to gain even more than the recommended 25 pounds. If you are in your teens, he or she probably will place you on a special diet, because nourishing a new life while your own body, is still growing can severely tax your system. Even if you are overweight to begin with, the doctor will probably want you to gain, or at least not attempt to lose weight until after pregnancy, lest the baby's development be jeopardized.

More important than how much you gain is how you gain it. As the chart on page 31 shows, a pregnant woman normally will gain less than three pounds in the first three months of pregnancy; she may actually lose weight or remain stationary. She then should gain about 11 or 12 pounds in each of the next three-month periods. During the last 24 weeks, she should be gaining at the rate of about a pound a week, bringing her to the 25-pound optimum. This even and regular rate of growth shows that the pregnancy is progressing normally and that the baby is developing on schedule.

A *sudden* spurt in weight, however, should be regarded as a danger signal. It may mean your body is retaining fluid, a condition sometimes associated with pregnancy complications. Always discuss with your doctor any abrupt change in weight.

THERE ARE STILL LIMITS

You shouldn't interpret the new thinking to mean you can eat all you want and pile on the pounds. Gaining weight beyond the recommended limits still can be hazardous to your health. An excessive weight gain overloads the heart and circulatory system, causing the heart to work harder at pumping blood through the extra tissue. The back and leg muscles may be strained, too, by the heavy weight.

And for the sake of your own figure, you'll want to stay as close to a gain of 25 pounds as you can. Losing weight after pregnancy is never easy, but it's more manageable if the gain is kept as low as possible. Weight gains beyond 30 pounds will take plenty of work to lose afterward.

EATING THE GOOD FOODS

Unless your doctor directs otherwise, you need no longer count calories during pregnancy. "Let the calories count themselves," advises a publication of the ACOG Committee on Nutrition, "If you are taking enough protein and supplementary foods and are avoiding foods that have little nutrition value, you will not need to worry so much about calories."

Good eating in pregnancy can be summed up in a sentence: Eat a balanced diet plus a quart of milk a day. A balanced diet means daily portions of each of the Basic Food Groups.

Protein—mainly meat, fish, poultry, or eggs. Organ meats, such as liver or kidneys, are very good. These also provide iron, B vitamins, and certain minerals. Shellfish, particularly oysters, often are overlooked as a source of protein. Dried beans, peas, nuts, and other legumes are good vegetable sources of protein.

An adequate amount of protein comes from two or three ounces of meat—an average-size hamburger patty or a small chop. Two eggs, a cup of cooked dried beans, dried peas, or lentils, a quarter cup of peanut butter, or two ounces of cheese contain as much protein as two ounces of meat. You should have three servings of protein daily.

Milk and milk products provide calcium. A pregnant woman requires four cups of milk (one quart) daily in the form of whole milk, skim milk, 2 percent milk, buttermilk, or reconstituted nonfat dry milk. Other milk products that can replace one cup of milk include: 1 1/4 cups cottage cheese, 1 1/2 slices American cheese, 1 1/4 cups yogurt, or 1 1/2 cups ice cream or ice milk.

Some of the dark, leafy green vegetables, such as collard, mustard, and turnip greens are very high in calcium, too.

Vegetables and fruits provide vitamins A and C and are subdivided into three groups. You should make it a point to have four servings from this category daily.

Group 1 includes foods rich in vitamin C—citrus fruits, cantaloupe, strawberries, papaya, and such vegetables as tomatoes, broccoli, brussels sprouts, peppers, cabbage, potatoes, and cauliflower. A medium-size orange or a four-ounce glass of citrus juice is considered a normal adult serving. A medium tomato supplies half the daily amount you'll need.

Group 2 includes foods rich in vitamin A—dark, leafy greens

such as beet, collard, and mustard greens; romaine; and spinach. Also included are yellow fruits and vegetables such as squash, carrots, yams, apricots, and peaches.

Group 3 includes most other vegetables and fruits, including lettuce, radishes, zucchini, cucumbers, corn, eggplant, green and wax beans, peas, beets, turnips, and such fruits as apples, peaches, cherries, berries, bananas, and pears. A half cup of vegetables or an average-size apple or pear is a normal adult serving.

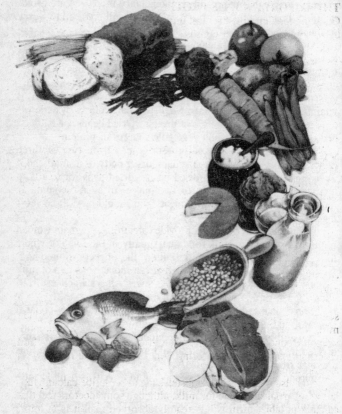

Good eating is a question of balance—daily meals with portions from each of the four Basic Food Groups: protein, milk and milk products, vegetables and fruits, and grains and grain products.

Grain and grain products provide thiamine, niacin, riboflavin, iron, phosphorus, and zinc. Whole-grain products provide more minerals than enriched breads and cereals, crackers, macaroni and spaghetti, tortillas, waffles, and pancakes. A normal serving is a slice of bread, a bowl of ready-to-eat cereal, or a half-cup of spaghetti. Include four servings a day in your diet.

THE IMPORTANCE OF PROTEIN

Of all the food groups, the most important to you and your growing baby is protein, whether consumed in meat, milk, or in vegetable form. Protein provides the actual building material for fetal tissues. The recommended daily intake is 80 to 100 grams.

Actually, most Americans—pregnant or not—probably consume sufficient amounts of protein in their diet, if it's balanced. You can assure yourself plenty of protein by eating two servings of meat and two eggs every day, plus the recommended quart of milk.

MILK FOR BONES AND TEETH

Milk and milk products furnish the minerals—especially calcium—that build your baby's bones and teeth. That's why you should sharply increase your intake of milk during pregnancy. Milk is the primary source of calcium, but it also provides other important nutrients, including proteins, carbohydrates, and vitamin A.

If you're not a milk drinker and find the consumption of a quart a day utterly unpalatable, there are trade-offs in the form of cheese, cottage cheese, and yogurt, as noted on page 33. You may substitute skim milk, buttermilk, low-fat milk, or diluted evaporated milk for the whole variety.

Remember, too, that you can use milk in cooking. Creamed soups, custards, and puddings or sauces are other ways to include milk. Ice cream can be substituted for milk, although it is more weight-producing. If you really "can't stand the taste of milk," add chocolate syrup or other flavoring. But remember, you're taking on additional calories.

You also might ask your obstetrician to prescribe calcium tablets as a partial substitute for milk, although some doctors feel that calcium in tablet form is less readily absorbed than it is in milk. Calcium tablets may be substituted in case you are allergic to milk.

In any case, milk is one of the key items in a pregnant woman's diet and should not be reduced or eliminated.

THE NUTRIENTS:
WHAT, WHY, AND HOW

Nutrient	Why we need it	Sources
Protein	Builds and repairs all tissue; synthesizes hormones, antibodies, and enzymes; provides sources of energy (expensive and inefficient).	Plant: Legumes, nuts, cereal grain products. Animal: Meat, fish; poultry, eggs; milk and milk products.
Fat	Provides concentrated source of energy; carries fat-soluble vitamins (A, D, E, and K) and essential fatty acids.	Plant: Vegetable oil, margarine, salad dressings. Animal: Butter, cream, fat meats.
Carbohydrate	Provides economical and efficient sources of energy and fiber or roughage.	Plant: Cereal grain products, starchy vegetables, sugar, fruits. Animal: None.

Important minerals

Calcium	Forms bones and teeth; clots blood; maintains muscle contractions.	Plant: Collards, kale, mustard greens; legumes. Animal: Milk and milk products, canned fish.
Iron	Forms hemoglobin; supplies various energy-producing enzyme systems.	Plant: Legumes, prune, juice, leafy green vegetables. Animal: Liver, red meats (beef, pork, lamb).
Zinc	Maintains growth and reproductive functions; produces blood cells; promotes enzyme reactions.	Plant: Whole-grain products. Animal: Shellfish, meats, liver, eggs.

Important vitamins/fat soluble

Vitamin A	Maintains mucous membranes and inner organs; enhances resistance to infections; promotes nerve and eye development.	Plant: Deep green and yellow-orange fruits and vegetables, margarine. Animal: Liver, egg yolk, butter.

Vitamin D	Facilitates absorption of calcium for strong teeth and bones.	Exposure to direct sunlight. Animal: Fortified milk and milk products, eggs, fish.
Vitamin E	Prevents oxidation of essential vitamins and fatty acids.	Plant: Vegetable oils, green leafy vegetables. Animal: None.
Vitamin K	Maintains normal blood clotting and prevents hemorrhage.	Plant: Leafy greens, cereal grain products. Animal: None.

Important vitamins/water soluble

Thiamine (B_1)	Promotes use of carbohydrates; provides energy and promotes good appetite and digestion.	Plant: Whole-grain cereals, nuts, legumes. Animal: Meat, milk.
Riboflavin (B_2)	Maintains healthy skin and eye tissue; produces energy in cells.	Plant: Whole-grain cereals, fortified grain products. Animal: Milk, fish, eggs, meat.
Niacin	Promotes use of carbohydrates; synthesizes fatty acids; maintains healthy nervous system; aids digestion and appetite.	Plant: Peanut butter, whole-grain cereal, fortified cereals, leafy vegetables. Animal: Meat, poultry, fish.
Pyridoxine (B_6)	Metabolizes protein; synthesizes hemoglobin.	Plant: Cereals, green leafy vegetables. Animal: Meats
Folic acid (folacin)	Produces blood cells; sustains growth.	Plant: Leafy vegetables, fruits, soybeans. Animal: Liver, eggs.
Cobalamin (B_{12})	Produces blood cells; metabolizes energy; maintains functions of central nervous system.	Plant: None. Animal: Meats.

| Ascorbic acid (C) | Forms connective tissues such as collagen; helps heal wounds and broken bones; metabolizes other important vitamins (folic acid, for example); maintains elasticity and strength of blood vessels. | Plant: Citrus fruits, dark green leafy vegetables, potatoes, broccoli, cabbage, tomatoes, cantaloupes, strawberries, peppers. Animal: None. |

VITAMINS AND SUPPLEMENTS

Your doctor may or may not prescribe daily doses of vitamins. Both you and the baby need vitamins, but your requirements will be satisfied if you follow a balanced diet like the one described above. However, some doctors prefer to play it safe and prescribe vitamin capsules, too.

An iron supplement is almost always required, however, because iron is not readily available in most diets. Iron gives blood its red color and is an absolutely essential mineral, because it is used in the production of hemoglobin, the blood component that carries oxygen to the cells. A woman takes in iron in small amounts throughout her life and stores them in her tissues; the baby draws on this storehouse to build his or her own blood supply. Thus, you must take in much more iron during pregnancy. Some iron is present in foods such as milk, meat, leafy vegetables, and fruit, but most doctors prefer to bolster this natural supply with an iron supplement.

Another supplement that may be prescribed is folic acid. This nutrient, found mainly in leafy vegetables and in vegetable sources of protein, helps to enrich the blood supply and prevent anemia. Some doctors prescribe a single capsule containing folic acid, vitamins, and iron.

WHAT YOU SHOULDN'T EAT

As a category, you should avoid "junk foods"—potato chips, pastries, candy, cookies, and other snacks that fill you up without providing nutrition. Occasional snacking isn't harmful, however. You also may find that certain foods make you uncomfortable because they produce gas that presses on the abdomen.

Fad diets should not be followed during pregnancy; indeed, some are downright dangerous. However, a vegetarian regimen including milk (lacto-vegetarian) is all right for both mother and fetus, provided sufficient protein is obtained in the choice of foods eaten.

SALT: NO LONGER A NO-NO

As long as your pregnancy is progressing normally, you can salt your food to taste, a marked departure from past obstetrical practice. Doctors formerly felt that salt caused the tissues to retain water, thus increasing the rate of complications. They urged that it be eliminated during pregnancy. Some doctors prescribed diuretics to flush the salt and accumulated fluids from the tissues.

Another statement of the ACOG Committee on Nutrition reversed this position. Instead of a sodium-free diet, the committee said women with a problem-free pregnancy should consume their normal amount of salt, because sodium is essential to the baby's development. The committee recommended the use of iodized salt, which provides the essential nutrient iodine. If fluid does begin to accumulate or in cases of elevated blood pressure, the directive said, obstetricians then may wish to reduce salt intake.

For your kidneys' sake, drink fluids in addition to milk every day, especially if you substitute milk products for milk itself. Doctors differ in the recommended amount, but four glasses of water or soft drinks, or cups of tea or coffee are probably sufficient. Liquids must be increased to remove wastes, because the kidneys now function for both mother and fetus.

CHANGING YOUR EATING HABITS

Space your meals so you eat small amounts six times a day instead of three. You'll like this schedule better in early pregnancy when you may not feel like eating, and again in the final months when the growing baby presses on the digestive system and reduces your stomach's capacity. Try to eat the same quantity at each of the three main meals, and balance the size of the snacks the same way. Breakfast is important, even though you may not want to eat much. Experiment with different foods to vary your own breakfast menu.

The easiest way to follow a balanced diet is to include one food from each of the four basic groups at each major meal. Then you can choose one food from each of the milk, vegetable-fruit, and bread groups for snacks.

Here, as recommended by the California Department of Public Health, is a sample one-day menu you might follow:

Breakfast:
½ cup orange juice
½ cup oatmeal with brown sugar
One cup milk (some of it on oatmeal)
Coffee or tea
Midmorning snack:
1¼ ounces cheese and crackers
Lunch:
Tuna fish sandwich on whole wheat bread, with celery, let-
tuce, and mayonnaise to taste
A small banana or dish of prunes, figs, or other fruit
One cup milk
Afternoon snack:
An apple
⅔ cup cottage cheese

Dinner:
Three ounces lean roast beef
$1/2$ cup buttered noodles
$3/4$ cup cut asparagus
Green salad made with spinach, sliced mushrooms, and radishes, with oil and vinegar dressing
$1/2$ cup milk
Coffee or tea
Evening snack:
Two oatmeal raisin cookies
$1/2$ cup milk

Avoid foods that fill you up but aren't nutritious (potato chips, pastries, candy). Snacking can be part of a regular daily menu: try cheese and crackers, cottage cheese, apples, oatmeal cookies, and milk.

RECORD WHAT YOU EAT

A daily food record can help you follow a balanced diet. Write in a notebook everything you eat, both by name and quantity, for two or three days. Carry the list in your purse so you can record lunches and snacks, too. Then evaluate it in terms of the four food groups.

Don't worry if you can't always be precise about ingredients or amounts. But don't skip entries because the meal was not typical. If you keep the list for several days, unusual meals will average out and you'll get a balanced picture of your intake. Then, if you see your diet is deficient in some nutrients, make changes to bring it more in line with the recommendations.

CARING FOR YOUR APPEARANCE

Obviously, you want to look as attractive during pregnancy as when you're not pregnant. Some women are said to be never so beautiful as during the nine months of pregnancy. That's not automatic, however, and you probably won't always feel beautiful. Sometimes you'll feel large, lumpy, and unattractive; you'll despair of ever getting your figure back. Those feelings will pass, however, as you anticipate the birth.

Your complexion and hair texture may be improved during pregnancy. Under the effect of certain glandular secretions, your skin probably will become drier. If you ordinarily have an oily complexion, you'll have better skin tone, rosier hues, and softer skin. If your skin is normally dry, use more moisteners. Rarely, the secretions cause a skin irritation resembling acne. This usually can be dealt with by washing in warm water.

You may note other changes in complexion. Because of stimulation of the cells governing skin pigmentation, you may develop dark spots on the cheeks and forehead, even a tinge over the whole face, sometimes called "the mask of pregnancy." These changes may require additional makeup, but you can be reassured they will disappear after delivery. You may also find your facial contours changing. You may have a rounder, fuller face, calling for a different hairstyle or makeup.

The amount of oil in your hair will decrease, too; the strands may become brittle and split, so you may need a daily shampoo to keep your hair fluffy and fresh. Your hair may become thinner, with less body; it may be time to change to a shorter, fuller cut. However, if you have oily hair ordinarily, the change may be a boon.

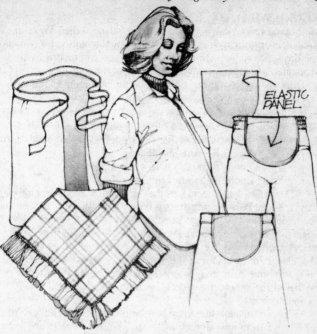

Your clothes will look good if they're simple, practical, and safe. Maternity clothes should fit your changing appearance. A whole wardrobe may be unnecessary; a few outfits will do nicely.

YOUR MATERNITY WARDROBE

Your choice of clothing should be governed by a few simple rules; keep it simple, keep it practical and keep it safe. Beyond that, you'll want clothes that are loose and comfortable, clothes that don't restrict you in any way.

You'll probably continue wearing your regular clothes until some time during the fifth month, at which point they'll begin feeling tight. Your new garments will have to allow for an expanding abdomen and for a waist that has all but disappeared. Blouses and dresses will have to hang from the shoulders instead of being gathered at the waist.

You probably won't want to buy a closet full of maternity clothes, especially if it's your first pregnancy, because they are expensive and you'll wear them only a few months. But you'll certainly want a few outfits for special occasions. Most cities have shops specializing in stylish maternity apparel. Also, department stores usually have maternity departments. If you plan to work throughout the pregnancy, you'll need more clothes than if you're not working outside the home.

For casual wear, maternity clothes aren't necessary. An oversized shirt will serve as a top, or you can make do with an unbelted dress. You can cut the front out of an old pair of jeans or skirt and replace it with an elastic panel that will stretch as the baby grows. A wraparound skirt can be worn during pregnancy, as can an unbelted jumper. In addition, a smock or tent dress probably will also fit your growing figure for the full nine months.

Maternity clothes come in the same sizes as street clothes. That is, a Size 10 maternity dress is designed to fit a Size 10 woman who happens to have a larger waistline. (You may, of course, need a bigger size if you've put on a lot of weight.) Most maternity clothes are designed to provide growing room for the developing baby, with tabs, elastic, or pleats for a better fit. Dark, solid colors usually are most attractive. You may want to pick designs with accents or touches at the shoulders or neckline to divert attention from your expanding waist.

Separates usually are your best bet in maternity clothes. You can choose from any number of shirts, blouses, tunics, and even T-shirts; all can be combined with skirts, jumpers, or pants. Many of them even can be worn after pregnancy. Look for slacks and jeans with a semicircular elastic panel at the waist to allow for expansion; they can be found in many fabrics and are both attractive and comfortable. Play outfits and even maternity bathing suits are also available. Essentially, you're limited only by your budget and taste. And if you can sew, a wide variety of patterns for both maternity dresses and blouses is available.

Underclothing must be chosen with care. It must not fit so tightly as to restrict circulation. You'll probably want snug underpants or briefs, but they should not limit blood flow in the legs. Panty girdles are taboo. A maternity girdle with an expanding panel is permissible if is has no reinforcing panels or stays. Avoid garter belts, garters, and stockings. Maternity pantyhose adapt to your movements and permit free circulation.

You'll probably wear a larger brassiere. If you regularly take a 34B, you may require a 36 or 38C by the end of the third month. Select a good bra, one that provides firm support but does not constrict the breasts nor press too hard on the nipples.

Pick shoes for comfort and safety. As your abdomen enlarges, you may lean backward and walk more flat-footed. The best shoes have broad toes and a heel not more than an inch high. Any higher heel will cause you to pitch forward and teeter precariously. Shoes need a full back rather than a sling. Especially in late pregnancy, you may wish to purchase shoes a half-size larger, because your feet will have a tendency to swell late in the day. Avoid sneakers, ballet slippers, negative-heel shoes, flopping sandals, and shoes with slippery soles.

A PREGNANT WOMAN'S CHECKLIST

While you needn't act like an invalid during pregnancy, you should observe certain sensible precautions to ensure a safe pregnancy. Here are the most important:

• Avoid anyone with a cold or other contagious diseases. Because a disease may be transmitted before a definite diagnosis can be made, stay away from anyone who seems to be coming down with an illness. Children's diseases are a particular hazard. Be especially careful if you have not been inoculated against rubella (German measles).

• Get plenty of exercise—and also plenty of rest. Complicated calisthenics aren't necessary; simply walking will do. Follow a nutritious diet with plenty of good foods.

• See your doctor at regular intervals, and notify him or her immediately of any unusual symptoms. Keep a close watch on yourself, and be aware of anything that seems unusual.

• Continue your outside interests and develop new ones. Keep working as long as you feel up to it.

• Learn all you can about pregnancy, childbirth, and childrearing. There's no such thing as knowing too much about parenting.

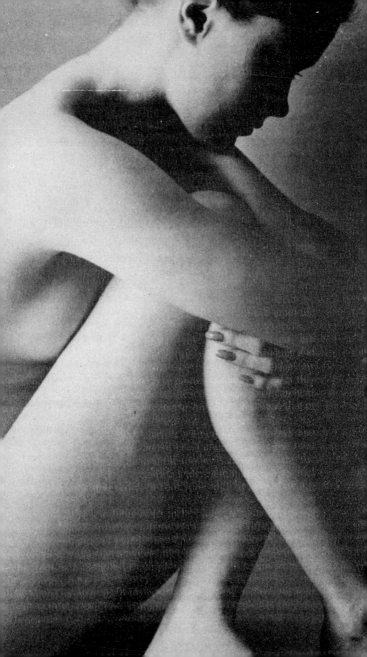

CHAPTER
3
Minor Discomforts
of Pregnancy

Some women sail through pregnancy and never feel better in their lives. Most, however, have brief, intermittent bouts of minor discomfort throughout the entire nine months—"a variety of aches and pains," one obstetrician has said, "throughout the area between the navel and the knees." Fortunately, problems usually cure themselves or can be cleared up with simple treatment. A few rare, serious prenatal complications require a doctor's attention.

"MORNING SICKNESS"
Nausea early in the pregnancy isn't inevitable; and if it occurs, it is more a nuisance than a serious problem. Mild stomach upset and queasiness may occur at any time during the day; a few women have several episodes, morning and evening. The condition seems to be caused primarily by increased amounts of estrogen acting on the smooth muscles of the stomach and intestinal tract.

Ordinary morning sickness, even with occasional vomiting, doesn't require medical attention. It's simply one of those passing annoyances pregnant women put up with. But if you vomit persistently, be sure to tell your doctor.

There's no sure cure for morning sickness, although women (and doctors) have been seeking one for centuries. Some women cut down on eating, believing the less you put down, the less will come up. However, you'll probably feel better with some food in your stomach. Try eating six small meals during the day, rather than three full ones. (You may have little appetite, anyway.) Keep dry crackers on the nightstand and eat them as soon as your eyes open, even before lifting your head from the pillow. (A glass of milk first thing in the morning also may help.) Stay in bed for 20 minutes after eating. Some women carry crackers in their purses to nibble on if they feel nauseated.

Change your diet to eliminate foods that are difficult to digest. Concentrate on starches—bread, crackers, potatoes, rice—and skip fried and fatty foods. Avoid butter, olive oil, and cream. Whole wheat toast and fruit are helpful, as are milk, tea, and carbonated beverages.

If your nausea occurs mostly in the morning, ask your doctor if you should take an antinauseant the night before. If the problem occurs later in the day, take the medicine as soon as you get up. Brief rest periods during the day also may help. Lie down or prop up your feet for 15 to 20 minutes until the nausea passes.

GAS, HEARTBURN, AND INDIGESTION

In the early months of pregnancy, you may feel bloated and uncomfortable after eating, burp embarrassingly, or bring up a little sour-tasting fluid. You also may have heartburn, that hot sensation in the upper abdomen or lower chest. This discomfort probably isn't primarily a result of your diet. Like morning sickness, it results from estrogen secretion.

Antacids may bring you some relief. So may a half glass of milk or a level tablespoonful of milk of magnesia about a half hour before eating. Baking soda, the standard remedy for indigestion, usually is ruled out by doctors during pregnancy, because of the sodium content.

Just as you might for morning sickness, you can lessen the effects of heartburn and indigestion by reducing your consumption of foods that produce gas or are difficult to digest. Cut back on beans, onions, and fried foods in favor of fruits and juices. Drinking enough liquids also helps. In addition, regular exercise and good bowel habits can speed digestion.

VARICOSE VEINS

Swollen, painful veins in the legs occur because the growing uterus presses on the major arteries and veins serving the lower half of the body. Circulation slows; the blood pools. The veins must work harder to return the blood to the heart. Their walls stretch and swell, causing the unsightly and throbbing blotches.

Varicose veins are rare in first pregnancies, but the risk in-

creases as each subsequent pregnancy further weakens the vein walls. The tendency appears to be inherited, and, fortunately, the problem does not afflict all women.

Presently, there are no methods to prevent varicose veins, but there are ways to gain relief. Support pantyhose, which look little different from ordinary pantyhose, reduce pressure and throbbing. Elastic stockings, put on before arising in the morning, may hold the swelling down. At work, you may wish to wear slacks to conceal the hose.

Exercise is often a helpful treatment (or preventive) for varicose veins, too. Don't stand in one position for extended periods of time. Walk around to keep the blood flowing. Or lie on your back, feet in the air, and pump your legs as if you were riding a bicycle. Try to sit with your feet higher than your legs to speed the blood's return to the heart. At work, prop your feet on another chair. If possible, lie down at intervals during the day.

HEMORRHOIDS

Another usually temporary consequence of reduced circulation in the lower part of the body is hemorrhoids, or "varicose veins of the rectum." The itching, enlarged veins may appear for the first time during pregnancy, or existing hemorrhoids may be aggravated by pregnancy. Constipation may make the condition painful. A diet of fruits and juices may help to relieve the problem, or ask your doctor to suggest a stool softener. Usually, hemorrhoids disappear after delivery. Surgery or more extensive treatment is seldom required; if it does seem indicated, it often is postponed until after delivery. The condition may not recur in subsequent pregnancies.

CONSTIPATION AND IRREGULARITY

Bowel irregularity is most common in the early months, another consequence of increased estrogen. Irregularity usually is relieved by mid-pregnancy, but may return in the final months when the baby's head descends and presses on the bowel.

Proper diet, plenty of fluids, and regular bowel habits will help promote regularity. Follow a balanced menu, with plenty of fruits and vegetables, and drink more liquids. Drinking two glasses of water before breakfast often stimulates bowel action. A regular time for a bowel movement also reduces constipation. Mornings after breakfast are usually best, although this time can be inconvenient if you're working or have children to pack off to school.

Eating laxative foods may help. Such foods include prunes, raw, stewed, or in juice; figs, dates, or other stewed fruits; baked apples; oranges; and cereals or breads with a high fiber content. Eating fruit before retiring at night may help to establish a morning bowel movement.

A mild laxative or stool softener may be helpful. Never use laxatives such as castor oil or enemas without consulting your doctor.

BLEEDING AND VAGINAL DISCHARGE

A few women may have one or two episodes of slight vaginal bleeding after conception. These episodes are usually of short duration with light flow, seldom lasting more than a day. A few women are said to "menstruate" throughout pregnancy, but such episodes are very rare. Any flow of blood from the vagina, no matter how scant, should be regarded as a possible danger signal. Report it to your doctor immediately.

Increased vaginal discharge is normal, however. Usually

white or pale yellow in color, the discharge represents increased secretions of mucus from the glands of the cervix and walls of the vagina. It can be washed off, although you may wish to wear a pad to protect your clothes.

If the discharge is heavy or causes itching, it may represent a vaginal infection. There are several types of infections, each with a specific treatment. Report the condition to your doctor for examination and care.

ITCHY SKIN
About one pregnant woman in five develops an annoying itch in the abdominal area, especially during warm, humid weather. The itching seems to be related to increased hormonal secretion, as well as stretching of the skin. It may worsen as the pregnancy progresses and the abdomen enlarges and may be further irritated if you wear a girdle or other tight-fitting clothing.

Choose loose, nonrestrictive garments that allow the skin to "breathe" freely. Do not use lotions containing cortisone.

Abdominal itching is not related to itching around the vagina. If an irritation develops in the vaginal or anal area, see your doctor.

MUSCLE CRAMPS
Cramps in the calf, or sometimes in the thigh, occur in middle or late pregnancy. The reason is obscure. Sluggish circulation, the swaybacked maternity posture, or the amount of calcium in the diet may be causes. Shooting pains in the legs may occur during the final months of pregnancy when the baby's head presses on nerves in the pelvis that run down the backs of the legs.

Massage is probably the best remedy. Hold the foot of the affected leg in your hand and bend it upward, to tense the calf muscle. Rub the muscle itself with your hands. If the cramp persists, you can apply a heating pad or a hot-water bottle. Liniments and lotions aren't necessary, however. Shooting pains can sometimes be relieved by shifting position, or by lying on your back and drawing your knees toward your chest for a few minutes. A maternity girdle and low-heeled shoes may help correct your posture and prevent leg pains.

SWOLLEN FEET AND ANKLES
Your shoes may feel tight and your feet and ankles puffy in the last two months of pregnancy, especially if you're working at a job that requires you to sit in one position or stay on your feet all day.

Again, the culprit is sluggish circulation. Fluid from the pooled blood leaks into the tissue, causing a condition called edema.

Exercise won't prevent swelling, but it will lessen it. Continue your daily walks. When sitting, prop your feet as often as possible—the swelling will probably decrease within 15 minutes. You may find that it's worse at night and improved by morning. If, however, the swelling persists through the night and especially if your hands and face also swell, be sure to notify your doctor.

SHORTNESS OF BREATH

Late in pregnancy you may find yourself gasping and short of breath after even the slightest exertion. One explanation for this sensation may be the expanded uterus pressing on the lungs. Fortunately, the problem will be relieved just before delivery, when the baby sinks lower into the pelvis.

For relief, always choose straight-backed chairs instead of upholstered ones. Try to stand and walk straight. If you can't sleep because of shortness of breath, prop yourself with pillows into a half-sitting position.

Shortness of breath is normal, but if it becomes so severe that you cannot climb stairs without puffing heavily, notify your doctor.

CHANGES IN YOUR SKIN

Skin changes may occur elsewhere than on the face. They include darkening of the nipples and the development of a dark vertical line on the abdomen between the navel and pubic hair. The facial changes usually disappear after delivery; the brown line may fade but never completely vanish.

Stretch marks—"striae"—are reddish, slightly depressed streaks on the lower abdomen and thighs. They result from tiny tears in the elastic layer beneath the skin as the abdomen stretches to accommodate the growing baby. The more weight you gain, the more the stretching. After delivery, the marks turn from red to white but do not disappear. The tendency to develop them seems to be hereditary. Stretch marks cannot be prevented, although bath oils and moisturizing lotions may keep the surrounding skin from drying out.

Vascular "spiders" are tiny red elevations radiating from a central point. They most commonly appear on the face, neck, upper chest, and arms and appear to be caused by high concentrations of estrogen. They normally disappear after delivery.

Regular exercise—walking, moderate jogging—may not prevent varicose veins or swollen ankles and feet, but such activity can help to relieve the discomfort they cause.

BACKACHE

Leaning backward to compensate for a growing abdomen may cause chronic backache or a "catch" just below the waistline. You may get relief from massage or heat. To prevent it, wear a light maternity girdle and low-heeled shoes. Exercises learned in pre-natal classes (see page 58) will also strengthen back muscles. Sleeping on a firm mattress also helps.

FOOD CRAVINGS

Folklore says you'll have sudden cravings for food you don't ordinarily like and in odd combinations—pickles and ice cream, hot dogs, coconut, persimmons. So long as the cravings are infrequent and the choices don't interfere with a balanced diet, go ahead and satisfy them. Very rarely, some pregnant women have bizarre cravings to eat such substances as laundry starch or even dirt. This condition, called pica, should be reported to your doctor immediately.

DIZZINESS AND FAINTING

Dizziness and fainting are most common in the middle months of pregnancy. You are most vulnerable when you have been sitting or standing in one position for a long period, restricting the return of blood from the legs and feet.

If you feel faint, sit down immediately and place your head between your knees, so that it will be lower than the heart. Don't be embarrassed to do so even if you are in a public place. Remember, it is better to sit down than to fall down. Carry a bottle of aromatic spirits of ammonia in your purse, and use it if necessary.

Wearing support hose helps to stimulate circulation and so does regular exercise. If your job requires you to sit for long periods of time, pump your legs—as if you were riding a bicycle—before standing. If the fainting sensation is frequent or if it is accompanied by blurred vision, be sure to tell your doctor.

CARE OF THE NIPPLES

About the fourth month of pregnancy, you may notice that a thick fluid, yellowish or whitish in color, called colostrum, has begun to drain from the nipples.

Drainage may continue throughout pregnancy, until milk begins to flow after birth. The substance is harmless, and if it cakes on the nipples, you may wish to wear pads inside your bra to protect your clothes.

Tender or sore nipples may be cared for by rubbing them with a skin cream. Some childbirth educators advocate massaging the nipples to toughen them as a prelude to breast-feeding, but La Leche League officials say massage is unnecessary, and some doctors believe stimulating the nipples may bring on uterine contractions.

INSOMNIA AND OVERSLEEPING

Some women say they "slept their way through pregnancy." Most pregnant women do sleep more, especially in the early months. Your nightly slumber may stretch from eight to nine hours, and you may also find that you want to take an afternoon nap.

By contrast, in late pregnancy sleep may not come easily. The baby's movements, muscle cramps, breathing difficulties, and the frequent need to urinate may combine to keep you awake. A short walk before retiring, a warm shower, or a glass of warm milk or cocoa may help you fall asleep more quickly. If insomnia persists, tell your doctor. Do not take sleeping medications unless prescribed.

You also may find you tire more easily. Be sure to rest after exercise.

MOOD SWINGS

You may have intermittent changes of mood during pregnancy—one day high, the next down in the dumps. On Monday you may feel overjoyed at the prospect of motherhood; on Tuesday you may feel depressed at how the baby will change your life. Some days you may feel big, cumbersome, and ugly; other days you may think that you have never felt so well and looked forward so enthusiastically to the future.

To some extent these moods have a hormonal basis; the increased secretion of estrogen and progesterone may be the cause of metabolic changes. Hormones notwithstanding, such swings are psychologically normal. Most women experience ambivalent feelings about motherhood—wanting children and the maternal role, while at the same time being aware of how profoundly different everything will be. Too, the relationship between the prospective parents undergoes a change or changes during pregnancy and thereafter. Fathers, like mothers, are ambivalent about parenthood, with its added financial and other responsibilities. A couple's relationship may deepen, enrich, and strengthen, but it is definitely not the same as before.

It's common during pregnancy to laugh one minute and cry the next. These mood swings will pass. Still, it is best to discuss your feelings with someone—your husband, your doctor, a friend. You may find your worries less troublesome than you thought. Don't be upset if there are times when you wish you'd never become pregnant—it's a normal reaction to a normal event, and one that normally ends happily.

IF YOU OWN A CAT

Toxoplasmosis is a mild and common infectious disease. Tests show that one-third of American adults carry antibodies to the toxoplasma organism, indicating that they have been infected at some time, often without being aware of it. If a pregnant woman acquires the disease, however, it can be damaging to her unborn child.

One of the primary ways the infecting organism is spread is through the feces of cats. If a pregnant woman has a pet cat, she should have a blood test for toxoplasmosis. If antibodies are detected. she has had the disease and there is no danger. If not, it is not necessary to dispose of the cat; other members of the household should empty the litter box, at least daily, and the litter should be incinerated or disposed of carefully. A woman should not garden in soil that may have been used by the cat or a neighbor's cat. In general, she should avoid contact with cats at least until a veterinarian has found the pet free of the toxoplasma organisms.

IF YOU'RE OVER 35

Most women give birth for the first time in their teens or 20s, and their families are complete before they are 30. But the average age of a first-time mother has been steadily rising. Many women do not have their first child until their mid- or late 20s, and an increasing number are past 30, or even 35.

With good medical supervision, there is no reason to fear a pregnancy at this age. You may require closer attention than a younger mother, but the pregnancy can be equally safe. Labor and delivery may be a little longer if this is your first baby. One study shows that first-time mothers 35 years or older labor $1^{1}/2$ to four hours longer than younger first-time mothers. However, their children are usually just as healthy.

There are certain risks to motherhood when you're over 35. The older mother is more likely to bear twins. And the possibility of conceiving a child with Down's syndrome (mongolism), a form of retardation, increases with age, being markedly higher at age 45 than 35. For this reason, your doctor may recommend a prenatal procedure called amniocentesis (see pages 82–83) to determine whether this possibility exists.

THE DANGER SIGNALS IN PREGNANCY

Most problems of pregnancy can wait to be reported to your doctor during your next visit.

Some symptoms can indicate an emergency and should be reported immediately. You should be sure to notify your doctor if any of the following occur: -

• Any bleeding or bloody discharge that comes from the vagina.
• Fever of 100 degrees Fahrenheit or more, not accompanied by a common cold.
• Severe nausea with vomiting more than three times in an hour.
• Swelling of the hands and face, especially if it is sudden.
• Dimness or blurring of vision, especially if you see spots or wavy lines before your eyes.
• Strong abdominal pains that are not relieved by a bowel movement.
• Continuous, severe headache.
• A sudden rush or trickle of water that comes from the vagina.
• Very frequent or burning urination.
• Any accident, hard fall, or other trauma.
• Regular, menstrual-like cramping before term.

HOW TO CALL YOUR DOCTOR

When you phone your doctor, make sure you get the most from the call. Follow these steps:

• If possible, call during office hours, when records are available to the staff. Report your condition to the nurse, who may be able to answer your questions or check for instructions; if the nurse can't help, leave a message for the doctor to call back.
• Always give your full name (there may be two Mrs. Joneses), the date when you last visited the doctor, and the stage (in months) of your pregnancy.
• Make the call yourself if possible; relaying information through your husband or a friend can lead to troublesome delay, confusion, and misinformation.
• Describe your problem in the most specific terms possible. How much blood is being passed? More than a heavy menstrual period? Lighter? Continuous or intermittent? How long have you felt nauseated? How many times have you vomited within an hour? Specific details will help your doctor to prescribe a treatment for the problem.
• Keep a pencil and paper near the telephone to write down the doctor's instructions. Don't trust your memory at a time when you are not feeling well.
• Be sure you know the name, address, and phone number of your pharmacy so you will not have to look them up if the doctor wishes to prescribe medicine.

PRENATAL EXERCISES

*Regular exercise before birth will make your delivery easier and help
you to feel better in the meantime. The exercises on these pages,
adapted from childbirth-education classes, offset the fatigue of
pregnancy and strengthen the muscles used in labor. Begin about the
fifth or sixth month, and continue until delivery.*

Breast support

Exercise in the tailor position off-
sets round-shouldered posture and
pain in the upper back caused by
heavier breasts and a larger abdomen; it also helps to open lungs and
make breathing easier. Sit on floor
in tailor, or Indian, fashion—legs
bent at the knees and tucked under
you. Lift arms to shoulder height directly in front of you. Rotate arms to
side, then extend directly overhead.
Return to original position. For variation, extend right arm to full
length overhead, until you can feel
the muscles stretch along right side
from shoulder to hip. Repeat for the
left side. Do the exercise 20 times
on each side, then return to original
position. The exercise may be performed daily during the middle
months of pregnancy.

General stretch

Muscle tone, hip and knee joints, and lower back all benefit from this general loosening-up exercise. Lie on floor, knees bent, feet flat. Inhale. As you exhale, draw your knee toward your chest as far as you can over the expanding abdomen. Inhale, straighten knee, stretch leg, and flex ankle. Then exhale and lower straightened leg until the foot is a few inches off the floor. Return to starting position, then repeat exercise with other leg. Do this exercise five times on each side at the beginning of your daily exercise period.

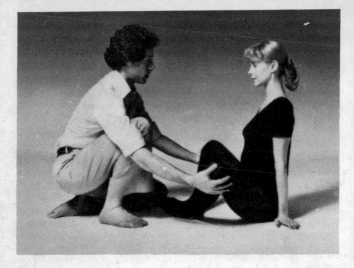

Thigh strengthener

This exercise husband and wife can do together helps strengthen the important inner thigh muscles that help the mother push during natural delivery. It also reduces fatigue if the mother's feet must be elevated in stirrups during delivery. Wife sits on the floor with knees bent, soles of feet pressed against each other. Husband kneels opposite, placing hands under wife's knees. Wife slowly pushes knees toward floor against resistance of husband's hands and holds position for a count of five. The exercise may also be done alone, with woman placing her own hands under her knees.

Thigh strengthener: a variation

In a variation of the thigh strengthener, sit on floor with legs extended in "V" position. Raise arms to shoulder height. Stretch slowly forward from the waist, keeping arms parallel to the floor. Don't try to touch the toes. Repeat exercise.

Thigh strengthener: another variation

Another way to strengthen inner thighs is to sit on the floor. with legs outstretched in "V" position. Extended arms to the sides as high as shoulders. Raise left arm directly overhead. Bending from the waist, reach with the right hand toward right foot, grasping the arch if possible, the ankle or calf if arch is beyond your reach. Hold this position for a count of five, then return to original position. Repeat the exercise to left side, with your right arm extended over your head.

"Kegel" or pelvic-floor exercises

This simple exercise, right, improves control of pelvic-floor muscles, which must be consciously relaxed during delivery.

Begin this exercise by sitting on the floor Indian fashion or with soles of feet together, keeping back straight. Relax the muscles of the genital area as if urinating. Slowly tighten the muscles and hold for a count of five. It may help to think of your muscles as an elevator: bring them slowly to the third floor, then back down. Then take the elevator to the basement, and return it to ground level.

Exercises to promote good circulation

Exercises to improve circulation are important late in pregnancy, to off-set swollen feet and ankles.

Begin by sitting with back straight, legs extended. Lift the left leg, knee bent, and support it with hands behind your thighs. Alternately flex the foot backward from the ankle as far as possible, and point it forward. Flex and point 50 times with each foot, then rotate each ankle 25 times to the left and then 25 times to the right.

For a variation of this exercise, lie on the floor with a pillow under the ankles. While pointing with the left, flex the right foot 50 times. Change, and repeat exercise 50 times. Then rotate ankles 50 times—25 times to the left, 25 to the right for each ankle. Exercise should be performed morning and evening during the final months of pregnancy.

In the lying position for the pelvic tilt, right, lie on your back with the bent knees together and feet flat on the floor. Inhale and relax. Then exhale and push the small of your back toward the floor, causing the pelvis to rotate. To be fully effective, this pelvic exercise should be performed daily during the final months of pregnancy.

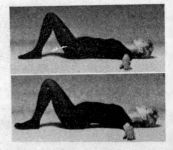

Pelvic tilt (or "rock")

This basic prenatal exercise is designed to build the back muscles, which are stretched and easily tired by the forward lean caused by the expanding abdomen.

In the "table" position, below, hands should be under the shoulders, knees under hips, with back straight. Inhale. Then exhale while arching back upward. Repeat this exercise ten times.

In the pelvic tilt exercise from a sitting position, at bottom, left, sit against a wall, with your legs extended in front. Inhale. As you exhale, flatten the back against the wall, which will rotate the pelvis forward. Relax, then repeat the exercise. The pelvic tilt also provides better support for the baby within the uterus and strengthens the mother's abdominal muscles.

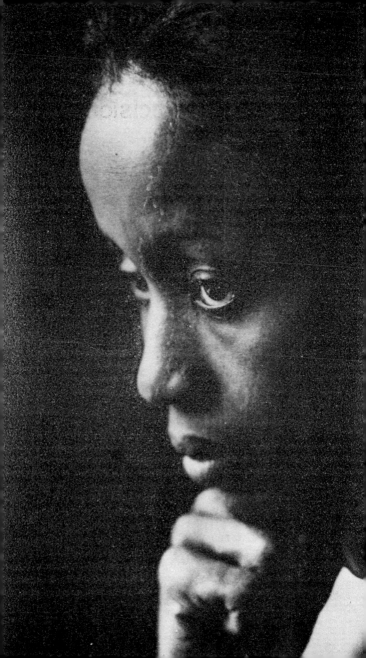

CHAPTER
4

A Time for Decisions

Each generation seems to have a different philosophy about the events leading up to that final, glorious moment of childbirth. When your parents were having children, the ideal childbirth was painless and perfunctory. A woman was sedated during labor and woke up with a baby in her arms; the father paced the floor outside the delivery room. Trusting that "doctor knows best," parents left major decisions to the obstetrician.

This attitude still prevails among some parents, some doctors, and in some places. But a great many other parents seek greater participation and fulfillment in what certainly is a momentous event in their lives. Thus, you'll probably want a voice in where and how the birth takes place, who'll be there, and whether the mother will be conscious during the delivery. Furthermore, you probably want doctors and hospitals to respect and be guided by your wishes.

These important decisions should be made early—not at the last minute on the way to the hospital. Fortunately, you'll have plenty of help in making them. Hospitals and other groups in almost every city now offer childbirth-preparation classes where parents can learn about the birth process, delivery techniques, and how to deal with pain. Such prenatal instruction groups will gladly furnish details on their particular methods or philosophy. And talk to your doctor. Your obstetrician may not agree with all your suggestions, but he or she will take time to discuss them, tell you why they make sense (or why they do not), and offer sound, practical advice.

THE ROLE OF THE FATHER

Fathers today play an important role in bringing a pregnancy to a successful conclusion, just as they did in its beginning. Most couples now recognize that childbirth is not simply the mother's domain, as it once was, but one in which parents have an equal stake. All of the many decisions about bringing a life into the world should be arrived at jointly, and parents often make a cooperative plan during pregnancy for caring for the child after birth.

Recognizing this trend, most hospitals provide childbirth preparation classes in which both parents participate. They also make provisions for the father to be at the mother's side, providing encouragement and support during pregnancy, labor, and delivery. Instead of restricting the father to passing out cigars and paying bills, some hospitals provide a guest room or even the same room where he may remain overnight while the mother is in the hospital.

Many fathers accept and enjoy the change that has come with the generations—but not all. Still, many matters of childbirth, such as the use of pain relief and the father's presence in the labor and delivery rooms, need to be brought out and discussed fully beforehand. It's easy at the time of childbirth for the father to feel shunted aside. Remember that pregnancy and childbirth are a time of stress for both parents. The least stressful pregnancies are those that grow from mutual cooperation and responsibility—themes that cement the relationship, rather than the separation.

A VISIT TO THE HOSPITAL

Now's the time to select the hospital where you plan to deliver the baby. Usually, your choice is limited by your obstetrician's practice, although some doctors have staff privileges at more than one hospital. Discuss with your doctor his or her—and your—preference.

A customary procedure is to make an orientation visit to the hospital, usually about the fifth month of pregnancy. Both prospective parents are expected to attend. You'll probably be shown a typical labor and delivery room (or possibly a film or slides) and given a briefing on what to expect. Such tours usually are held at regular intervals, mostly in the evening for the benefit of couples working outside the home.

On the tour, you'll probably visit the admitting office to provide basic information about yourself, so that it won't be necessary to repeat the process when you arrive for the delivery. The hospital will want to know name, address, telephone, occupation, and a limited personal and family medical history; you'll be asked your religious preference. You may also be asked to make a cash deposit or provide evidence of hospitalization insurance.

Take this opportunity to ask about certain hospital policies. (You'll want to discuss them with your doctor beforehand, too.) Among questions you may wish to ask:

• May the father remain in the labor room during all stages of labor?

• May he be present in the delivery room?

• May photographs be taken, and movies or videotapes made during the birth? Are there any special rules to follow?

• What, if any, alternative birth methods are available?

• Will the hospital respect our wishes about alternative birth methods?

• May our baby remain in the room with the mother after birth?

• May other children, friends, or relatives visit us in the hospital and see the new baby?

• How long will the mother remain in the hospital after a normal delivery?

• Can a husband remain overnight in his wife's hospital room?

Even if you're planning a conventional delivery, be sure to ask if certain specialized childbirth facilities (described below) are available. You may want to avail yourself of some features without taking advantage of the entire package. If not included in the tour, ask to see the maternity ward, labor and delivery rooms, patients' quarters, and the nursery. If you haven't already done so, now is a good time to ask if the hospital offers prenatal classes for parents or if they recommend childbirth instruction elsewhere.

You'll probably be pleasantly surprised to find the hospital more flexible—and more cheerful—than you anticipated. And so as long as your obstetrician approves and your pregnancy is considered normal, with minimum risks, the hospital probably will try to accommodate any sort of delivery you suggest. You'll probably find a welcome attitude and a desire to serve.

Stung by criticisms of traditional maternity service, many hospitals have established new guidelines for maternity care. Birth is treated as a natural, rather than a medical, happening and is conducted in a homelike, rather than an antiseptic, environment. You're treated as a guest, not a patient, and your wishes followed just so long as your own and your baby's health aren't jeopardized.

ALTERNATIVE BIRTH CENTERS

The whole family takes part in the birth in an alternative birth center. This concept, spreading rapidly, transfers the home atmosphere into the hospital itself. You and your family are housed in a special hospital room that resembles a hotel suite. There's usually a double bed, sleeping space for the children, cooking facilities, a television set, stereo, and other amenities.

A few steps away, however, is an intensive-care nursery and a standard delivery room, ready for use in case they're necessary. You can be whisked out of the room in seconds if complications arise. All the hospital facilities and staff are available to you.

In an uncomplicated birth, both labor and delivery take place in the room. You'll be under the care of a nurse or nurse-midwife, who will remain with you throughout labor. Your private obstetrician or the nurse-midwife may deliver the baby, as you prefer. While you're waiting, you can get up and move around or even have guests. The father-to-be also will be invited to participate in the process and to be at your bedside throughout labor. Or you may ask a friend to serve as labor "coach."

Following the delivery, the baby remains in the room. A nurse stays to assist and provide a short course in baby care. The whole family, including the newborn, can go home within 48 hours and sometimes on the same day.

NEIGHBORHOOD BIRTH CENTERS

In a neighborhood birth center, you will find a kind of halfway house between hospital and home, combining the cozy casualness of a residence with the reserve medical facilities needed for an emergency. Reserved for low-risk patients, these centers are patterned after institutions that have operated successfully for centuries in some European countries. Most are situated in big-city or suburban neighborhoods and function as satellites of larger hospitals, to which the mother may be transferred if necessary. About one in five first-time mothers is transferred.

Delivery in a birth center usually is conducted by a nurse-midwife; in some states an obstetrician must be standing by. The father is encouraged to be present and may be permitted to help in the delivery if he wishes. Drugs and medical equipment aren't used routinely but are available if needed. Afterward, you're taught how to care for the baby. You may be allowed to go home with the new baby the same day.

HOME BIRTH VERSUS HOSPITAL BIRTH

Even a few years ago, the idea of giving birth at home might not have occurred to you. Ninety-five percent of babies were born in hospitals, and the proportion was rising. Recently, the trend has reversed itself slightly. Births at home are still few in number, but they have grown, even though the practice is restricted in some states. Thus, one question that may occur to you is whether the baby *should* be born in a hospital or in your own home.

In a home birth, you should be under the care of a nurse-midwife, who is trained to handle routine obstetrical deliveries. She should be affiliated with a nearby hospital or work under the supervision of an obstetrician. (Sometimes, obstetricians themselves deliver the baby.) The midwife arrives when labor begins and remains with you until the baby is delivered. In the event of an emergency or other than routine delivery, she will summon help from the affiliated hospital. Afterward, she helps you care for the baby until you can take over yourself.

The argument for home birth is that eight or nine of ten deliveries are normal—and advocates say the rare complicated pregnancy can usually be identified in advance, in time to transfer the mother to a medical facility. Proponents insist that the vast (and expensive) facilities of a hospital aren't needed in most cases. Worse, they say, the hospital atmosphere is often cold, impersonal, and frightening. Nurses may be too busy to provide individual attention, leaving mothers alone and tense. By contrast, at home with a nurse-midwife, a woman gets one-on-one care in a relaxed surrounding.

Medical studies done in Europe, where home births are more common, and at least one U.S. study appear to show that the risk of complications is no more frequent in home than in hospital births— at least when cases are identified as low-risk in advance. The American College of Obstetricians and Gynecologists (ACOG), however, opposes the practice of home delivery. The ACOG says the most serious emergencies during childbirth arise very quickly, often with little warning, and the immediate medical backup of a hospital is needed to deal with them.

ROOMING-IN

In many hospitals, your newborn can now live in your room, in a bassinet beside your bed, almost from the time of delivery. He or she needn't stay in a nursery down the hall to be brought to you only at feeding time. With rooming-in, you can feed, care for, and get to know the baby on your own terms.

Rooming-in arrangements vary from hospital to hospital. Some require that the practice be limited to daylight hours, especially if several women share a room. The baby remains in the nursery at night, under the observation of the nursing staff. You may actually prefer this arrangement because it lets you get more rest and gives the nurses time to spot any problems.

If this is your first baby, you'll find rooming-in an important learning experience. A nurse will spend much of the first day with you, demonstrating how to care for the baby. Under her supervision, you'll sponge-bathe the baby, change diapers, and put the baby to bed. She'll also help you to begin breast-feeding (if you choose this method). A major advantage to rooming-in is that you can feed the baby at your (and the baby's) convenience, rather than at a rigid feeding time.

Another advantage for a first-time mother is that rooming-in helps build confidence. You get practice caring for the baby under experienced supervision, so you're almost a veteran by the time you get home.

Too, in many hospitals the father also may participate in rooming-in care, so that he also gets the kind of training that will be helpful later on when the baby comes home.

FAMILY VISITING

A growing number of hospitals now permit other children in the family to visit you and see their new brother or sister in the nursery. They usually must be accompanied by another adult, and may not be permitted to hold the baby. The length of family visits may be limited. In many hospitals, the father usually can visit any time he chooses. If you have a private room, he may be permitted to sleep in the hospital overnight.

IN THE LABOR AND DELIVERY ROOMS

Labor and delivery aren't something you have to go through alone, as they used to be. Now parents may remain together throughout labor and during delivery, the father providing help and support and coaching in breathing exercises—and sharing in the triumphant moment of birth. Some hospitals even permit the father to watch a cesarean delivery. An additional person, such as a sibling, relative, friend, or prepared-childbirth instructor also may be permitted to observe the routine delivery in some hospitals.

Natural-light photography, movies, or videos also may be permitted in the labor and delivery rooms, so that you have a permanent record of the happy event. The use of floodlights and flash may be prohibited because of the very slight danger of excessive heat or anesthetic explosion touch off by a spark. The American Society for Psychoprophylaxis in Obstetrics (ASPO), the leading prepared-childbirth organization, has suggested that this danger is remote and more hospitals should allow delivery room photography. Any danger is almost nonexistent using modern equipment and fast film, ASPO says.

Ask your local camera or video dealer for advice on which type of film to use. The special "spotlight" used in hospital delivery rooms, combined with fluorescent lighting and perhaps even daylight, may necessitate the use of special filters. Well in advance, check with the hospital about the lighting.

Like the captain of a ship, however, your obstetrician will be the person who has the final say over who's on board. Whether visitors (or photography, for that matter) are allowed in the labor room is considered to be a medical question. The doctor usually reserves the right to clear the room or prohibit spectators in case of emergency or if in his or her judgment their presence or action interferes with sound obstetrical care.

CLASSES FOR PROSPECTIVE PARENTS

Childbirth education grew out of the natural-childbirth movement, but prenatal classes will benefit you regardless of the delivery method you choose. Many obstetricians strongly recommend that prospective mothers and fathers take these classes as a means of preparing themselves for the labor and delivery process.

If your hospital doesn't offer classes as part of its prenatal service, you may find them at a local YWCA, adult education center, or community college. You usually take six classes, beginning in the seventh month of pregnancy. (A few places also offer early-bird courses, so you can practice special breathing and relaxation techniques even further ahead of time.) Both mothers and fathers attend, usually in groups of 20. The teacher is a specially trained childbirth instructor.

The philosophy of childbirth education stresses learning about labor and how to deal with it so you can overcome many of the fears associated with the process. It is said women fear labor because they have been convinced it is painful. Thus, when contractions start, you grow tense, hold your breath, and fight back. This starts a vicious circle. The tighter you grit your teeth, the stronger the pain becomes and the more difficult the labor. To carry through the whole process most effectively, you must relax and breathe normally.

Childbirth preparation fosters a different attitude, advocates say. Once you've learned what's happening to your body during labor, you're able to see the experience positively—each contraction a step forward, advancing the moment when your baby will be born. Labor will no longer be a series of pains to be endured; you'll look forward to the next contraction with anticipation, not dread. And you'll want to help in the birth process, rather than fight against it. Trained to relax and work with your contractions, you'll want to forgo drugs that might dim your sensations and perception of delivery.

Classes usually include the basic lessons in the anatomy and physiology of conception and labor, followed by instruction in breathing techniques and exercises to help with the labor. In the most common, the ASPO method, the following techniques are taught:

• Relaxation, to reduce tension and permit your body to function at maximum efficiency.

• Breathing geared to the phase of labor and aimed at teaching you to concentrate on breathing and thus reduce the perception of discomfort.

• Abdominal exercises to help you "push" and deliver more efficiently.

• Physical exercises designed to prepare the body for birth.

• Instruction for a birth "coach" or partner, usually the father.

"BREATHING" EXERCISES

Proper breathing makes labor and delivery easier. Breathing exercises can be learned by enrolling in a childbirth education class. Four types of breathing are learned, corresponding to the various stages of labor. Husbands learn the exercises to coach their wives. Start exercises six weeks before due date.

Start breathing exercises from one of three basic positions:

1. Lie on back, two pillows under head, one under knees.

2. Lie on stomach, with head lower than abdomen, pillows under head, legs, abdomen.

3. Sit comfortably in chair, legs relaxed, knees bent.

Exercise 1 teaches breathing for early labor. Wife lies on back, husband kneels alongside. At his cue, "Contraction begins," she inhales deeply and exhales in a long "cleansing breath." She then begins rhythmic breathing from the chest—in through the nose, out through the mouth. The husband (or a labor "coach") times the breaths. When a rhythm of six to nine breaths per minute is achieved, the partner starts abdominal massage. Placing his cupped hands on her abdomen just above the pubic bone, he brings fingertips upward along the sides of the abdomen, across the waistline to the midpoint, and then down the center of the abdomen to the starting point, timing the upward stroke to the inhale, downward to exhale. Massage continues until husband signals that contraction has ended, about one minute.

Exercise 2, for well-established labor, may be performed either on the back or in a sitting position. A deep, cleansing breath is followed by rapid, shallow breathing in the throat, chest barely moving; practice until it can be done for one minute. In the second stage, take a cleansing breath, then take shallow breaths at a slow rate. At the cue, "accelerate," gradually increase to rapid rate, hold pace for 30 seconds, then "decelerate." Follow with a cleansing breath. Massage may be added, timed to the breathing rate.

Exercise 3 is for transitional labor, the period of actual delivery. On back or in a sitting position, take a cleansing breath, then follow with rapid, panting breaths—four to eight in succession—steady exhaling, followed by blowing out, as if trying to extinguish a candle. Follow the first sequence with a second pant-blow sequence, and continue for 60 seconds. Practice three times daily for four to five "contractions" of 60 to 90 seconds each.

Exercise 4 is for pushing, as the mother voluntarily helps the baby come into the world. In the sitting position, couple this exercise with the pelvic-floor exercise (see page 61). Inhale and exhale normally; follow each exhalation by forcing the remaining air from lungs, while contracting the abdominal muscles and those of pelvic area. Hold for several seconds; take a deep, cleansing breath; relax; then begin exercise again.

NATURAL AND PREPARED CHILDBIRTH

Childbirth with a minimum of medication is better for you and the baby; it enables you to remain fully conscious and perceive the whole experience unhindered. Here are the most popular methods:

The Lamaze Method of Prepared Childbirth was originated in the Soviet Union by disciples of Ivan Pavlov. It was refined by a French obstetrician, Dr. Ferdinand Lamaze, and has become widespread in the U.S. through the efforts of the American Society for Psychoprophylaxis in Obstetrics (ASPO). ASPO prefers the phrase "prepared childbirth" to "natural childbirth," which the group thinks gives mothers the idea they can't have medication if they wish or require it. If the techniques are followed, however, medication frequently is not needed. Instead, discomfort is overcome by breathing, relaxation, and dissociation techniques.

Four types of breathing are taught:

• Deep-chest breathing is used in the early stages of labor. It consists of a deep, cleansing breath, taken in through the nose until the lungs swell and the abdomen rises, then exhaled through the mouth. Deep-chest breathing should be timed to coincide with contractions, which may be up to 60 seconds long. The breathing rate then should be about six per minute.

• Shallow, accelerated breathing is used as the contractions

become more intense, it begins with deep breathing, followed by short, shallow breaths from the chest only. They should be fast, light, effortless, in through the nose and out through the mouth. As the contraction subsides, the pace of breathing should be slowed, followed by a deep breath.

• Panting is used when the delivery is imminent and enables the woman to hold or resist the urge to push until the appropriate time—usually when the doctor asks. Breaths are taken in and out through the mouth, in a regular panting rhythm. Exhaling should be forceful but not too forceful—like blowing out a candle. After the urge to push has abated, return to deep breathing.

• Expulsion or delivery breathing is used during pushing. It consists of two slow, deep breaths, followed by a push. During the push, the breath is held as long as possible, after which another deep breath is taken. Pushing is done only during a contraction.

The Bradley Method of Natural Childbirth differs from the Lamaze method in that it stresses abdominal (deep) breathing and teaches the woman to focus on what is happening during labor, instead of dissociating herself from it. The method, named for Dr. Robert Bradley, a Colorado obstetrician, stresses that discomfort is more tolerable when a woman participates in the whole birth process. Bradley followers also say that the woman must be totally prepared, mentally and physically, for pregnancy and delivery. Thus, Bradley also has a more intensive program of classes, beginning in the early months of pregnancy, including nutrition and exercise as well as breathing techniques. About 95 percent of "Bradley babies" are said to be delivered without medication.

The Read Method of Natural Childbirth is the forerunner of other "natural" methods and now has been largely supplanted by them. It is based on the teachings of the British obstetrician, Dr. Grantly Dick-Read, who believed that because all childbirth is natural, medical intervention should be minimal. Advocates of the Read method stress education, believing the mother will favor natural delivery once she understands what the natural process is. The Read method also emphasizes breathing and relaxation as an alternative to pain-reducing medication.

PAIN AND PAIN KILLERS

Probably, you'll want to limit the use of pain-reducing drugs and anesthetics during labor and delivery. A growing number of women now wish to remain fully conscious, alert, and in command of themselves throughout childbirth, so they can see, feel, and recall every aspect of the experience. Many parents are concerned, too, about the possible effects of drugs and anesthetics on mother and baby. In some hospitals, as many as 50 percent of deliveries are conducted totally without medication, and in many other births only mild pain-reducing agents or local anesthetics are used.

But pain is individual. Indeed, if you brought five women together to describe labor, you'd probably hear five different descriptions. There *is* pain associated with labor—after all, that's how nature tells you that a new life is on the way. But how much discomfort you'll personally feel is impossible to predict. And the amount of pain one woman can tolerate cheerfully, another may find utterly unbearable. Indeed, the discomfort you felt when you delivered an earlier child may not be felt during this delivery.

There's another aspect, too, expressed by the American College of Obstetricians and Gynecologists (ACOG). "Pain relief during labor and delivery is an important aspect of modern obstetrics," states a technical bulletin published by the ACOG. "It consists of more than providing personal comfort to the mother; it is a necessary part of good obstetrical practice. Thoughtfully chose analgesia (pain-reducing agents) can improve labor, and proper anesthesia permits difficult deliveries to be accomplished with safety."

Thus, keep an open mind about pain relief. However much you want to avoid drugs and anesthetics, remember that childbirth isn't an endurance contest. If during your labor, the pain seems too great—and only you can be the judge of that—it's better to ask for relief than to go on grimly enduring what seems unendurable. And if your doctor suggests that analgesia or anesthesia might smooth the delivery, hear him or her out and respect the opinion. Remember, healthy babies were born and enjoyed in the days when their mothers were completely anesthetized. You may have been one of them yourself.

EFFECTS ON THE BABY

But will analgesia or anesthesia harm you or your baby? The answer is that no one knows precisely—so the tendency is to play it safe. Drugs given to the mother cross the placental barrier and reach the fetus. Some depress the baby's heart rate—although the lasting effects of the depression, if any, are not known. Some doctors say that babies born to mothers given even mild medication are sluggish and not fully alert for several days after birth. Others believe drugs may cause subtle nerve damage that may not appear for years, but their opinion has been strongly challenged. For all these reasons, however, a committee of the American Academy of Pediatrics has stated that in childbirth, probably less medication is better, and none may be best of all.

It's pointed out reassuringly, however, that millions of babies have been born to sedated mothers, and widespread effects have not been detected.

A DIRECTORY OF DRUGS

Most doctors believe that the most important pain reliever a woman can receive is the emotional support of her husband and the obstetrical team. One widely used obstetrical text declares, "In ordinary circumstances, about 60 percent of women can go through labor with psychologic assistance and a minimum of pain-relieving drugs in a manner satisfactory to both them and their obstetrician."

However, at times either analgesics (for reduction of pain) or anesthetics (which deaden sensation) may be called for. Here are the most commonly used methods:

Analgesics

• *Tranquilizers* don't actually relieve pain, but they may ease the anxiety and tension some women feel during contractions. If administered, they are usually offered early in labor.

• *Demerol,* the commercial name for meperidine, is a well-known pain killer used in many situations other than labor. It is said to be give to as many as 50 percent of women during the first stage of labor. Demerol reduces pain but leaves the mother conscious and able to participate in labor. Its use may depress the fetal heart rate, especially if labor is prolonged.

• *Nisentil,* the commercial name for alphaprodine, is often used instead of meperidine because it has a more rapid onset of action, a shorter duration, fewer side effects, and an equally effective impact on maternal pain. It, too, may produce depression in the infant, but the effects seem not to persist beyond 30 minutes.

• *Talwin* (pentazocine) is said to have pain relief comparable to that of meperidine but with fewer maternal side effects. It is rapid-acting, and passes the placental barrier to a lesser extent than meperidine, thus is less likely to cause depression of the heart rate in the child.

Anesthetics Local and regional anesthetics are administered to reduce sensation in a circumscribed area of the body. They are primarily given in the late stages of labor. A variety of drugs may be used.

• *Pudendal block* is the primary local anesthetic method. It anesthetizes the immediate birth area via a simple injection, usually of novocaine. A pudendal block allows the doctor to make a small incision that widens the birth canal. It does not affect the mother's ability to feel contractions nor to "push," and it does not affect the baby's heart rate.

• *Perineal block* is the traditional method of anesthetizing the birth area, but is less commonly used because greater amounts of anesthetic are needed to produce loss of sensation.

Regional anesthetics affect a larger area of the body.

• *Caudal epidural anesthesia* is given near the base of the spine, in the epidural space where a network of nerves emerges from the spinal cord. After the injection, there is no sensation in the pelvic area, but muscles are not affected, so the mother can push when the doctor instructs her to do so. The method appears not to affect the baby's heart rate. Caudal epidural anesthesia was once the most popular form of regional anesthesia, because of its simplicity and long-lasting effect. It is still used in routine delivery, but lumbar epidural anesthesia is preferred for more difficult early labors.

• *Lumbar epidural anesthesia* often is substituted for the caudal method because it can be administered in stages, anesthetizing only limited areas of the body at a time. During the first stage of labor, an injection blocks the upper pelvic areas, while allowing the muscular mechanisms of labor to continue; later, a larger dose may be given to block the lower lumbar area, and finally, an injection in the immediate birth area in labor's second stage. Like caudal anesthesia, the lumbar method appears not to depress the infant's heart rate, and has the additional advantage that smaller doses are needed, with surer and faster results.

• *"Saddle block"* is a form of spinal anesthesia that deadens sensations below the waist by means of an injection directly into the birth canal. It gets its name from the part of the body anesthetized, although one doctor has written that "the area is considerably greater than that which would be in contact with a saddle." The drug is given after the cervix is fully dilated; it often is used to facilitate a forceps delivery. As with other regional anesthetics, the woman remains conscious and the baby's heart rate seems unaffected.

• *General anesthesia,* usually thiopental sodium but sometimes a combination of nitrous oxide and oxygen and rarely other anesthetics, is now mainly reserved for cesarean delivery (although sometimes spinal anesthesia may be used for this purpose). The method anesthetizes the woman completely. In past years, general anesthesia was the most common method, even for normal deliveries, but is seldom is used in routine cases today.

TESTS YOU MAY HAVE

Medical tests are a routine part of pregnancy management: You may have some on each visit to the doctor, others only once. The doctor may send you to a laboratory to have certain procedures performed. Tests seldom are a matter for concern—strictly a precaution or an effort to gain additional information about the progress of the pregnancy. Here are some common tests:

Urinalysis. You'll usually furnish a urine sample on each visit, collected at home on arising or in the doctor's office. The urine is checked for human chorionic gonadotropin (hCG), for evidence of how the pregnancy is progressing. The urine also will be tested for the presence of glucose, which could indicate a diabetic condition; protein, which might signal that toxemia or preeclampsia, two common but manageable complications of pregnancy, are developing; white blood cells, which might indicate a kidney or urinary infection; or red blood cells, which might mean a kidney problem. If any of these conditions are discovered, the doctor may decide to conduct additional tests.

Blood pressure will be measured on each visit. Elevated blood pressure also may be a warning of toxemia.

Blood tests. A small sample of blood will be taken, usually at the first or second visit. The blood will be typed, and a number of tests made from this sample.

Hemoglobin concentration. Your blood will be checked for the percentage of hemoglobin it contains; a low count indicates anemia, which could require treatment.

Serological tests will be conducted to determine if you have or have had a previous hepatitis infection, since this disease could be passed on to nurses or to the child at birth; and for syphilis, a test that is mandatory in most states, even if you're sure you could not have contracted the disease. Syphilis in the mother can present grave danger to the unborn child, and because the disease frequently shows few if any symptoms, the test is important to permit prompt treatment and thereby reduce the risk.

Rubella titers. Rubella, a mild virus infection also called German measles, causes severe damage to a fetus if contracted by the mother during the first six weeks of pregnancy. For this reason, all women in the childbearing years are urged to be immunized against the disease prior to becoming pregnant.

Once pregnant, it's too late for immunization, however, because injecting the vaccine might have the same consequences as contracting the disease itself. Thus, if an uninoculated woman conceives, the doctor will check her blood for rubella-fighting antibodies. Chances are she may have been immunized as a child and forgotten it, or she may have had a mild case of rubella, conferring immunity without realizing it. Studies have shown that seven out of eight women are immune.

Immunization is customarily done when the woman is not pregnant; contraception is advised for two or three months after immunization. However, in instances where immunization has been carried out inadvertently when the woman was pregnant, there have not been any verified instances of fetal infection.

Rh factor. A general antibody titer will be conducted from the blood sample, particularly to test for the Rhesus, or Rh, factor in the blood. This blood constituent is found in 85 percent of the white population, who are called Rh positives. It is lacking in others, the Rh negatives. If a woman is found to be Rh negative, the father's blood may be checked, too.

When an Rh-negative woman conceives by an Rh-positive man, the child is likely to be Rh-positive, too—its blood incompatible with that of the mother. Although their bloodstreams are separate, some fetal blood may cross the placental barrier into the mother's body, which identifies it as an invader and produces antibodies to destroy it. The antibody production is gradual, but the transfer of cells may occur at any time during pregnancy, particularly when the process is disturbed, as at the time of delivery. The antibodies may then remain after delivery, and, if the mother conceives again, cross into the new fetal bloodstream, ravaging the red blood cells. The condition is called erythroblastosis, or Rh disease. The amount of damage varies, but can threaten the baby's life.

Fortunately, a substance called Rh-immune globulin can be injected into the mother to protect the fetus. Rh-immune globulin contains Rh antibodies which attach to and destroy the Rh-positive cells before they have an opportunity to turn on the mother's own antibody production. The Rh-immune globulin antibodies are then absorbed so that none are present at the next pregnancy.

A very few women carry antibodies against the Rh factor without being aware of it. Some have received transfusions of Rh-positive blood during surgery or after an accident; other have had an early miscarriage of an Rh-positive fetus, without an injection of Rh-immune globulin afterward, or, rarely, without knowing that the miscarriage occurred. For these reasons, it is important for an Rh-negative mother to furnish her obstetrician a complete medical history, including all previous miscarriages.

Vaginal cultures. Fluids obtained from the vagina may be tested for gonorrhea, herpes, or other infections that might harm the infant at birth. In many states these tests are mandatory.

Ultrasonography, which resembles marine sonar, is now the most commonly used method of visualizing the fetal growth and position, because it involves no exposure to radiation. High-frequency sound waves are transmitted through the mother's abdominal wall. Bouncing off the fetal form, their "echoes" translate into images on a screen, according to distance traveled, and form a discernible outline of the fetal body. Ultrasound tells whether or not the baby is developing normally; it may also be used to establish whether the fetus is sufficiently mature for cesarean delivery.

A **stress test** begins by injecting the hormone oxytocin or by stimulating the nipples to induce mild uterine contractions similar to those of labor. The contractions and the baby's heartbeat are then monitored electronically to determine whether the baby can withstand normal birth or be better delivered by cesarean section.

Lung-maturation tests determine whether an unborn baby's lungs are sufficiently mature for delivery. There are several types of lung-maturation tests, of which one of the most common is called the shake test. In this test, amniotic fluid is removed by amniocentesis, diluted with alcohol, then shaken by hand or machine. After 15 minutes, bubbles at the top of the sample are examined. If they have formed a complete ring around the edge of the test tube, safe delivery is possible; if there are no bubbles, the fetal lungs are not yet mature.

Amniocentesis is not a test but a procedure for obtaining amniotic fluid, which may then be used to obtain information about various conditions. Usually performed in the doctor's office and relatively quick and painless, the procedure is normally safe for the fetus and does not markedly increase the likelihood of miscarriage.

Under local anesthesia, a long, thin needle is inserted through the abdominal wall to extract a small amount of the amniotic fluid surrounding the fetus. In the laboratory, cells from the fluid are examined chemically or microscopically, depending on the information being sought.

The procedure is most commonly performed in mid-pregnancy, about 15–18 weeks. A primary purpose is to conduct chromosomal studies to determine if the fetus carries a chromosomal abnormality that lead to Down's syndrome, a form of retardation; the chances of the abnormality are markedly increased in mothers over 37 years of age.

The sample also may be used to reassure parents that a fetus is free of certain blood or enzyme abnormalities that "run in the family," and may be used to determine the baby's sex in cases where a sex-linked hereditary disorder, such as hemophilia, must be considered.

Nearly 100 hereditary conditions, mostly very rare, can be detected prenatally by amniocentesis. Genetics counselors say that the test should always be conducted when family history points to disorders such as hemophilia, certain disorders of the nervous system, inborn errors of metabolism such as Tay-Sachs disease, and muscular dystrophy. They say that finding the child free of the condition brings a great relief to worried parents, and when a defect is disclosed, the doctor is alerted to the need for prompt treatment.

Amniocentesis also may be performed later in pregnancy when the mother has suffered infection which could have damaged the fetus, or to determine the fetal stage of development before a cesarean delivery is attempted. In those cases a lung-maturation test also may be performed to determine the risks of delivering the infant.

A final use for amniocentesis may be to treat suspected conditions in the fetus until it is mature enough for delivery. In those cases, medication may be injected into the amniotic fluid via the amniocentesis procedure.

Chorionic Villus Sampling (CVS), available since the end of the 1980s, has the potential to replace amniocentesis for most prenatal diagnoses.

Like amniocentesis, CVS takes place in the doctor's office and causes little discomfort. Using ultrasound as a guide, the obstetrician either uses a needle through the abdomen or inserts a special catheter through the cervix, applying gentle suction to obtain a sample from the chorion, finger-like projections of the placenta attached to the uterine wall.

Women undergo CVS much earlier than amniocentesis: at seven to nine weeks rather than four months. An additional advantage: Technicians test the tissue immediately and deliver results in a few days. Fluid from an amniocentesis contains only a small number of fetal cells; these must multiply in culture for several weeks before testing is possible.

Both procedures seem comparable in diagnostic accuracy. Perhaps because CVS disturbs the fetus at a much earlier date, bleeding and miscarriage are slightly more common than with amniocentesis.

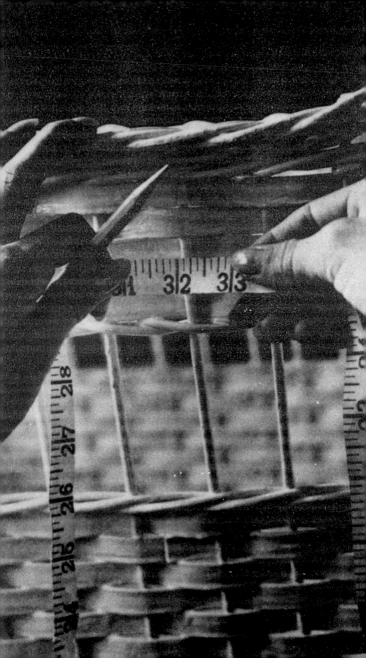

CHAPTER
5

Getting Ready for the Baby

Outfitting a newborn can be expensive, but, fortunately, you don't have to buy everything beforehand. Beyond some basic equipment and a small wardrobe, most items can wait until the baby has arrived. In fact, it's sensible to limit your clothing purchases at first, because they're often outgrown before they're outworn.

Most cities have stores specializing in furniture and clothing for infants. And you can usually find a baby section in large department or discount stores. An experienced clerk can best answer your questions and give you advice on how to get the most for your money.

You need not buy everything new, of course. If you're penny-wise or on a limited budget, a little searching may turn up serviceable used equipment and apparel. Garage sales can be excellent sources of inexpensive nursery furnishings. With luck, they'll need only a little sprucing up or repair. School or church rummage sales are good places to pick up secondhand clothing. Classified advertising sections often include baby furniture for sale. Some communities now have stores specializing in used baby equipment. And, of course, you can expect hand-me-down items and gifts from friends and relatives.

Try not to spend your money on frills. Furniture, in particular, should be bought to last for several years; don't be seduced by Mother Goose motifs. Choose items that are easy to take care of: clothing that is simple and easily laundered and furniture that is sturdy, safe, and easily cleaned.

A ROOM FOR THE BABY

Your first impulse may be to keep the baby in your bedroom at night, to simplify feeding or just because you're worried you might not hear nocturnal cries. Resist it. A room of the baby's own is important both for parents and for child. A baby sleeps more soundly where he or she will not be disturbed or interrupted.

Meanwhile, you should live normally without tiptoeing about. During the day, you can close the door to the baby's room while he or she is taking a nap and continue with your own activities. At night, you'll still be able to hear the baby while retaining your own privacy.

The nursery needn't be large. All that's required is enough space for a crib or bassinet, a dresser for clothing, and a lamp. The room should be well ventilated, not drafty, and not too hot. Seventy to 72 degrees Fahrenheit is about right. In cold weather, especially, proper humidity is important, so the baby's throat and nasal membranes don't dry out—30 percent humidity is recommended. If you have a forced-air furnace or other form of dry heat, a humidifier for the furnace or a room-size humidifier may help.

The decor in the nursery is up to you, of course, but it should be kept simple for ease of care. Pastel colors such as pink, blue, and yellow are traditional, but any lively hue will do in this age of washable, easy-to-clean paint. Babies actually prefer bright primary colors, some tests of perception seem to show. Vinyl tile, sheet vinyl, or a rug of synthetic fiber is best for the floor. Paint walls or secondhand furniture with a washable enamel.

BABY'S FURNITURE

A tiny newborn requires only a tiny bed. Most parents today begin with a portable crib, a scaled-down model of a full-size crib. It's made of fabric over an aluminum frame, with mesh sides. Most models fold flat and will fit in a car trunk, to be taken along when traveling or on visits to relatives. Leg height is adjustable, allowing the crib to double as a playpen. The standard size portable crib is 24 by 38 inches, large enough for a baby to use for seven to nine months.

The traditional "first bed" is a bassinet, a wicker basket on wheels, and it's still a popular choice. A bassinet is hip high, just right to bend and lift the baby, and can be wheeled easily from one room to another or even outdoors for naps or airings. The most useful model comes in two parts; a wheeled stand that is collapsible and a basket that can be lifted off and carried.

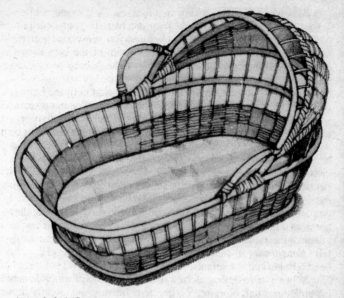

A new baby's first rest stop may well be a bassinet. About 16 inches wide and 32 inches long, it's a convenient, temporary bed for the baby. If you don't want to buy a bed, you can easily make one from a drawer, laundry basket, or box.

A bassinet probably made sense in the days when people had large families and there was always a temporary occupant. Today it may not be economical. The standard-size bassinet is 16 inches wide and 32 inches long. Because the average newborn is about 21 inches, you can see a bassinet won't be used for any length of time. After about three months, the baby will be too large, with too many kicks and squirms. Also, a bassinet is top-heavy and older children, in their eagerness to see the baby, may yank on the edge and tip it over. The cost of a bassinet is about three times that of a portable crib.

Of course, you needn't buy a bed; you can improvise one. A well-padded, good-size laundry basket makes a perfectly adequate baby bed. Or use a dresser drawer or cardboard box, lined and padded with a folded blanket. You won't have a movable platform, of course, but you can set the box or basket on a table to reach it more easily.

Now also is the time to buy an infant seat for the automobile—a rear-facing, inclined, dynamically tested model. (See pages 194–195 for carseat safety standards.) Even on a first trip home from the hospital, an infant should never be transported in the parent's arms. If you purchase a secondhand model, read the label to be sure the seat complies with government standards.

You may want to acquire a crib now or wait until the baby is ready for it. This will be your baby's bed for three or more years, so choose wisely. New cribs must now meet government safety regulations. The mattress and the inside dimensions of the crib must be the same for a snug and safe fit; $27^1/2$ inches by $51^7/8$ inches has become the standard mattress size. Slats can be no more than $2^3/8$ inches (six centimeters) apart, so a newborn's head cannot be accidentally wedged between them. (Those antique brass cribs seldom meet these standards, so be sure to insert a padded bumper). The two-stage locking device in the drop rail must be secure against accidental opening, and the dropside panel, when lowered, must be at least nine inches above the mattress so the baby cannot accidentally tumble over it. In addition, all the hardware on the crib must be safely beyond the infant's reach.

When you're buying a crib, also look for one in which panels on both sides can be raised or lowered. Be sure the lever is in a place where the baby cannot reach it from inside as he or she grows older. A model with an adjustable mattress height is preferable because the mattress may be kept raised for convenient lifting while the baby is small, then lowered when he or she is larger.

If you've bought or been given a secondhand crib, check it carefully for safety features. Be particularly sure the latches on the side panels are secure and won't pop open if the baby leans on the top rail or if the crib is bumped from below. Replace all hardware that seems worn, and mend or replace broken slats or rails.

Buy a foam-rubber bumper at least six inches high and install it around the perimeter of the mattress. The bumper should be tied tightly in place. Make sure the mattress fits snugly.

WHAT YOU'LL NEED FOR THE BABY'S BED

Baby's bedding needs are few. Both a portable crib and a bassinet usually are equipped with a standard-size, waterproof mattress. For a portable crib, you can buy full-size crib sheets for use later, and tuck the excess fabric under the mattress. Fitted sheets for bassinet mattresses are available, or you can use a pillowcase from your own bed. A flannelette or rubberized pad under the baby protects the sheet or pillowcase. For a crib, here's what you'll need:

Mattress. Be sure it's firm—a baby's bones are still somewhat soft in the early months and good support is needed. Most new mattresses are designed with steel innerspring coils under a thick layer of foam rubber and a waterproof plastic covering. Small vents on the sides of the mattress allow air to circulate and prevent moisture from collecting. The reversible mattress should be about four inches thick.

Like cribs, new mattresses must meet government safety regulations. They must be of standard size, made of flame-retardant materials, and must maintain their shape. Hypoallergenic materials (those not likely to cause allergies) are recommended. Remove all plastic packaging material and destroy immediately.

Mattress pads. A quilted mattress pad of cotton or synthetic fiber between mattress and sheet allows the mattress to "breathe" and keeps the baby cooler. You'll definitely need a quilted pad if you have an older, cotton-filled mattress.

Sheets. Crib sheets, like full-size bed sheets, come with mitered (fitted) corners. Choose a soft synthetic or cotton fabric that launders easily and requires no ironing. A government regulation requires that crib sheets be flame-retardant. You can buy them in many decorative patterns and designs.

Small moistureproof pads. One of these goes between baby and sheet for added protection. They also can go on laps, on furniture, or beneath the baby when diapers are being changed. You can buy them in several convenient sizes or in a large sheet, which you can then cut to suit your needs. A handy size is about 12 by 14 inches; it will protect most of the area around a newborn. You'll need about six.

Cotton blankets. You'll need four to six, large enough to cover the baby. They need not be tucked under the mattress.

Heavier blankets. Two are sufficient. Buy lightweight or thermal blankets or a down- or acrylic-filled comforter.

OTHER NURSERY FURNISHINGS

As mentioned earlier, a good crib will have the following features: panels (with secure, two-stage latches) on each side that can be raised and lowered; an adjustable mattress height; an inside dimension matching the mattress size; constructed so that all hardware, latches, and levers are out of the baby's reach; and manufactured with slats that are not more than 2⅜ inches (six centimeters) apart, so a newborn cannot accidentally wedge his or her head between them (see page 86 for more information).

Babies are small, but they need frequent changes of clothing.

A chest of drawers should have at least three roomy drawers to accommodate a growing wardrobe. If you're buying a new one, choose a durable model with washable paint and a mar-proof top that you also can use when changing the baby's diapers. Some are available with a padded top that can be removed when the child is older.

A comfortable chair (many mothers and fathers prefer a rocking chair) allows you to feed the baby, nurse the baby, or just spend some relaxing moments together. A footstool placed nearby lets you prop your feet up. Add a small table beside the chair to place items needed for feeding.

A dressing table or other surface for changing the baby is handy if the dresser top isn't practical. It should be padded and moistureproof. A bathinette-dressing table with convenient compartments below for diapers and clothing is nice but may be an unnecessary expense. Make sure that whatever you choose is the height of your hip, so bending and lifting are easier.

You'll want a shaded lamp or night-light so you can occasionally peek in at your sleeping baby without disturbing him or her.

A covered pail for soiled diapers may be kept in the nursery or bathroom. A diaper service, if you decide to use one, usually furnishes a deodorized container. If you launder diapers at home, buy a pail that will accept a standard-size plastic bag for soiled diapers. Even if you do neither and use disposable diapers, a container should be used. You should fasten the plastic bag securely before

disposing of it in the garbage. The nursery also should have a hamper for soiled clothes and a wastebasket. And you'll probably want some pictures, mobiles, or other decorations to catch the baby's eye.

THE BABY'S BATH NEEDS

Now is a good time to choose a place to bathe the baby. Using the bathtub for a newborn is neither convenient nor safe. It requires more water than necessary and you must kneel to use it, so that you are in an awkward position if the baby slips. Some parents use the kitchen sink or buy an oval-shaped plastic baby tub, big enough for the baby to kick and splash in. There's also an inflatable type of tub, which can be deflated and stored between baths.

Buy a fitted sponge liner for the sink, available in most baby equipment stores. The sponge provides a soft cushion under the baby and reduces the possibility of slipping, allowing you to hold the child with one hand and wash with the other. It also serves as a nonskid surface for sponge baths. You can clean it periodically by washing in the top rack of the dishwasher. A large folded towel in the bottom of the sink also helps to steady the baby.

A small tray or basket is handy to keep all the bath articles together, so they can be carried from place to place. Here's a list of bath necessities:

• Mild, pure soap. A castile-based soap is least drying. Liquid soap in a bottle or tube is less wasteful.

• A soap dish or jar.

• Diaper pins with plastic heads. You may wish to use diaper clips, which are easier to open and close. (Even if you don't use cloth diapers you'll occasionally reclose a disposable diaper.)

• Cotton balls.

• Soft, terry cloth washcloths—at least two.

• At least four bath towels large enough to wrap the baby completely. Receiving blankets also may be substituted for towels.

• A bath apron. Babies will splash.

Baby powders, lotions, oils, and creams are a matter of personal choice, but aren't necessary. Powder may be dangerous because it can be drawn into the baby's lungs, and cornstarch, sometimes used as a substitute, can be a medium for yeast infections. A baby's skin is naturally soft. Adding oil or cream may prevent air from keeping skin dry and may promote rash.

You'll want to stock a small medicine chest, including a rectal thermometer (a child's temperature is taken rectally until the age of four) and a nasal aspirator with a two-inch bulb. Most doctors discourage the use of cotton swabs to clear a baby's nose and ears because the sticks may damage delicate membranes.

THE WELL-DRESSED BABY

The baby's basic wardrobe will be partly determined by where you live and what time of year he or she is born. A baby arriving in June in Atlanta obviously won't need as many clothes immediately as a child born in December in Minneapolis. Don't overstock; babies grow quickly. To start, buy the six-months size for maximum wear.

Be prepared to bathe the baby in the kitchen sink or a plastic tub. Necessities: mild soap and soap dish or jar; diaper pins; cotton balls; washcloth; bath towels; an apron (for you to wear). Baby oil, cream, powder, or lotion are not recommended.

Buy clothes because they fit the baby's needs, not because they're cute. A basic wardrobe for the well-dressed baby may include: diaper and plastic pants, undershirt, a one-piece jumpsuit, booties, and light sweater.

Because most homes today are centrally heated, it's unnecessary to swathe a baby in layers and layers of clothing. Most of the time, the basic outfit consists of a diaper and plastic pants (or a disposable diaper with its own plastic cover); an undershirt; and a nightgown, sacque, kimono, or one-piece jumpsuit. On hot days, you may even discard the outer layer. For trips outdoors or in cooler weather, the baby will need a light sweater and a blanket wrapper.

In buying, remember the objective is to keep a baby comfortable, not hot. Wrapping warmly won't prevent colds—infections result from exposure to other persons, not from being chilled. And overheating causes perspiration and skin rash, especially in the diaper area.

Pick clothes for convenience, not because they're cute. They should be easy to put on and remove, equipped with snaps or zippers, and readily turned back or opened for diaper changing. A full-length kimono or hip-length sacque both leave the feet exposed, so you'll need socks or booties; the shorter sacque lacks a skirt and thus cuts down on the amount of wet fabric. A nightgown tied beneath the feet will keep the baby covered completely. A blanket sleeper with zipper will keep the baby warm even when he or she is active enough to kick off blankets.

A popular baby garment is the one-piece jumpsuit that snaps from neck to ankles, allowing it to be opened completely for diaper changing.

Buy these in stretch fabrics, which will expand somewhat as the baby grows and can be worn when he or she is old enough to crawl.

There will be a lot of spilling, spitting up, and soiling, so choose clothes that can be laundered easily. Synthetics, washable cottons, and permanent-press fabrics are best. Blankets should be acrylic. Choose hypoallergenic materials when available.

If you are able to do the wash daily at home, you'll need fewer garments than if you're sending clothes to a commercial laundry or taking them to a self-service laundry.

Here is a suggested first wardrobe:

• Six undershirts—opening at the front, with side snaps, or pullover with adjustable neck and short sleeves.
• Three kimonos, long-sleeved, with snaps.
• Three sacques, short-sleeved, with snaps.
• Six jumpsuits, full-length, with snaps.
• Sweater, synthetic and washable. (You'll probably get one as a gift.)
• Six receiving blankets.
• Four plastic pants.
• Two treated cotton or silk waterproof pants for dress occasions.
• A dozen diaper pins, with plastic heads, or diaper clips.

For an outer wrap, a wool or acrylic blanket usually is handier than a baby coat or baby bunting, which a newborn quickly outgrows. A baby hat is cute but seldom fits properly and won't stay on. Instead, wrap the baby in a blanket and cover the head. A quilted zipper bag with a hood will completely cover the child and protect against cold weather.

WHAT KIND OF DIAPERS?

The baby won't care about the style of diapers, but you will. Disposable paper diapers are popular because they keep the baby drier and eliminate laundering, but present a disposal problem; legislation banning their use has been proposed by environmentalists. A diaper delivery service is usually more costly but particularly handy in the early months when you're especially busy. Some parents find it less expensive and more convenient to own and launder their own diapers, especially if more than one child is wearing them.

Whether you choose paper or cloth, however, you'll want some of the other kind for emergencies; even if you choose diaper delivery, you'll need about a dozen of your own.

Disposable diapers are used more than any other kind, according to their manufacturers, and can be bought in almost any drugstore or supermarket. They're made with a plastic outer liner to retain moisture and protect the clothing and an inner thickness of soft absorbent paper next to the baby's skin. The manufacturers say the paper layer can be shredded and flushed down the toilet, but the plastic must be removed and discarded, for environmental reasons. (If placed in a refuse bin, they should always be sealed in a plastic bag.) Disposables come in a variety of sizes, fitting newborn to toddler. Most brands are made with self-adhesive fasteners that eliminate the need for pins.

A diaper delivery service will bring freshly laundered diapers to your home once or twice a week, usually three dozen at a time, and will furnish a deodorized diaper container with a fitted plastic bag. Some services will wash the rest of the baby's laundry, too, for an additional fee. Diaper services now operate even in small communities, although in some places, there may be a waiting list for their services. Ask your friends which services they've been pleased with, or consult the yellow pages of the phone book.

For your own diaper supply, you can choose from three basic styles—flat, stretch, and prefolded. The first two are made of a thin oblong fabric, which can then be folded and refolded to fit the baby. You change the folding pattern as the baby grows. Prefolded diapers are a single sheet of cloth, with an extra thickness in the diaper area.

Automatic washers with presoak cycles and special diaper rinses now simplify home laundering of diapers. It's important, however, to be sure that all detergent is rinsed from the diaper during the cycle, because some detergents can cause a skin rash.

6

Your Part Before and After Delivery

The last few weeks of pregnancy are a time of eager anticipation and busy preparation. Whether the mother is still working outside the home or is at home counting down the days, there are a lot of last-minute chores to be completed before the baby arrives to take a place in the family circle. It's a hectic period, but parents will be buoyed by the realization that the countdown has almost reached zero and the nine months will soon be over.

Of course, you'll have weary times when you wish the baby would please hurry and end your discomfort; the ninth month often brings breathlessness and sleepless nights. And during these last weeks both parents may begin to have waves of trepidation. How will we know when real labor starts? Will it be painful? What if I'm out shopping or traveling when labor starts? Can I be sure to reach the hospital in time?

Be reassured. Although most women fear labor will start in the middle of the night, only about one in four pregnancies actually requires an early-hour trip to the hospital. Studies show the number of hospital admissions is approximately evenly spaced around the clock. As many women in labor arrive between the daylight hours of noon and 6 p.m. as appear between midnight and 6 a.m.

We already know the baby arrives at the baby's convenience, not yours, because only one baby in ten is born on the presumed due date. You probably won't be warned very far in advance, so the best idea is to be ready for a summons at any moment.

GETTING READY TO GO

About the beginning of the ninth month; pack a small suitcase for your trip to the hospital. Then, if there's a hurry-up call, you won't have to rush about looking for things at the last moment.

Hospital stays after uncomplicated delivery now last only one or two days; except in cases of cesarean delivery you won't need to take many items to the hospital. Even if you do overlook something, it can always be brought to you. The essentials are a comb and brush, toothbrush and toothpaste, robe and slippers, bed jacket, and cosmetics. At first, you may wear hospital gowns, but you'll probably want to discard them as quickly as possible in favor of something more attractive, so bring a gown from home.

If you're planning to breast-feed, you'll need a nursing brassiere. The size is sometimes difficult to gauge in advance, however; ask the hospital if brassieres can be fitted and purchased there. If not, buy the adjustable kind. You might need sanitary napkins and a belt; they're usually provided by the hospital.

Wear a wristwatch (which can be checked for safekeeping during labor and delivery), but otherwise leave valuables behind, especially credit cards and more than a few dollars in cash. You may wish to bring a checkbook, tissues or handkerchiefs, address and phone directory, pen, stationery, and stamps. Take that book you've always wanted to finish, although with caring for the baby, rest periods, visitors, and television, you'll have plenty of activities to occupy you.

Pack a coming-home bag for the baby beforehand, too. Hospitals may provide disposable diapers and an undershirt or gown. Depending on climate and time of year, you'll also need a shirt, sweater, receiving blanket, and perhaps a heavier blanket. If you haven't already done so, buy a car seat for the baby, who should *not* be brought home in your arms.

You also may want to select in advance those clothes you'll wear home from the hospital. They can be brought to you on the date you're discharged. Remember that you won't yet have regained your pre-pregnancy figure, so the maternity clothes you wore early in your pregnancy probably will be the best fit.

If it's your first baby or you haven't a family physician, arrange now for a pediatrician to examine the baby. The pediatrician also will care for the child after the hospital stay, so you'll want to choose carefully.

If you're planning to use a diaper service, sign up now. You'll need a supply waiting when you and the baby return home.

If you're planing for a friend, relative, or visiting nurse or homemaker to live in and assist you for a few days after you return home, make arrangements at this time.

After that, there's little to do but wait.

LIGHTENING

Probably the first sign your baby is *really* on the way is one you'll greet with relief. One morning, after weeks of puffing like *The Little Engine that Could,* you'll wake up to find your breath comes easily again. If you observe yourself in the mirror, you'll see your figure has changed—the bulge is lower in the abdomen.

"Lightening" has occurred, to use the popular term. The baby has descended in the pelvic cavity. (You also may feel shooting pains down the legs, the result of pressure on nerves in the pelvic area.) A first-time mother may experience lightening at any time during the last four weeks before birth, although sometimes it does not occur until labor has started. Women who've previously borne children usually do not lighten until the last week or ten days and frequently not until just before delivery.

LABOR

If you've attended childbirth classes, the mechanics of labor probably have been explained to you. In labor, the uterine muscle contracts, like the contractions of any muscle. The contractions squeeze the baby and the bag of waters downward toward the cervical opening. Here, the tissues have become thinner as the result of a process called effacement (see page 18), during which tissues of the cervix are drawn up into the uterine walls. Normally, the opening is about the diameter of a pencil lead. The pressure of repeated contractions widens the opening to many times that size to allow the baby's head to pass through. Dilation of ten centimeters, or four inches, is considered the proper measure. Your doctor or the nurses in the labor room may speak of it in terms of fingers—each finger representing two centimeters of dilation.

The process of labor sometimes is compared to putting on a turtleneck sweater. The opening is smaller than the head, but the head steadily pushes until it gradually widens the opening, progressing farther and farther until it ultimately pops free. As with the sweater, the opening afterward reverts to its former shape, but the process will never be so difficult again.

Labor is said to occur in three stages, although they actually blend together, coming one after another in a continuous sequence of events.

The first stage of labor is the longest, covering the period from the time the cervix begins to dilate until full dilation has been reached. It sometimes is further subdivided into early and late labor. Early labor is somewhat like an athlete's warmup. The muscle contracts at long intervals, loosening up for the real work during late, or hard labor, which pushes the baby little by little down through the cervix and into the birth canal. The initial contractions during this first stage of labor may be weak and 20 or more minutes apart, but they gradually become longer, stronger, and more frequent, with each one inching the baby slightly farther along the road to birth. The length of this stage is partly determined by the number of previous births. Twelve to 15 hours is not an uncommonly long period of time for the first baby. Later labors often are considerably shorter.

The second stage is sometimes called "transition" labor. It includes the period from full cervical dilation until the baby has passed through the birth canal and into the outside world. Contractions now are about two to three minutes apart and last 45–50 seconds each. The contractions are involuntary, and the mother assists, almost by reflex, in pushing with her abdominal muscles, as in a bowel movement. In a normal birth, the baby's head is forced out first, followed by one shoulder, then the other, then the body and legs. For a new mother, this stage of labor may last an hour or more. In later deliveries, transition labor may be over within a few minutes.

Labor's third stage also is known as placental labor. The placenta, which has nourished and supported the budding life for nine months, is cast off by the uterus now that it is no longer needed. The placenta often is called afterbirth. There is little or no pain at this stage, and it lasts only a few minutes. The doctor may hurry the process by massaging the uterus through the abdomen just above the pubic bone. Some bleeding may follow, but loss of blood throughout delivery seldom exceeds one pint.

HOW TO KNOW YOU'RE GOING INTO LABOR

Three distinct signs indicate your labor is about to begin. They may occur in any order, and you may be unaware of the first two. They are:

"Show." A small amount of reddish or pink mucus tinged with blood is passed from the vagina. This material represents the plug of mucus that has closed off the uterus during pregnancy. Dilation of the cervix dislodges the plug and pushes it out the birth canal. Show may precede or accompany the initial contractions of labor. Once it occurs, labor commonly begins within 72 hours.

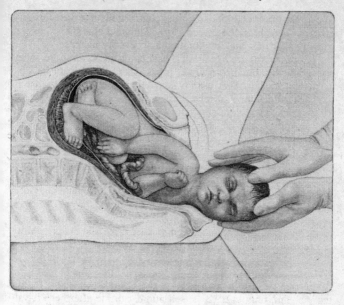

"Transition" labor ends with the baby's grand entrance into the outside world. Pushed along by involuntary uterine contractions and the mother's voluntary use of her abdominal muscles, the baby usually arrives head first.

Breaking of the bag of waters. Pressure from the early contractions may rupture the amniotic sac of fluid surrounding the baby; or the rupture may actually precede contractions. Depending on the size and location of the tear, there may be a gush or a trickle of water from the vagina. Labor usually follows within a few hours. If this happens, you should phone your doctor, or, if you are not at home, proceed to the hospital and phone from there. The need for notification doesn't mean that ruptured membranes are dangerous; many normal labors begin this way. The reason to get you under observation because the baby is no longer protected against infection.

Contractions. Everyone has these, the unmistakable signs of labor. You feel them as labor pains, but that popular term is less commonly used today because people believe it exaggerates the discomfort. Contractions first make themselves felt as a mild backache, accompanied by a weak cramp in the abdomen, somewhat like a menstrual cramp. The initial contractions may last for only 10 to 20 seconds and be spaced 20 to 30 minutes apart. The interval steadily shortens, and the duration and severity increase.

Contractions are like the surf beating on an ocean shore. They rise gradually, build to a crest, break, then die away to be succeeded by another. They usually signal their coming by a twinge in the back, which then switches to the abdomen and becomes steadily stronger, holds a crescendo for a brief period, and then ebbs. In the transition stage of labor, sensations are closer together, with brief letups between.

A mother giving birth for the first time should call her physician when contractions are about five minutes apart—depending on how far she lives from the hospital. A woman with previous children should call when she feels contractions at 10-minute intervals.

If any of these signs should occur before the thirty-sixth week of pregnancy, they should be brought to your doctor's attention immediately, as they may indicate premature labor and the possibility of premature birth.

FALSE LABOR
About one woman in ten rushes to the hospital with labor seemingly begun, only to have the sensations subside after her arrival. These false alarms often resemble genuine labor, because they are uncomfortable, with pain occurring at intervals. You may be able to distinguish them from true labor, because they occur irregularly, not predictably, and do not increase in intensity. You may even find that they disappear when you change position in bed or get up and walk around—which does not happen during true labor. But don't rely on your own judgment to decide whether your labor is true or false. If there is any doubt in your mind, phone the doctor.

OFF TO THE HOSPITAL
Once you're fairly sure you're in labor, time your contractions. Wait until they've reached the appropriate interval, and then seek your doctor's instructions. Don't take medication for the pain or eat solid food, which could complicate matters if you require anesthesia later.

And don't worry—you'll reach the hospital in time. Babies arrive in the family car or the backseat of a taxi so rarely the occurrence rates coverage by the local paper or a spot on the television news. And on those infrequent occasions, a husband who's attended childbirth-preparation classes (or a police officer or paramedic) is qualified to help with delivery. So just keep the car's fuel tank filled, plan your route to the hospital beforehand, and set off without delay—but not at a breakneck speed.

As Chapter 4 showed, today there are several types of childbirth care available in modern hospitals; what'll happen when you reach the hospital depends partly on which method you've chosen. Probably, you'll be met with a wheelchair and taken to a "prep" room. If you haven't preregistered, your husband or whoever has accompanied you may be asked to see that you're registered.

First, you'll be checked to be sure you're in labor. Your doctor or another member of the obstetrical team will conduct the first of many abdominal examinations to determine the baby's position and will listen by stethoscope to the heartbeat. Your vagina also will be examined to determine the extent of cervical dilation.

You'll be issued a hospital gown, and your temperature, blood pressure, and pulse will be taken. You also may be given an enema, although this is not always routine. Intravenous feeding also may begin at this time.

IN THE LABOR ROOM

When preparations have been completed, you'll be transferred to a labor room, usually a small, simply furnished cubicle equipped with a bed, nightstand, chair, and sometimes a television. You may share the room with others. Most hospitals now permit a husband, friend, or "labor coach" from your childbirth-preparation classes to remain with you in the labor room.

You'll be comfortable here. Nurses or other members of the obstetrical team will visit regularly to determine how you're progressing.

Between contractions, you'll be able to converse with your visitors or even read; it's a time, too, to practice your breathing exercises (see page 72). You may even doze off between contractions. If you wish, the doctor may now give you a sedative or pain-reducing drug.

Occasionally, the doctor may choose to insert a small tube or catheter through the cervix into the uterine cavity to more accurately measure the frequency and intensity of contractions. This is particularly true if it becomes necessary to administer medication to increase uterine activity. The procedure isn't uncomfortable and you'll probably be unaware of the catheter's presence.

ELECTRONIC FETAL MONITORING

To provide an additional set of eyes and ears, some hospitals routinely use an electronic fetal monitor in the labor room. Although monitoring helps in managing a difficult pregnancy, experts continue to debate whether it improves the outcome of a normal pregnancy. Obstetricians are also divided, so some use a monitor on all women while others limit it to those having problems. With this device, electronic sensors are placed on your abdomen and connected to a monitor at the bedside; sometimes, the signals are sent to the nursing station, too. The machine continuously records the contractions and the baby's heartbeat. If the heartbeat falters, which might indicate a decrease in the oxygen supply or that squeezing of the umbilical cord has reduced blood, an alarm sounds and attendants come.

Monitoring is not painful, and does *not* necessarily indicate that yours is a problem-filled delivery, calling for extra vigilance. Usually, the electrodes are held in place by a strap circling your abdomen, but in another system they are tucked inside a stockinette, which resembles a pair of pantyhose with the feet cut out.

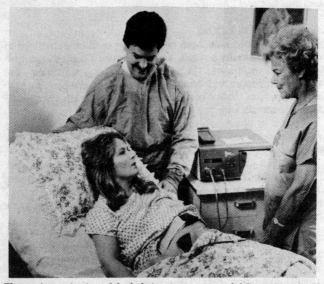

Electronic monitoring of the baby's progress toward delivery is a routine procedure in some hospitals. Sensors on the mother's abdomen monitor and record contractions and the infant heart beat. Most hospitals allow fathers and friends to be present during monitoring.

Contractions may temporarily diminish blood flow to the uterus, so you may be asked to lie on your side rather than your back during part of labor. This position provides better blood flow to the uterus and thus more oxygen to the fetus.

Another system of monitoring sometimes is used when a better signal is needed. When dilation has reached about four centimeters, the bag of waters is broken, and an electrode is applied directly to the baby's scalp. This technique is more sensitive and may be substituted when a clear impulse cannot be received through the abdomen. It is also sometimes used for closer surveillance of prolonged or premature labors.

IN THE DELIVERY ROOM

When the cervix is fully dilated and you have entered the transition stage of labor, you'll be moved to the delivery room—unless, of course, you've chosen a birthing-room delivery. A delivery room will look like any operating room you've seen in the movies—bright lights, a long table, and nurses and doctors in masks and gowns. An anesthesiologist may be standing by. Your own obstetrician will be there and perhaps one or more hospital staff physicians.

Your husband, friend, or labor coach may be present, too, in most hospitals, to offer encouragement and support. They may be required to wear caps and gowns, also. The number of visitors probably will be limited, and the hospital may reserve the right to ask them to leave in the event of an emergency.

Again, what happens next depends on the method of delivery you've chosen. If you received a spinal or general anesthetic or an epidural block, you'll lie on your back during delivery. Your legs will be elevated and covered with white cotton stockings. A sheet will be draped over you, so that only your hands, face and the birth area are visible.

Or you may assume a semisitting position, back resting against a portion of the table that has been partially elevated. This posture enables you to push more easily.

This is your big moment. Your husband or labor coach will encourage you to thrust downward with the pelvic muscles, as you've learned, to help the baby emerge from the birth canal. If no companions are present, you'll get the same encouragement from nurses and medical staff.

At the moment of birth, the doctor will ease the baby out with gentle pressure. If you're lying down, your newborn will be lifted high for you to see and to hear the first cry. The baby will receive a name bracelet; the umbilical cord will be double-clamped and the eyes washed out with silver nitrate or antibiotics to offset possible infection. The baby's nose will be aspirated to clear it of mucus, and you may be able to hold your baby in your arms for the first time right at the place of delivery.

INDUCED LABOR

If labor is prolonged or delayed, the doctor may take measures to start or expedite the process. Such intervention may be particularly called for if there are indications that the length of the labor is causing distress for the baby. Induced labor doesn't mean that you can have a delivery to order. It does not succeed (and, in fact, can be dangerous to both mother and baby) unless labor has already begun or is clearly about to.

Rupturing the bag of waters surrounding the baby usually will bring on labor within about 12 hours. The membranes are broken by the doctor in the hospital by puncturing them with a sterilized instrument. A few doctors perform this painless process routinely to speed up labor, but most prefer to do so only if necessary, because, as one obstetrician says, "There's no turning back once the bag of waters breaks." That's because breaking the waters destroys the sterile environment, allowing for possible infection. Also, the bag of waters appears to serve as a cushion for the baby's head during the contractions of labor.

An intravenous method of inducing labor uses a synthetic version of the natural hormone oxytocin. Oxytocin itself is one of the hormones that increase in quantity around the time of birth, although its exact role and interaction with other substances never has been established completely. The administration of oxytocin usually will bring on labor (if it is imminent) within minutes, and it will dramatically speed up the strength and frequency of contractions if they have already begun. It also may be used to stimulate or augment labor that has slowed.

Some doctors believe that births may be more difficult for both mother and baby if labor is induced. At least one study has shown more heartbeat irregularities occur when oxytocin is administered, and another indicates that the hormone hurries the labor to completion before the mother's systems are coordinated. On the other hand, hundreds of thousands of births have been initiated with oxytocin, with success and safety for both mother and child. In any case, a doctor is likely to use induced labor only as a last resort, and in no case should a woman attempt to bring on labor herself.

EPISIOTOMY

The vagina, which doctors describe as a "potential space," can open wide to accommodate the emerging baby, thanks to accordionlike pleats of tissue making up the vaginal walls. But the perineal muscles controlling the vaginal opening may not relax sufficiently to permit an untraumatic birth. The result may be a jagged tear in the perineum, between the vagina and the rectum. To prevent this, the doctor may make a straight incision about two to three inches long in the perineum, using a local anesthetic such as novocaine and closing the incision afterward with absorbable sutures, which need not be removed later.

This procedure, called episiotomy, occurs more often in the U.S. than abroad. Many doctors believe that a clean, straight incision heals more normally than an irregular tear. Others say that such tears are too rare to justify a routine episiotomy. Ask your obstetrician to explain his or her policy.

FORCEPS DELIVERY

Forceps—two metal blades that, joined together, look like the tongs used for serving salad—often have been called the "woman's best friend." When a labor is particularly difficult and prolonged, and natural forces seem unable to expel the child through the cervix, the doctor may remove the baby with the aid of the forceps. The two blades are shaped to fit the curve of the baby's head. First one blade is inserted into the birth canal and placed on one side of the head; the other then is placed on the other side and the handles brought together at a central joint. The doctor applies firm but gentle pressure on the handles and draws the baby from the canal.

Forceps cannot be used unless the cervix is fully dilated and the baby's head is visible; under these circumstances, forceps delivery is considered safe, but it is not recommended simply as a means of shortening labor. With forceps, the baby may be born with pressure marks on the cheeks, but these disappear within a few days.

CESAREAN DELIVERY

Birth through the abdominal wall rather than the vagina—a surgical procedure called cesarean section—is much more common than in the past. One of six babies in the U.S. is now born this way, and in some hospitals the proportion is even higher.

A cesarean section may be undertaken for a number of reasons. Failure to progress in labor is one of the most common. The mother's pelvis may be too small to permit passage of the baby's head, and both dilation of the cervix and descent of the head may cease. Excessive vaginal bleeding also may require prompt delivery for the sake of the mother, the baby, or both. Occasionally the baby's life may be endangered by a reduced oxygen supply during labor, and the operation may be necessary to save the child's life. And, when the baby "presents" abnormally—lying crosswise in the uterus, for instance—the doctor will frequently need to deliver by cesarean section. For example, in a so-called breech presentation (buttocks first), the umbilical cord may be kinked, twisted, or extruded during labor and may cause a diminished oxygen supply during this difficult delivery.

A cesarean section usually requires about an hour to an hour and a half. Under a regional or general anesthetic, an incision is made in the lower abdominal wall, usually at or near the pubic hair line, so the scar will be less noticeable afterward. An incision then is made in the lower portion of the uterus and extended until it is large enough for the baby's head to emerge. The surgeon then lifts out the baby, head first, then shoulders, trunk, and legs. The uterine incision is repaired, followed by that in the abdominal wall. Both usually heal quickly enough for the woman to go home within three to five days.

One reason for the increase in cesarean deliveries is that they are considerable safer than in the past. A cesarean now is considered less risky than a difficult vaginal delivery, although less safe than a normal birth. The procedure still is not considered routine, however, because of the attendant risks of general anesthesia and major abdominal surgery.

The wider use of electronic fetal monitoring also partly accounts for more cesareans. Medical personnel now are alerted to the first indications of fetal breathing difficulties and can intervene in a hurry to save lives that might be jeopardized by allowing the labor to continue. Most hospitals now are prepared to spring into action quickly if a cesarean is needed. The American College of Obstetricians and Gynecologists' list of community hospital standards requires that a maternity ward be equipped to set up and perform a cesarean within 30 minutes.

In the past, women who had undergone one cesarean received cesareans for all further deliveries because doctors believed that the uterine scar was a weak point, likely to rupture during contractions. During the 1980s experts concluded that this was not so and began to encourage a trial of vaginal delivery. Many obstetricians have adopted this approach for women who have had a cesarean, although others continue to advise surgery.

AFTER THE BIRTH

Your first stop will likely be a recovery room, where you can be watched closely for several hours. Your baby will be taken to the nursery, cleaned, and bathed. You'll probably see the newcomer within a few hours and may be able to assist in caring for the baby then.

The first hour or two after delivery is critical, and you'll be visited frequently by nurses and other attendants, some of whom will wish to examine or massage your abdomen. They are checking for delayed hemorrhage, a serious postnatal complication, and to be sure that the healing process has begun. You may wear a sanitary napkin to absorb blood.

Even without drugs or anesthesia, you'll probably feel woozy and tired after the delivery; having a baby is hard work. Within a few hours, however, you should feel refreshed and strong enough to take a few steps, and by day's end, you'll be able to sit up and have visitors—or even to go home.

SECTION

2

Birth to Two Years

Now you are parents. It is
an experience as old as time
yet ever new. No one can predict
exactly how it will be for you—
how great the difficulties, how
rich the rewards. Right now the
task may seem insurmountable.
You may feel overwhelmed
and unprepared. But with time
will come skill and confidence,
fed by love, understanding,
and concern.

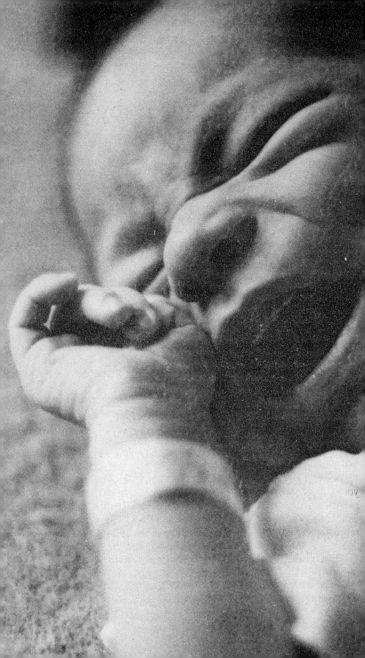

CHAPTER
7

A New Life for Baby— and You

After nine months of eager anticipation, your first reaction to your new baby may be one of absolute shock. All along, you've pictured a rosy-cheeked, brightly scrubbed infant like the one on the baby-food jar, but your newcomer will be, to put it charitably, a mess.

The baby will be wet, blood-spattered, and coated with a white, waxy substance (vernix caseosa, or cheesy varnish) that protects the skin and lubricates passage through the birth canal. Fine, downy hair—lanugo—may cover cheeks, ears, and back. Vernix matted in the lanugo may give the baby a strange, pasted look.

You may note that the baby's head looks misshapen. It may seem pointed at the back or lopsided. There may be lumps, protrusions, or swellings. The ears may look pinned back against the head or forward against the cheeks. The nose may look flattened. If yours has been a forceps delivery, there may be red marks on the baby's cheeks or temples.

Whether your own race is white, black, yellow, or brown, your baby's complexion may be mottled with a bluish tinge. It'll be particularly noticeable around the lips, nail beds, palms, and soles; whte babies may be bluish from head to foot. The skin may be wrinkled and loose, perhaps with scaling in the creases of the arms and legs. The baby's legs may be so bowed that the soles actually face each other or the feet may be pointed inward, as in pigeon toes.

And the breathing! It will probably be a series of snorts, snuffles, rattles, and sneezes, punctuated by shallow breaths coming about three times as fast as your own. Small wonder parents often think, "Did we do this?"

Relax! All these characteristics are normal reminders of what the baby's been through for nine months. The vernix will dry and flake off within a few days. (Some hospitals bathe the baby within the first few hours, but others leave the vernix to protect the baby's skin during the transition to the outside world.) The lanugo will disappear within a few months.

An asymmetrical head shape is caused by the tight squeeze through the birth canal, a passageway that is about a centimeter narrower than the diameter of the baby's head. Because the skull bones have not yet joined (hence the "soft spot" on the baby's crown), they can flex and overlap enough to facilitate the baby's passage. It can be a week or two before the skull returns to a normal configuration, a year or more before the bones join together.

The lumps and protrusions result from the head pushing against the cervix during contractions; they're harmless and gradually disappear, along with any marks from the forceps. The bluish tinge will vanish, too, as the baby's circulatory system matures and delivers more oxygen to the tissues. The legs are bowed because they've been curled up for nine months; they'll straighten over the next year or two. As for the noisy breathing, it will continue intermittently for three or four months because of the baby's small nasal passages and insistence on breathing through the nose even when it is partially plugged. Breathing will gradually quiet down, although several years will pass before its rapid pace slows to the adult rate.

THE BABY'S APGAR SCORE

One minute after birth and again at five minutes, a member of the obstetrical team assesses the baby's "Apgar score" and may call it out for you to hear. Named for the late pediatrician, Dr. Virginia Apgar, this score is simply a quick gauge of the baby's condition at birth. The baby is given a rating (from 0 to 2) on each of five measures: heart rate, respiratory effort, muscle tone, color, and response to stimuli. The maximum total for a normal baby is 10.

A very low score, especially when duplicated in the second assessment, calls for immediate medical intervention, but a score of 4 to 7 at one minute is not necessarily a cause for alarm. It simply warns the pediatrician to keep an eye on the baby during the coming days and weeks. Even if the score is low at five minutes, with prompt medical attention the long-term outlook is good. Few babies achieve a rating of 10 even at five minutes (one doctor jokes that he only gives a 10 to children of colleagues as a professional courtesy); 8 or 9 is normal and does not indicate any deficiency in the baby.

Not all hospitals voluntarily disclose the Apgar score, but most will do so if you ask. They stress, however, that the score is not a competition and that parents should not misinterpret a less than perfect score.

WHAT IS THE BABY THINKING?

You may find your baby alert and ready to socialize from the very first minute. Although newborns vary, and some are sleepy at birth, many enjoy a quiet alert phase in which they observe and absorb this bright new world so different from the darkness left behind. If placed in your arms or on your chest in the delivery room, he or she may stare right into your eyes.

Babies used to be compared with newborn kittens, their senses unresponsive to their surroundings. A series of ingenious tests has shown that newborn children are much more aware of their environment than previously had been believed.

Your baby can see you, for one thing. It used to be thought that babies couldn't focus until eight weeks because they didn't smile until then. Now, tests show that even babies less than 24 hours old can discriminate clearly between images. In one test babies were propped in a box so their visual field was limited. Two images were projected, with a doctor studying the reflection of the image on the babies' pupils. The test showed that newborns preferred watching some images more than others, usually choosing bright colors and bold patterns. Above all, they were attracted to the human face.

Your baby also can hear. Ring a bell and the baby will be startled and perhaps try to locate the sound. He or she will respond to

the sound of a human voice. Films of children in the first weeks of life show that they move their arms and legs in a predictable manner when the mother speaks but not when others do so. Your baby can smell, too. He or she will react to a strong and unpleasant odor; by five days, the sense of smell is discriminating enough to distinguish mother's breast from another. Reflexes are developing, too. If you prick a baby's foot, the other foot comes over and attempts to kick the offending needle away.

MOTHERING AND FATHERING

Within minutes of birth, both parents may be encouraged to hold and nuzzle the newborn right in the delivery room—the first step in tying the lifetime knot that unites child to mother and father.

This get-acquainted time is important—as well as enjoyable— for all three of you. It may last a few minutes up to an hour, if the baby is in what doctors call the "quiet alert" phase. You'll find your baby responds to touch, warmth, skin-contact, a soft voice, and gentle handling. That's why mothers the world over sing to their newborns and croon lullabies to them.

Don't feel disappointed, though, if this idyllic first meeting doesn't occur for you. Some babies are born sleepy, or if yours was a particularly difficult delivery, several hours may pass before you and your baby meet for the first time. Doctors now agree that there is no critical period for parent-child bonding and that the lifetime bond is just as strong if that first meeting is delayed for hours or even days—even if the delay is for years, as in the case of adopted children.

Tender loving care comes naturally to most people, but some are more spontaneous about expressing it. Parents sometimes feel that newborns are very fragile and perhaps should be handled only gingerly or not at all. It's true babies can't support their heads at birth—that's why you cradle yours in your arms—but they're surprisingly durable creatures who thrive on physical affection. Some doctors believe that babies in institutions suffer most from lack of flesh-to-flesh contact, and other studies have shown that newborns prefer physical contact to food.

WHAT WILL THE BABY LOOK LIKE?

Your newborn seven-pounder will offer some clues at birth— though not many—to his or her appearance as an adult. The arrangement of facial features, the set of the eyes, the shape of the head usually won't change drastically with the years. If your baby resembles father, mother, or cousin Sally at birth, that resemblance may still be noticeable in adulthood.

Other features, though, are less reliable—coloring, in particular. To predict the baby's future complexion, look in a mirror, because it will probably resemble the parents'. Ruddiness tinged with blue at birth will lighten gradually; by the third day, the complexion and eyes actually may appear yellow—a kind of jaundice caused by an immature liver not yet completely able to excrete a chemical from the blood. By the first week's end, the yellow will have given way to pink.

Your child's hair may be dark, blond, or red, thick or sparse—depending partly, of course, on ancestry. That won't mean much either. Baby hair will begin to drop out by the fourth month, and for a time he or she actually may appear bald. Your baby will be nearly a year old before baby hair has been replaced totally by a more permanent crop. As for future eye color, most white babies are born with blue eyes, a few with brown; brown eyes retain their color, but blue ones may change sometime during the first six months. You may get a clue to the probable change by the presence of dark flecks in the iris.

It'll be some time before the baby resembles a miniature—but well-proportioned—human being. At birth, the head comprises one fourth of the baby's length; the chest is narrow, the limbs foreshortened. Even if the baby appears fat, it's no clue he or she will be fat in maturity.

TESTS AND BIRTH CERTIFICATES

By law, your baby's birth must be recorded with state authorities. It's a simple procedure: A nurse or aide will visit your bedside and obtain pertinent data, including parents' names, nationality, citizenship, and the child's given name, length, and weight. Your obstetrician or attending physician signs the form to certify his or her presiding at the birth, and the application is filed, usually by computer, with the state central registry. There is no fee.

You'll receive a certified copy of the document by mail, usually within a month. Always review it to be sure the information is correct, then store it in a safe place. A birth certificate is an important document in your child's life. It's required for enrolling at school, proving citizenship, and obtaining a passport, among other formalities. If you lose it, fortunately, you usually can obtain a duplicate for a few dollars.

About an hour after birth, the baby's eyes will be treated with

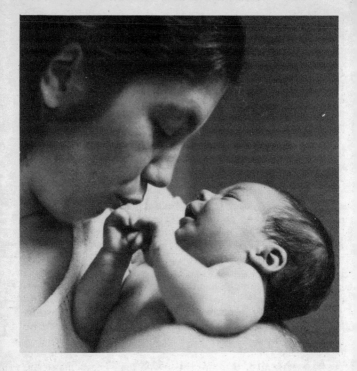

Getting to know you. The parent-child attachment called bonding begins early. Many doctors and hospitals encourage both parents to hold the baby only minutes after delivery.

silver nitrate or erythromycin. This treatment is compulsory in most states to prevent potential blindness if gonorrheal infection is present at birth. It does not suggest that either parent has a venereal disease. Silver nitrate may cause the baby's eyes to redden and swell, which is why the procedure now usually is delayed until the baby has passed the "quiet alert" phase (the first hour after birth). In most states, the baby also receives an injection of vitamin K, which aids blood clotting.

Some states also require other tests to detect several types of inborn defects of metabolism that can cause retardation and death if not detected. Any problems usually can be prevented with a treatment begun shortly after birth. These simple tests involve nothing more than obtaining a small blood sample from the baby's heel for immediate testing.

CIRCUMCISION

For religious or other reasons, you may wish to have your baby boy circumcised. In this minor operation, the foreskin, or movable fold at the end of the penis, is trimmed away. The operation usually is performed within three days of birth.

Circumcision has been practiced for centuries, and the majority of American male babies today are circumcised. But, religious strictures apart, circumcision's medical value still is questioned. Advocates maintain that circumcision helps to keep the penis clean and reduces the chance of infection; that it protects against cancer of the penis; that it lowers the risks of adult prostate cancer; and that women married to circumcised men have less cervical cancer than the general population. But these claims have largely been refuted.

In 1971, a committee of the American Academy of Pediatrics, investigating circumcision, concluded there was "no valid medical indication for routine circumcision." Four years later, the committee reviewed the subject and found no reason to change its original conclusion. The 1975 report agreed that infection and penile cancer had been shown to be lower among circumcised boys in primitive populations. Teaching uncircumcised American boys to keep their penises clean avoided the risks of surgery and was as effective or nearly as effective, the committee reported. The pediatricians found no convincing evidence that circumcision in infancy protected against prostate or cervical cancer decades later.

The committee said that circumcision should never be performed on premature babies, those with congenital defects, or those with known bleeding problems, and the committee advised that circumcision be delayed until the boy was at least 12 hours old. The committee suggested that parents discuss the topic with the physician in advance so a thoughtful decision could be reached before delivery.

IN THE HOSPITAL

Unless delivery was by cesarean section, you'll probably remain in the hospital only one to three days and perhaps go home in a matter of hours. You won't be bedfast. You're likely to be on your feet within an hour or two of birth and ambulatory most of the time you remain in the hospital.

Most hospitals are liberal about visitors and visiting hours, but you'll still find some restrictions. The father usually can visit without restriction throughout the day, but other visitors may be limited in number and to specified hours; they may be able to see the baby only in the nursery through a glass partition. These rules are to protect the baby against germs and infections. Children under 16, if they are permitted to visit, usually are restricted to areas outside the maternity ward.

You may not want many visitors. Although you'll rapidly regain strength, you'll probably find that you tire easily and need to rest frequently during the first few days. You may wish to postpone visits with friends until you return home.

ZIGZAGGING BACK TO NORMAL

As soon as your baby is born, the uterus begins a most remarkable vanishing act. Its function temporarily ended, this organ, which has sheltered the young life for nine months, shrinks to its normal size in a process called involution. After birth, you can feel it through the abdominal wall—a large, hard, globular mass about the size of a volleyball. Six weeks later, it will have shriveled to a mere two ounces and reverted to its normal dimension.

For four or five days after delivery, you will have a heavy discharge of blood mixed with castoff by-products of the delivery. The flow, called lochia, usually will be deep red and about as profuse as your heaviest menstrual day. Gradually, the color will turn from red to brown; after about ten days, it will have a yellow or white tinge and will be considerably lighter. Lochia usually stops within two weeks, but there is great individual variation among women and, indeed, among deliveries. A flow of four weeks isn't unusual, but if it persists longer than this, resumes after it has stopped, has a bad odor, or exceeds your heaviest normal menstrual flow, tell your doctor.

Involution usually is painless, but some women have menstrual-like cramps that persist for a few days. They are less common among first-time mothers than among those who previously have borne children. The pains result from attempts by the uterus to expel small blood clots remaining after delivery. Afterpains are seldom serious, but if they continue more than a week, notify the doctor.

If an episiotomy was performed to widen the birth canal, the stitches may make sitting a bit uncomfortable for a few days until they're absorbed by the body. You may wish to sit on an inflated cushion for comfort. Rarely, the area swells. An ice pack may reduce the swelling.

Even before you leave the hospital, you may wish to begin exercises to strengthen the abdominal muscles and help regain your figure. Your physician or a nurse may demonstrate very simple exercises you can perform within a day or two of delivery. Those to be performed at home are demonstrated on page 122. You'll want to continue daily exercises at least through the first six weeks. (For more on postnatal exercises, see pages 133 and 135).

THE AFTER-THE-BABY BLUES

An unexplainable bout of the blues strikes two-thirds of new mothers sometime in the first six weeks after delivery. One minute you seem happy, on top of the world; the next, you may burst into tears or be plunged into what seems like bottomless gloom. Later, the episode will subside as mysteriously as it began. "It just came over me," you may explain.

Anxiety, depression, mood swings, crying, and easy distraction are some of the ways the blues manifest themselves. And when you think about it, these emotional upheavals aren't really so mysterious. You've been through quite an ordeal. A psychiatrist once compared so-called postpartum depression to combat fatigue.

There also may be a physiological explanation. After birth, secretions of the female hormones, estrogen and progesterone, drop dramatically. The amount of hormones circulating in the bloodstream affects the emotions; not coincidentally, some women feel similarly depressed when the production of female hormones drops during menopause. There is an obvious link between hormonal secretions and emotions—a link which isn't fully understood.

WHEN WILL MENSTRUATION RESUME?

The resumption of menstruation is irregular. Periods usually begin no sooner than four to eight weeks after delivery; three to four months aren't uncommon. If you breast-feed your baby, menstruation may be delayed even longer (see page 127)—perhaps for six months or as long as the baby is fed only with breast milk. Periods usually start two to four weeks after nursing stops.

The first period after childbirth may be unusual—shorter or longer or heavier than you have been accustomed to. The second period—which may not occur at your regular interval—will be more normal. Several months may pass, however, before periods occur as regularly as they did before pregnancy.

Don't be fooled by the mistaken idea that you can't become pregnant until menstruation resumes or as long as you're nursing. Many women have learned to their dismay that both are incorrect. Your first menstruation signals that ovulation—the fertile period—already has taken place. Breast-feeding (see page 127) does seem to inhibit both ovulation and menstruation but usually only so long as the baby is breast-fed completely, and it is not uncommon for a woman to ovulate while breast-feeding.

EXERCISES AFTER THE DELIVERY

Exercising is important to tighten the muscles and restore your figure. You can begin the exercises on this page one or two weeks after delivery.

Abdomen strengthener (below)
To firm the abdomen, lie on your back with your knees bent. Inhale gradually, expanding the chest and abdomen. Pull in the abdomen, spreading the ribs. Then exhale. Now pull in the abdomen again, and press the lower back against the floor or bed. Hold the position for a few seconds, then exhale and relax. Repeat each phase of the exercise ten times. The exercise may be done in your hospital bed.

For the back and abdomen
Two exercises for back and abdomen (top, next page) begin on hands and knees. First, lift your head and look at the ceiling, creating a hollow in your back and letting the hip muscles go slack. Repeat three times, then rest your head on your forearms. Repeat three times, four times daily. In the second exercise, pull your abdomen up toward your spine, arching the back and tightening the hip muscles. Tuck head down to look at your knees. Keep your back completely rounded. Repeat five times. Alternate the two exercises four times daily after birth.

Midriff firmer (above and right)
The exercise helps to tighten the muscles in this area. On hands and knees, swing hips from side to side. Turn your head in the same direction with each swing, so your waistline is tucked in on the side to which your head is turned.

For exercises after six weeks see pages 133 and 135.

RESUMING INTERCOURSE

The old rule about resuming intercourse was: "not for six weeks." A more common view today limits the period to two weeks, because the cervix remains dilated for that length of time and intercourse might introduce germs to the area. (For the same reason, you should not use tampons during the first two weeks after delivery.) After that, the resumption of intercourse is strictly up to you, to resume when you feel ready. Intercourse may be uncomfortable until an episiotomy has healed. Decreased vaginal wall thickness and lubrication during nursing also may cause discomfort. You may wish to use a lubricant. Some form of contraception should be used. If you are nursing, however, avoid oral contraceptives. Substitute another form of contraception.

BREAST-FEEDING IN THE HOSPITAL

You may be invited to put the baby to your breast in the delivery room. Although your breast milk won't appear for two to four days, the baby still will find the nipple and nurse through his or her rooting reflex. Immediate nursing isn't just for the baby's welfare. Nursing stimulates the secretion of oxytocin, which helps to contract the uterus, forestall hemorrhage, and promote the return of the organ to its normal size.

According to figures reported to the U.S. Surgeon General, 61 percent of American women now plan to breast-feed their babies, and the figure is more than 90 percent among certain population groups and in certain parts of the U.S. Even nearly half the women returning to work outside the home said they planned to nurse their newborns. These figures are all considerably higher than during the decade of the 1960s, when breast-feeding was at its low point.

The pendulum has swung strongly in favor of breast-feeding, and most authorities would agree that this natural method of infant nourishment has benefits for both mother and child. Still, some women prefer *not* to breast-feed and others feel themselves unable to do so, or quickly stop. And the American Academy of Pediatrics, while strongly endorsing breast-feeding (see p. 125), has noted that children can grow up healthy without human milk.

Like many other aspects of childbearing and rearing, there are strong and emotional arguments on both sides, and in the end breast-feeding is a matter for individual decision—or rather, one to be decided by mother and father jointly. Listen to both sides before entering the hospital, and make up your mind for yourself. You may feel strong pressure from family or friends to breast-feed or not to breast-feed; in some hospitals and communities it may be simply assumed that you will do so. Don't be swayed by others. Instead, think out for yourself how breast-feeding may affect your and the baby's life. And feel free to change your mind and stop nursing if the experience is less than successful.

WHAT IF YOU DON'T BREAST-FEED?

The American Academy of Pediatrics encourages breast-feeding as a matter of policy but adds: "Normal growth and development are possible without it." Many babies have been formula-fed from birth and have thrived on it—you may have been one of them. Obviously, adopted babies, whose new mothers have no milk supply, also grow up healthy.

Some women strive valiantly to breast-feed but aren't successful despite their best efforts. Others simply don't feel able to breast-feed or don't wish to do so. Some feel they'll be tied down by breast-feeding.

There's another important reason some couples today favor bottle-feeding: it includes the father. Bottle-feeding gives parents an opportunity to share equally in this important part.

In these cases, the hospital nurses will introduce the baby to formula-feeding and show you how to give the baby a bottle, so that once you've gone home you'll be fully prepared.

Whether you feed by breast or bottle, be sure the baby gets plenty of affection. Cradle, nuzzle, talk to, and allow the baby to cling to you for support. Love and the emotional bonds of parenthood are at least as important as the nutrients contained in the milk.

BREAST-FEEDING AND HEALTH

"Human milk is for the human infant; cow's milk is for the calf." With those words, the late nutritionist Dr. Paul Gyorgy once summed up the pro-breast-feeding side of the continuing controversy over the comparative value of breast milk and its most common substitute.

Even the commercial manufacturers of formula acknowledge that breast milk is the most appropriate nourishment for newborns. And despite conscientious efforts, manufacturers never have been able to duplicate breast milk, although their products contain all essential nutrients.

But are breast-fed babies healthier? They certainly are in less developed countries, where hygiene, water purity, and refrigeration aren't up to Western standards. In the U.S. the picture is less clear, with some studies seeming to show fewer health problems among the breast-fed, and others showing no difference in the health of breast- vs. formula-fed babies when such variables as economic status are considered.

The La Leche League International, the organization that has done most to foster the return of breast-feeding in the U.S., firmly advocates breast-feeding for infant health reasons and cites these purported advantages:

• **Fewer infections.** Breast-fed babies appear to have fewer intestinal infections and fewer respiratory infections, according to research conducted by several investigators. There also is said to be less diarrhea, spitting up, and constipation. Breast-feeding seems to protect against enterocolitis, a condition that is common among bottle-fed babies. Natural immunity to polio, measles, mumps, and other viral infections appears to be prolonged among the breast-fed.

• **Fewer allergies.** Eczema and other common skin rashes of infancy are less frequent among breast-fed babies, the La Leche states on the basis of several research studies. The breast-fed babies also have fewer allergic sensitivities in later childhood and adulthood. Of course, those babies who are breast-fed exclusively also are free of infancy's most common allergy, a sensitivity to cow's milk.

• **More consistent growth.** Human milk is utilized more quickly by the body, one reason breast-fed babies are fed more frequently than bottle-fed babies. Breast milk also provides the exact nutrients, in the proper quantities, that the baby needs for growth. Because breast milk is digested easily, it can be used immediately.

Other doctors question these conclusions, saying that carefully designed studies have failed to support them.

The American Academy of Pediatrics (AAP), however, has suggested that bottle-fed babies may have more problems with obesity later—a concern in overweight America. The AAP statement said that formula-feeding parents may push babies to consume the full amount offered, which can pile up unnecessary ingredients the body cannot use immediately, and lead to poor eating habits in adulthood.

IT'S NOT JUST MILK
When it was first reported that breast-fed babies had fewer infections, it was thought they were healthier because their supply of food was protected against contamination. More recent investigation shows that breast milk transfers disease-fighting antibodies

from mother to child, including white blood cells that combat infection.

The flow of antibodies begins even before the milk itself arrives. Colostrum, the yellowish fluid that comes from the breast before delivery and continues after the baby is born, is a chief source of immunizing substances. It also contains a substance that has a mild laxative effect on the baby, to clear the young digestive system of meconium, the fetal waste. And it has the proper proportion of proteins and fats for the baby's early feedings.

PSYCHOLOGICAL BENEFITS

Nursing sometimes is called the very essence of mothering, and the benefits to both mother and child may go well beyond merely providing nutrition.

At the mother's breast, a baby not only satisfies the need for food, but apparently the equally universal need for warmth, security, and love. And in a subtle way, the rhythm of the mother's movements introduces the baby to the rhythm of life. For the mother, breast-feeding fulfills her own need to nurture and love. The two-way exchange of gratification helps to cement the bond between mother and child that continues for a lifetime.

The bond formed in breast-feeding is not something unique to American women and their infants. It extends across a wide spectrum of primitive and sophisticated societies, according to Dr. Derrick Jelliffe, of the University of Southern California School of Medicine, who has studied nursing practices in cultures and countries throughout the world. For both mother and child, Dr. Jelliffe says, breast-feeding seems to satisfy a universal emotional need.

Of course, there are more prosaic advantages to breast-feeding: it's inexpensive, it's convenient, and it's easy. You don't have to prepare formula, sterilize bottles, or clean up afterward. The supply is always on hand in the right amounts and at the right temperatures. When you travel, you don't have to pack anything—the supply travels with you. And the La Leche League estimates that you could hire cleaning help for six months with the money you save on commercial formula and baby food!

CAN ANYONE BREAST-FEED?

The size of a woman's breasts has nothing to do with the ability to nourish her child. Milk production isn't determined by the amount of breast tissue, but by a network of vessels and canals within the breast. The woman who wears a small bra has just as extensive a network as does her more amply endowed neighbor. Some women believe they cannot breast-feed because their nipples are flat or are turned inward. Patience and special care—augmented by some relatively simple exercises—usually can overcome these difficulties for most women.

The production of milk is an intricate and self-regulating process, but almost every mother produces enough milk for her baby. Interestingly, in France before World War II, 38 percent of mothers breast-fed their babies; but during the war years when other forms of milk were scarce, 90 percent found themselves able to do so. Also, the milk you produce will almost always be rich enough for the baby's nutritional needs.

BEGINNING TO BREAST-FEED

Your milk will arrive about the third day after delivery—a little earlier if you've previously had children, later if the baby is your first. (In another of those miracles of timing, the schedule will be exactly the same, even if your baby is premature.) Before the milk itself arrives, the substance colostrum will drain from the nipples, and it will continue to be an ingredient in the breast milk for about ten days.

If you're not planning to breast-feed, your doctor may give you an injection to dry up the milk. Indeed, such injections are routine in some hospitals but apparently do not seriously impair your ability to breast-feed if you continue to put the baby to your breast. When the milk arrives, your breasts may feel full, swollen, and sore. The milk may leak from the nipples onto your clothes, so you may wish to wear a folded handkerchief or pad inside your bra. Although an inconvenience, this drainage is not a hindrance to nursing.

You'll probably begin nursing the baby well before you have milk to deliver. Babies usually are put to the breast within four hours of birth—and, of course, sometimes immediately after delivery. You'll probably feed the baby every two to three hours after that, more frequently than if the baby were bottle-fed.

Breast-feeding comes naturally, but you'll get some advice and instruction from the nurses. Or you may wish to read La Leche League books or pamphlets beforehand. Many of these are available through the hospital or doctor's office, or can be obtained by mail from La Leche League International, P.O. Box 1209, Franklin Park, IL 60131.

At first, you'll probably want to nurse the baby lying down. (Later, this will be your choice for night feedings at home, so you

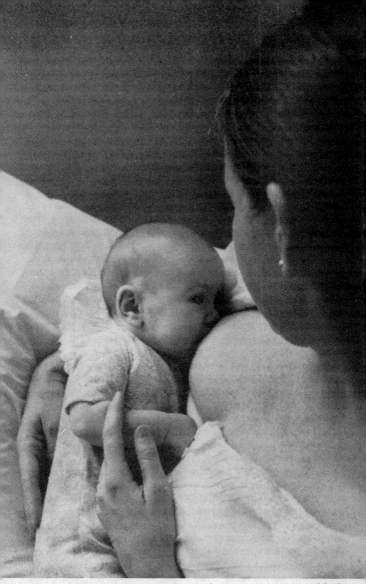

Breast-feeding is the most popular—and most nutritious—way of feeding an infant. Nursing offers both psychological and medical advantages, but babies flourish on formula-feeding, too.

can doze while the baby nurses.) If you're feeding from the right breast, lie on your right side and place your right arm over the baby's head or under it, whichever is more comfortable. Use your left hand as a steering hand. Pull the baby toward you until his or her cheek touches your breast near the nipple. The baby will turn toward it instinctively, but you can give a little assistance by holding the nipple between your thumb and forefinger and guiding the baby toward it. Lift your breast from beneath, so the nipple is directed toward the mouth, and see that the baby takes the brown area around the nipple into the mouth as well. Then pull the baby's feet toward your body so the angle allows him or her to keep the nose free.

If you nurse sitting up, choose either a low, comfortable chair with arms or the corner of a sofa. Remember, you'll be there awhile, so arrange yourself in a relaxed position that takes the strain off the muscles in your arms, neck, and back. A rocker is often a good choice. Sit well back in the chair, and place a pillow under your elbow on the feeding side; or double a pillow under the baby so that he or she can reach your breast without your bending forward. Hold the child in the crook of your elbow in a semisitting position, guiding the baby toward the nipple with your free hand. When you change breasts shift the pillows and support to the other side.

When the baby has finished or you're changing breasts, gently press your breast away, inserting your little finger into the corner of the baby's mouth to reduce the suction on the breast. Don't yank the baby away from the breast; this may cause sore nipples. If the baby shows little interest in feeding or begins to doze, stroke the mouth or cheeks to stimulate the rooting reflex. If you can't wake the baby with gentle handling, don't worry; it won't hurt if he or she sleeps through a feeding.

At first, your baby may not show much interest in feeding. Appetite usually picks up when the milk itself arrives after a few days. As you gain more confidence, too, the baby may begin to eat more, because you will produce more milk. Nurses may suggest (or even automatically provide) a supplementary bottle of formula. Breast-feeding advocates discourage this practice because they say the baby becomes accustomed to the easier feeding by bottle and because the mother's milk supply is affected. The less you feed, the less milk you have and the more chance of sore or fissured nipples.

Like many aspects of mothering, breast-feeding is an individual matter. You'll probably work out your own techniques after a little practice. Usually, it's a good idea to offer both breasts at each feeding. Start the baby on one side, then stop for a rest or a change of diapers, then switch to the other breast. At the next feeding, first offer the breast used last. You might attach a small safety pin to your bra to remind you which one it was.

HOW MUCH AND HOW OFTEN?

Some babies are gourmets and some are barracudas. The gourmets nurse daintily, seemingly savoring every drop, while the barracudas greedily latch onto the nipple and never let up. That's true whether the baby is breast-fed or bottle-fed. Babies' eating habits, like those of adults, are strictly individual.

Babies will tell you when they are hungry. In the hospital, he or she may be brought to you for feeding every four hours, but that interval is set more as a convenience for the staff than for any nutritional reason. Breast-fed babies usually want to be fed more often than their bottle-fed contemporaries, because breast milk is assimilated more quickly. Fed on demand, a breast-fed baby usually will nurse every two to three hours, sometimes with one longer interval during the day.

How much depends on how soon the baby is satisfied. You'll soon be able to gauge that for yourself. About three to five minutes on each breast is a good beginning while you're in the hospital and until your nipples have become conditioned. Later, you'll probably offer the first breast for about ten minutes, the second for at least that period and perhaps longer.

Don't worry that you won't have enough milk for the baby. Nature has its own self-regulating mechanism. The more milk the baby takes, the more the mother supplies. If you have twins, the body produces enough milk for twins. If the baby's appetite drops, the milk supply drops, too. If it drops too far, the baby will nurse more often and production will pick up again.

About a week after your milk comes in, you may lose the full feeling in your breasts, and the spontaneous leaking of milk may stop. You may think you have lost your milk. But this is simply evidence of supply adapting to demand. As nursing begins, there may be an oversupply of milk until the baby has established a daily quota. Then the supply drops to meet the demand.

At first, even though your breasts feel terribly full, you may find the baby is dissatisfied, cries, and turns away from the breast. That's because the breasts are so full the area around the nipple is swollen. The nipple then is depressed and cannot reach the baby's hard palate, which it must do in order for the baby to feed properly. You may correct this problem by hand-expressing milk from the nipple until the breast reaches a more normal configuration. Nurses can demonstrate hand-expression, or you may try it for yourself; hold the nipple between your thumb and forefinger and squeeze gently, but do not pull. Remember that hand-expressing milk also affects future supply.

Your milk supply is governed by what is called the let-down or milk-ejection reflex. It's a psychosomatic reflex, affected by how you feel. If you're anxious about your ability to nurse, this tension interferes with milk supply and the amount the baby can receive. Doctors say anxiety is the leading cause of unsuccessful breast-feeding. On the other hand, confidence and eagerness to breast-feed enhance the milk production.

WORKING AND BREAST-FEEDING

One reason you may decide not to breast-feed, or may discontinue the practice early, is a desire to return to your career. According to the La Leche League, it's possible, however, to continue breast-feeding while working, and a rapidly growing number of mothers are doing so.

How this works for you will depend upon the convenience for you and baby to be united during the working day. Some women are able to breast-feed right at work, either because the employer operates an affiliated child-care center or because the person caring for the child brings him or her to the mother at feeding time. If you're working near your home, of course, you may simply return there during your lunch period.

Even if you can't be with the baby at feeding time, you can continue to provide breast milk simply by hand-expressing into a relief bottle that then can be given to the child by the person caring for him or her. Many women perform hand-expression during working hours, so that breast milk continues to be produced on schedule. The milk is then refrigerated or kept in a chilled vacuum bottle.

Women who plan to breast-feed usually do not resume their jobs until the baby is at least six to ten weeks old, by which time he or she may have reduced the number of feedings, and others wait until four to six months, when the child may obtain some nourishment from solid foods. But some women hold jobs and continue to breast-feed the child exclusively until one year or older.

THE HUSBAND'S ROLE IN FEEDING

If your baby is formula-fed, father automatically takes part. Mother and father can alternate feedings, depending on who's available. The baby isn't likely to complain.

Breast-feeding, of course, is different. But a hand-expressed relief bottle allows the father to feed the baby, especially if you're planning to go out alone, or if the father cares for the child during the day. For nighttime feeding, it can be the father's responsibility to get up and bring the child to you. Another role for the father, breast-feeding advocates say, is to provide moral support and companionship, and to encourage you to continue with this natural form of nutrition. The father also can take over a larger share of the household duties and spend more time with the other children. That leaves you free for nursing and for the routine of baby care.

EXERCISES TO BE STARTED AFTER SIX WEEKS

Routine exercises begun after six weeks will restore firmness to your midriff and abdomen, if they are performed regularly. It may take six to eight months to get your figure back.

Back builder
Sit on the floor with your right knee bent and your foot flat on the floor. Clasp your hands around the knee. Then using your back muscles, stretch your body toward the ceiling. Be sure to keep your abdomen pulled in and shoulders loose. Repeat this exercise ten times, alternating the knees after each five repetitions.

Trunk tightener (right and below)
Take position on hands and knees. Swing right arm under left side of body, reaching as far up the back as possible. Turn your head in synchronization with arm. Repeat five times per side. In second exercise (above right), swing arm under body, then raise toward ceiling. Lift head to look at arm. Repeat each five times daily.

Sit-ups (right)
Lie on your back, knees bent, feet flat on floor. Raise your head and shoulders off the floor. Reach forward with hands outside the left knee, then outside the right knee. Repeat three times. In second phase, lift head off floor slowly, then lower gradually. Try to raise your entire back.

High stretcher

Sit on stool against the wall, with back, buttocks, and head touching wall. Tuck chin in; keep feet flat on the floor, arms at your sides. Raise arms over your head; pull in your stomach until your lower back touches the wall. Be sure your arms touch your ears on each side of the head. Repeat exercise five times.

Touch the chest (below)

To do this exercise, lie on your back with your knees pulled up and hands clasping your bent knees. Pull the knees toward your chest, touching it if possible. Hold this position, then lower your legs very slowly until your feet touch the floor. Now relax and repeat the exercise. Do the exercise six to ten times. Practice it until such time as you are able to touch your chest with your knees on each movement.

Camel walk (right)

Take a "table" position, placing your palms and feet on the floor, feet 12 to 18 inches apart. Keep your knees and elbows straight, and walk around on all fours. Repeat the exercise at least five times daily, moving around the room in this manner once on each attempt. This exercise strengthens the abdominal muscles and helps to reduce the sag that usually occurs in these muscles following delivery.

CHAPTER
8

A New Routine at Home

The tiny bundle you bring home from the hospital can shake up your style of living far out of proportion to its modest size. The first three weeks of parenthood have often been called by new parents the longest and most depleting period of adult life. Considering the adjustments that have to be made in your family routine, that may be no exaggeration.

The family circle may be turned topsy-turvy. Sleeping, eating, and working may be governed by when the baby wants to sleep, eat, and socialize. Family relationships, attitudes, and feelings can be knocked off stride. If the baby is your first, the household may crackle with nervousness and anxiety.

Such strain isn't surprising. For perhaps the first time in your life, another human being will be totally dependent on you. You may face a dozen crises a day: Are we feeding enough? Are we feeding too much? Why is the baby crying? Should we pick him or her up? Is a pin sticking the child? Is the baby too warm? Is he or she too cold? Do diapers need changing?

Looking at your robust infant a year from now, you'll laugh at your beginning jitters. Babies thrive despite their parents' inexperience. The main casualties of the first six weeks are mothers' and fathers' nerves. Just relax, follow your instincts, and enjoy the baby. If you're in doubt about some detail of care for your newborn, *ask* for help—and keep asking until you get an answer that satisfies you. That's what doctors, nurses, clinics, more experienced parents, and baby books are for.

THE LARGER FAMILY CIRCLE

Whether or not you get additional help from a friend, relative (your mother or mother-in-law, perhaps), visiting nurse, or housekeeper to assist you during the first few weeks after you return from the hospital is up to you.

Some parents are made even more nervous with another person in the house; they consider a father's help plenty. But an extra pair of hands can be a godsend. First, although mothers aren't invalids, their energy levels may still be below normal. Second, temporarily delegating the household chores to another person gives parents time to get acquainted with the baby and to practice caring for the child.

These first few weeks are important for both parents and infant; don't waste your limited energies doing the family laundry or dusting the furniture while someone else cuddles the baby. Make sure that you have a considerate helper and not a houseguest.

THE OTHER CHILDREN

To you, the arrival of a new baby is a happy event, but an older—and up to now an only—child's feelings may be mixed. Once the sole occupant of the family limelight, he or she now may feel rudely shouldered aside by a demanding newcomer whose every cry brings parents running. No matter how much you reassure the older brother or sister, there's keen competition.

There are no easy answers to what psychologists call sibling rivalry. Preparation helps; before going to the hospital, explain about the baby to the other children, and try to emphasize that the arrival of the newcomer will not lessen your love for them. For children old enough to read, books about the arrival of a new baby are available. Buy younger children a doll to feed and diaper. And if the new baby was born at home or in the presence of the family in an alternative birth center, perhaps the lesson already has been reinforced. Yet the feeling of jealousy is a natural one for a small child, and the actual event may evoke some strong reactions.

A three-year-old may now insist on being treated like a baby—and behave like one. He or she may demand the bottle that had been given up months before. It's not uncommon for children long since past such stages to begin wetting their pants or sucking their thumbs again.

Fortunately, children adjust. You can't ignore their feelings, but don't chide or punish them. All you can do to ease the situation is assure them of your love for them, spend as much time as you can exclusively with them, and try to include them in caring for the new

baby. A small gift for the older child may help when someone
brings a gift for the baby. If the other child is under three, a word of
caution: he or she should never be left alone with the baby.

THE SHARING OF PARENTHOOD

Most fathers today expect to take a full role in child care, and,
according to one survey, in about one-fourth of homes, the father,
rather than the mother, will be the primary care provider. About
half the enrollment in hospital baby-care classes is male. This division of responsibilities means that in many homes decisions about
child care are mutually arrived at.

*Fathers today often take an equal—or even primary—role in child
care with mothers. In an increasing number of households, it's the
man who stays home with the children during the day.*

Still, this "new" parenthood doesn't apply to every household. Many men have never had the opportunity to change diapers or bathe an infant. Even today, some grown men have never held a baby in their arms. Part of the new mother's role may be to impart her own, possibly limited, knowledge to her spouse. The first few weeks may be a time of learning together.

Meanwhile, don't forget you are partners as well as parents. The stress of parenthood strains your relationship, too, as each of you may concentrate on the baby and neglect the other. Fathers often feel jealous of the little being who may monopolize the mother's time, while mothers seethe at the paternal pride that focuses on the offspring as it downplays her contribution.

These feelings are normal, and they can be overcome. As soon as you can possibly do so, spend some time with each other. Leave the baby with someone you can trust, and go out for the evening—even if it's only to the nearest fast-food spot.

BABY SETS A SCHEDULE

The first few days and nights with the baby will pass in one big blur, as one feeding blends fuzzily into the next. But soon you'll see that the baby's life (and therefore yours) falls into a regular routine.

In more dogmatic days, infants were fed every four hours, whether they were hungry or not. Now most doctors recommend a more flexible schedule. Babies eat when they announce they're hungry.

Baby's whims, unfortunately, aren't always convenient for you. Observe the baby's own pattern of eating and sleeping for a few days, and then construct your schedule accordingly.

Usually, a newborn will want to be fed six to eight times a day, about two to five hours apart. If you feed the baby at 6 a.m., you may expect to do so again at roughly 10 a.m., 2 p.m., 6 p.m., and 2 a.m.

But few babies are that regular. A baby may be fed at 6 a.m., ask for more at 9 a.m., then go without eating until 2 p.m. One the average, a breast-fed baby requires more frequent feedings than a bottle-fed infant; eight feedings daily at intervals of two to three hours is typical, and some even wish to be fed every hour. But appetite is as individual in babies as in adults. Your bottle-feeder may feed just as frequently or infrequently as the breast-feeder next door. And some babies simply seem to be hungry all the time, eating regularly every three hours around the clock. All these patterns are normal.

As for sleeping, a newborn averages 16 hours a day and may be drowsy or half-awake several additional hours. However, some babies sleep as little as eight hours and yet are not at all deprived of sleep.

Eventually, one nap lengthens and the number of feedings falls to five a day. This usually occurs at about five weeks or when the baby's weight reaches 11 pounds. With luck, the longer nap comes at night, and the periods when the baby is alert come during the day, when you can enjoy them.

Once you understand the baby's schedule, sometimes you can influence it. If the baby seems to sleep through a daytime feeding, wake and feed on schedule; he or she *may* take a longer nap. If the baby dozes during a feeding or falls asleep before it is finished, nudge the child so that he or she does not wake up again in two hours for refueling.

You may want to schedule the baby's bath in the morning, after the early feeding, then put the newborn to bed until another feeding is necessary. Afternoon is a good time for an airing or a stroll, when the sun is higher and the air warmer. By letting the baby catnap during the day, you may be able to keep the child awake at dinner time to socialize with the family.

Remember that the baby's welfare is important, but it can't completely dominate the family's life. When it's time for a nap, put the baby in a crib or bassinet in his or her own room, close the door, and go about your business. Do not tiptoe or caution the other children to "Hush!" Artificial silence only conditions the newcomer to wake at the slightest noise.

YOUR OWN RECOVERY

Legend says pioneer women gave birth in the morning and plowed the back 40 in the afternoon. If so, they must have been exhausted by evening. Bearing and caring for a baby are fatiguing activities.

During these early weeks, take advantage of every opportunity to rest, preferably with your feet up. Keep strenuous work to a minimum; don't set out to do the spring cleaning. Take naps when you can, because it may be difficult to get eight hours of uninterrupted sleep at night. Family finances and the strictures of your maternity leave may dictate when you return to work outside the home, of course, but a customary minimum is six weeks.

The exercises on pages 133–135 will help restore your figure by tightening the abdominal muscles that stretched to accommodate the expanded uterus. Physical activity also will help trim any excessive poundage you may have accumulated during pregnancy. A girdle helps support the abdomen. If you're breast-feeding, wear a supporting brassiere during the day and while you're sleeping.

Watch your diet carefully. Breast-feeding requires that you eat for two, but if you limit junk foods and unnecessary calories, your figure won't suffer. If you're not breast-feeding, limit the food you eat. You may have eaten larger meals during pregnancy; now try fewer than 2,000 calories daily. Proper eating and exercise can restore your figure to normal within three months.

WHEN THE BABY CRIES

Babies have only one way to communicate at first: they cry. Your job is to interpret your baby's cries and decide how to respond, if at all.

In time, translation will become second nature. You'll learn to distinguish the tired cry, the hungry cry, the I'm-lonely-someone-come-and-pay-attention-to-me cry. But at first all cries may sound alike: what *is* that child crying about?

Usually, a child cries because another feeding is in order. If the clock shows the baby hasn't eaten in three or four hours, you almost can be sure the message is "Come feed me."

When babies continue to cry after eating, it may mean they're not getting enough to eat. If you're breast-feeding, allow time for a longer feeding, or offer a supplementary bottle. If the baby is bottle-fed, increase the amount.

Sometimes the cause of crying is obvious. It may be something as simple as a soiled diaper or the discomfort of diaper rash (see page 165). A few babies cry at sudden change, or are startled by a loud noise. Some cry when they are too warm or too cold.

Older babies may cry because they're lonely. The infant, wanting to see faces and hear voices, may call for a visitor.

The cry seldom signals a real emergency. Despite parents' fears, an open diaper pin is seldom the cause. A medical explanation is equally rare and is usually indicated by other signs, such as fever, decreased appetite, nasal congestion, vomiting, and diarrhea. Thus you seldom need to drop what you're doing and respond to the baby's cries. But don't let crying continue for more than a few minutes without investigation.

THE CRYING HOUR

Some babies cry persistently without explanation. In fact, about one-fourth of the parents who visit well-baby clinics report their infants fall into this category. The crying is harmless for the baby, but nerve-wracking and exhausting for parents, particularly when they seek an explanation and cannot find one. The problem seems to be most persistent around six weeks. It may stop shortly thereafter, and seldom lasts more than three months.

For many of these babies, a daily "crying hour" develops, mostly in late afternoon, but sometimes in the morning or late at night. The baby often reddens, draws knees up to chest, and kicks and screams loudly. As each cry subsides, another begins. The length of the "crying hour" varies. Some normal infants cry six to seven hours a day.

This regular, persistent crying is sometimes called "colic," because it was previously believed to result from intestinal cramping. Most doctors now doubt this explanation. It is based on the observation that "colicky" babies draw up their legs, distend their abdomens, and pass gas. But babies do this at other times, too.

Intolerance of formula is sometimes blamed for colic, but changing the ingredients seldom lessens crying. (And breast-fed babies cry, too.) Other theorists, noting that the crying hour often coincides with late afternoon when parents are likely to be most frazzled, attribute the baby's crying to family emotional stress. Emotional stress may indeed exist when babies cry for hours on end, but it is difficult to determine which came first, crying or stress. Moreover, babies of experienced, calm parents are not immune from crying.

The most logical (and comforting) explanation for persistent crying is a developmental one. Babies cry because their nervous systems are still maturing. The regular daily pattern and the fact that the baby seems to "grow out of it" by the age of three months, no matter what steps are taken, supports this point. It is further substantiated by folklore parents have known for centuries that soothing, rhythmic sounds and motions have a calming effect on a crying baby.

To soothe a crying baby, the first step is an age-old one. Try rocking to and fro in a rhythmic, tick-tock way. Holding the baby in an upright or semisitting position seems to work better than cradling him or her in a horizontal posture. Other rhythmic motions in a sitting position may help. Some parents find that a car or bus ride—even a short one—will halt the crying. At home, try a mechanical wind-up swing, which will keep the baby rocking for 10 to 15 minutes.

The rhythm of music and sound helps, too. You sing to the baby—that's where lullabies originated—or play the radio or stereo. Even the regular, continuous noise of a vacuum sweeper or vaporizer may be soothing.

However, no harm is done if you simply let the baby cry until he or she stops, as he or she eventually will. Persistent crying does no physical damage. That presupposes that you can tolerate it, and that it does not disturb the neighbors.

The "crying hour" can be a great strain for parents. It is normal and natural to feel frustrated and angry at a tiny child who continues to shriek hour after hour despite your most solicitous efforts. It is particularly difficult for a parent who is left alone with the child and calls for plenty of mutual support.

THE BABY IS HUNGRY

Whether you feed by breast or bottle, baby's meals will consume time. At an average of 30 minutes per session, you'll devote three full hours to six or more daily feedings.

You won't have difficulty recognizing when it's time for a feeding. Even before the baby is fully awake, you'll hear fussing—a restless moving in the crib. Next will come a sucking, slurping noise as the baby tries to get fists into mouth and, succeeding, gnaws on them. Then there'll be a tentative cry or two, the cries coming closer together until—if you wait long enough—a series of lusty squalls will send the message in no uncertain terms.

Even if you're fast asleep, your subconscious will pick up the baby's signal. In fact, some nursing mothers say the baby's first cries unconsciously start the milk let-down reflex.

Round-the-clock feedings usually continue for approximately one to three months. Then the baby may begin to sleep through one of the feedings, lengthening that particular nap to six or more hours. Your baby may be erratic for a time, missing a feeding, then reverting to the old schedule for a night or two, then missing it again. You may try to induce a longer sleep by providing an extra large feeding in the evening or by waking the baby for feedings during the day, so the rest at night is a longer one.

BREAST-FEEDING AT HOME

It may not be so easy to breast-feed at home as it was in the hospital. You'll be faced by interruptions and conflicts when the baby's demands interfere with your other obligations. Many a nursing mother feels overwhelmed and gives up the project. One doctor recalls a mother whose milk dried up when she was welcomed home by a week's accumulation of dirty laundry!

For your part, this period calls for perseverance. It's a difficult time, for the baby's appetite may vary widely, leading you to feel inadequate and uncertain about your milk supply. And being solely responsible for the baby's feeding can make you feel terribly tied down. It's important to overcome these feelings and recognize that you really needn't restrict yourself.

If breast-feeding is to succeed, your family must help, too. Your milk supply will be enhanced if you are rested and relaxed, rather than fatigued and tense. Rest is essential. So is assistance with household chores. If you haven't hired someone to help and no relatives are available, the father and any other children must pitch in, or some tasks must be postponed for a few weeks.

THE NURSING MOTHER'S DIET

As the baby's sole source of nourishment, you must eat well yourself. As a general rule, a nursing mother needs about 300 calories more than when she was pregnant and 600 more than before pregnancy. She requires an even greater number if she is under 20 and still growing herself. Of course, telling you to eat more may be gratuitous advice. You'll probably find, perhaps to your dismay, that you have a ravenous appetite.

A well-balanced diet is essential, including daily servings from each of the basic food groups of protein foods, milk and milk products, grains, and fruits and vegetables. The diet differs slightly from the one you followed during pregnancy. You need less protein and more vitamin-rich foods. The doctor may prescribe that you continue your iron supplement and multiple vitamins. The baby also may be given supplementary vitamin D.

You also need a good supply of calcium. The easiest way to get it is via a daily quart of milk, which supplies this important mineral for the baby's bones and teeth as well as providing a liquid base for the milk supply and your digestive wastes. You should take in plenty of other fluids daily. Drink a glass of water before and after each feeding.

If you're concerned about your weight, substitute low-fat or fat-free milk. Or your doctor may suggest calcium tablets. You also may use milk in puddings, custards, or soups. Other liquids may be coffee, tea, juices, or broth. Avoid carbonated drinks.

Just about anything you eat or drink may find its way into your milk supply. The flavor of onions and garlic comes through almost unchanged. Some babies will refuse to nurse if the taste is particularly strong. If you eat chocolate, it is said the baby will have diarrhea, although the relationship never has been definitely established. A meal of beans or cabbage is said to cause indigestion in the baby.

Be sparing with drugs, cigarettes, and alcohol. Aspirin or mild laxatives probably are not harmful, although you may want to ask your doctor before using them. Barbiturates, tranquilizers, and other stronger medications should be taken only for good medical reasons. Some doctors oppose the use of oral contraceptives by nursing mothers.

The potential harm of cigarette smoking by nursing mothers still is being investigated. To be on the safe side, don't smoke. Some doctors approve an occasional glass of wine to relax after a tense day and stimulate the mother's let-down reflex. But they caution that too much alcohol can make the baby woozy after breast-feeding.

You may be tempted to reduce your weight during this period, but it is not a time for strict dieting. Both you and the baby may suffer. During nursing, priority goes to building up the breast milk.

The following is a sample menu to be used during nursing:

Breakfast
Small glass orange juice
1/2 cup oatmeal with brown sugar
Full cup milk (some may be used on oatmeal)
Coffee or tea

Lunch
Tuna fish sandwich made with 2 slices of whole wheat bread, 1/2 cup tuna fish salad
1 small banana
Full cup milk

Afternoon snack
1/2 cup peanuts
Full cup milk

Dinner
Six ounces of roast beef
1/2 cup egg noodles
3/4 cup cut asparagus
Spinach salad with oil and vinegar
Full cup milk
Coffee or tea

Evening snack
2 oatmeal-raisin cookies
Full cup milk

BREAST-FEEDING AND VISITORS

You may not want many visitors during the first few weeks you are breast-feeding. Company and excitement can hold back the milk flow and result in a less than satisfactory feeding. Guests shouldn't be allowed to interfere with the nursing schedule. For your own comfort, don't delay the feeding more than a few minutes.

Some mothers are embarrassed to nurse before other people— or feel their guests might be embarrassed. Writers who discuss etiquette divide on whether public display of this natural function is socially acceptable. But like many aspects of motherhood, the question doesn't involve protocol—just follow your own judgment. Nursing is natural and nothing to be ashamed of. Indeed, many offices provide places where employees may nurse their babies.

Regardless of your feelings, be sure to explain nursing to your other children. Make it clear that nursing is a perfectly natural phenomenon, a warm human experience between mothers and babies to be shared by the members of the entire family. In fact, it can be an early lesson in sexual difference for the older children, showing that mothers nurse babies and fathers don't.

Once you've established a regular nursing routine and feel more relaxed about it, you'll probably find no need to be isolated from the rest of the family; nursing can be a time to enjoy the other children. It provides the opportunity for conversation, for playing games with the other children, or for story-telling.

A TIME AND PLACE

With experience, you'll be able to nurse the baby anywhere. Some mothers say they can nurse while standing or walking. But your early nursing will be more successful if you establish a relaxed, regular routine. A quiet room is best. Pick a chair with arms, bolster your elbows with pillows, and prop your feet up. Use the time exclusively to cuddle and talk to the baby, not watch television or read. At night, take the baby into bed with you, so you can rest while nursing.

For your own comfort and the baby's, nurse when the baby is ready to eat. He or she will probably follow a three-hour schedule, but if the baby wakes early, don't wait for the three hours to pass. On the other hand, if the baby oversleeps, rouse the child and begin feeding. Otherwise, your breasts may feel full and sore; and milk may begin to leak on your clothing.

Once a routine is established, you'll probably nurse about ten minutes on each breast. More than that is probably fruitless. Even slow eaters get about four-fifths of their capacity in the first five minutes. Some babies are satisfied with just one breast. Remember that suckling itself is important; the baby may be kept at the breast a few minutes to satisfy this instinct. But prolonged suckling can cause sore nipples. You may wish to substitute a pacifier (see page 232).

WILL YOU HAVE ENOUGH MILK?

Only rarely does a woman have too little milk for her baby. The human breast normally manufactures one and one-half to two ounces of milk in each breast every three hours. A newborn requires only about two fluid ounces per pound of body weight a day. A seven-pounder thus needs 14 to 21 ounces a day, compared to a normal output of 24 to 32 ounces.

The milk will be rich enough, too. A seven-pound baby needs about 50 calories per pound of body weight per day—350 calories daily. Breast milk measures about 20 calories per ounce, so that amounts to approximately 80 calories per feeding.

Some nursing mothers become discouraged when they first see breast milk. It just doesn't look very nourishing. It's not foamy and white, like milk you pour from a bottle, but resembles skim milk—thin, watery, and slightly blue. But that color and consistency is just right for the baby's development.

A true gauge of your milk's quality and amount is how well the baby grows. If he or she seems to be thriving and filling out, you're furnishing an ample amount of nutrition. Most babies lose a little when they first leave the hospital, but then begin to gain at the rate of about a quarter of a pound per week—noticeable even to an unpracticed eye. In any case, the doctor will weigh the baby at the first checkup.

Another yardstick is how many diapers are used. More than six wet diapers a day usually indicates the baby is getting plenty of fluid.

Don't automatically assume that if your baby won't eat, there's something wrong with your milk. Bottle-fed babies also fuss, cry, spit up, or refuse to eat sometimes.

SUPPLEMENTARY AND RELIEF BOTTLES

If your baby still seems unsatisfied and continues to cry after being placed at the second breast, your doctor may suggest you offer a supplementary bottle immediately afterward. Regularly supplementing breast milk with formula is usually a last resort, however. As part of the supply-demand principle, your milk production will drop. And the baby may later resist the more difficult task of breast-feeding. Giving water isn't necessary except in hot weather.

After a few days, you may wish to provide a relief bottle, so the baby becomes accustomed to bottle-feeding and you can get an

For formula-feeding, take a prepared bottle from refrigerator, shake, and warm under hot-water faucet.

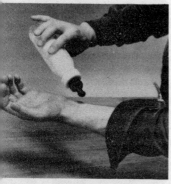

Test temperature by sprinkling a few drops on inside of wrist. It should feel warm, not hot.

Prop the baby in semi-sitting position in crook of elbow, for easier breathing and swallowing.

occasional respite. That's also a way to bring the father into the feeding routine and allow him a private period with the baby. Your own milk is the best supply. Hand-express milk from your breast, or use a breast pump to squeeze it from the nipple into a sterile bottle. Refrigerate until needed. This way you'll maintain your milk production.

When the baby is down to four or five feedings per day, relief bottles may be used more often. By then, the baby has become accomplished at nursing and may readily switch between breast and bottle; you will now be freer to leave him or her and resume working outside the home. When you are absent from home at feeding time, you always should nurse as soon as you return, so you can relieve the fullness in your breasts and continue to produce milk. Especially in the early weeks, some milk may leak from your breasts and retard the flow. If it occurs regularly, you may wish to wear a folded handkerchief inside your nursing bra.

BOTTLE-FEEDING

The majority of babies are bottle-fed, including many who started on breast milk. Babies brought up on formula thrive, too, so don't hesitate to feed yours by bottle or to switch from breast milk to formula if you find nursing unsatisfactory. The choice of feeding method is an individual matter.

On the average, bottle-fed newborns eat about six times a day, once every four hours. A newborn takes about two ounces at each feeding. The amount increases as the baby grows older, and the number of feedings decreases.

As with breast-feeding, bottle-feeding comes naturally. Because you'll be there for 30 minutes or more, pick a comfortable armchair or the corner of a sofa, with pillows to support your elbows. Hold the baby in your lap, the head in the crook of one elbow, the bottle in your other hand. The baby should be in a semisitting position, to keep the airway open and allow easy swallowing. Don't feed while the baby is lying on his or her back; gagging may result.

When you tickle the cheek or lips, the baby instinctively will turn, seize the nipple, and begin to suck. Hold the bottle at slightly more than a right angle to the baby's mouth, so the nipple and cap are filled with formula and not air, which causes a false fullness and makes the baby uncomfortable.

Keep the cap of the bottle slightly loose to allow air to enter. A line of bubbles will rise through the formula to indicate the baby is feeding successfully. Place a folded diaper or bib under the chin to catch dribbles.

Sometimes the baby may pull so hard that a kind of negative pressure builds up in the bottle. The nipple or plastic bottle liner collapses and shuts off the flow. The frustrated baby continues to suck but gets nothing for the effort. To prevent this, move the bottle in the baby's mouth from time to time to break the suction, or remove it entirely for a moment.

Your baby may not finish the entire bottle at each feeding. Just like adults, babies have the right not to be hungry sometimes. Don't coax him or her to finish.

On the other hand, if the baby repeatedly devours the bottle's contents and seems to want more, increase the next feeding by one-half ounce. When that amount no longer satisfies the baby, add another half-ounce. Try to keep just a little ahead in matching supply to demand.

Don't prop the bottle and leave. That practice not only denies the baby some necessary parenting, it can be dangerous. If the milk flows too quickly, it may cause the baby to gag or vomit, then choke by sucking matter into the lungs. And if the bottle slips away and the baby can't recover it, the experience can be downright frustrating.

PREPARING THE FORMULA

You can mix cow's milk or evaporated milk with other ingredients to make an acceptable substitute for mother's milk, but few parents follow this complicated procedure today. More commonly, they use commercial, premixed formulas, which are more nourishing and more convenient and save time.

Sold under various brand names in supermarkets and drugstores, the formulas come in three types:

• Powdered formula is mixed with warm water, a scoop of formula per two ounces of water. It is the least expensive variety.

• Liquid concentrate also must be mixed, usually one part of concentrate to one of water. It is available in 13-ounce cans and must be refrigerated after opening.

• Ready-to-feed formula may be used directly from the can, requiring no mixing. It is the most expensive kind. Disposable bottles, the ultimate convenience, require only a nipple to be used for immediate feeding.

Commercial formulas are said to contain the important ingredients of mother's milk in the correct proportions, and manufacturers improve them as knowledge is gained. Most use cow's milk as the basic source of protein. Others use vegetable protein, usually from soybeans, and may be recommended for babies with allergies or for babies born into families with allergic reactions to milk. The American Academy of Pediatrics recommends that formula fortified with iron be used by the age of four months.

Preparing formula isn't such a big deal, as it used to be when sanitation and sterilization methods were less sure than they are today. With improved hygiene, a relatively pure water supply, and presterilized formula, the elaborate sterilization measures are considered unnecessary by many doctors and parents, except in unusual cases. Instead, you simply prepare the formula as you need it, one bottle at a time.

If you own a dishwasher, rinse out the bottles after use and wash and dry them in the washer's bottom rack. Wash the nipples in the dishwasher, too, or sterilize them separately in a pot of boiling water, storing them in a jar until ready for use. If you use ready-to-feed formula, pour the prescribed amount into a bottle, cover with a nipple, and feed. Liquid concentrate or powder can be mixed with warm water directly from the faucet. Just add the right amount of liquid or powdered formula, cap with the nipple, shake the bottle, and feed.

If you don't have a dishwasher or aren't certain about your water supply, you may wish to follow another method. Wash and rinse the used bottles, nipples, rings, and caps by hand, then fill each bottle with the prescribed amount of water. Cover with nipples and caps, and boil in a sterilizer for 25 minutes. After the bottles have cooled, remove them from the sterilizer, and store them at room temperature until needed. Then add formula, cap, shake, and use without heating. An advantage to this method is that you open formula only as necessary.

You may also sterilize one bottle at a time. Wash and rinse the bottle and nipple after use, then place them in an uncovered saucepan of water; boil for five minutes. Remove with tongs, pour in the prescribed amount of water from the saucepan in which the materials were sterilized, add formula, shake, and use.

TERMINAL STERILIZATION
The traditional method of preparing formula is called the terminal method, which enables you to prepare a day's supply of formula at a time. It is still favored by many parents and pediatricians.

To prepare formula this way, you should have a set place in the kitchen, near stove, sink, and refrigerator. It should be equipped with the following, which may be bought as a kit:

• Eight eight-ounce glass or plastic bottles, with nipples, screw-on rings, and covers.

- Two or three four-ounce bottles for water.
- A quart measuring pitcher that is graduated in ounces.
- Punch can opener.
- Bottle and nipple brushes.
- Long-handle spoon for stirring.
- Funnel and tongs.
- Jar with lid for storing extra nipples.
- A sterilizer or a large pot with a tight lid. It must be deep enough so the bottles are kept off the bottom and nipples don't touch the lid.
- A rack for the sterilizer, to keep the bottles away from the bottom of the kettle.

After a bottle has been used, rinse the formula from it with clean water. Remove and rinse the nipples, squeezing water through them to remove scum or butterfat from the holes. When ready to prepare formula, wash bottles, nipples, caps, and nipple covers in hot, sudsy water, using a detergent, which cuts scum better than soap does. Use a bottle brush to clean the insides of the bottles, and a nipple brush to cleanse scum or dried formula from the nipples. Also wash the measuring pitcher, can opener, tongs, and other utensils, rinsing everything in hot, clean water.

With soap, wash the top of the can containing liquid formula and wash well.

Next, follow these steps:

1. Measure the prescribed number of ounces of warm water into the graduated pitcher.

2. Add a full can of concentrated formula, or specified amount of powdered formula, and stir with the long-handle spoon. Always add concentrated or powdered formula *to* the water.

3. Pour the mixture into the clean bottles—about one more ounce per bottle than you expect the baby to drink.

4. Put nipples, rings, and caps on bottles, leaving rings loose so steam can escape.

5. Place the bottles on the sterilizer rack or kettle. Add about three inches of water.

6. Bring the water to a boil, cover, reduce heat, and allow it to boil gently for 25 minutes.

7. Remove sterilizer from heat, and allow to cool until you can touch it.

8. Remove the lid and cool the bottles gradually by adding cool water. (Gradual cooling keeps scum from forming.)

9. Remove bottles and tighten caps.

10. Store in refrigerator until ready to use.

11. Before feeding, warm the bottle by heating it in a small saucepan of water, by placing it under the hot water faucet for a few minutes, or by using a bottle warmer. Shake a few drops on your wrist to test the temperature. It should feel pleasantly warm, not too hot or cold.

STORING FORMULA

Bacteria grow rapidly in milk. Don't give the baby an unfinished bottle of formula unless he or she is definitely hungry again within an hour.

Be sure to refrigerate the formula as soon as it has cooled after sterilization. It will then keep as long as ordinary milk. Canned formula must always be refrigerated after opening; cover the top with aluminum foil or plastic wrap. You might mark it with date and time.

DISPOSABLE BOTTLES

Disposable bottles are a definite convenience in busy households, and some doctors insist that babies fed with them are healthier, perhaps happier, and have less colic, too, although this has not been established scientifically.

Disposable bottles are narrow sacs of transparent plastic, bought in a roll, torn off for individual use, and thrown away afterward. A complete bottle preparation kit usually includes a roll of sacs, unbreakable plastic sac holders, nipples, retaining rings, and covers. If you've inherited an older kit, you may find a metal expander that was used before the advent of the plastic tabs that are now present on most disposable bottles.

Prepare either a day's supply or a bottle at a time. Wash and dry the retaining rings, nipples, and nipple covers in your dishwasher. You can buy a nipple holder that will fit the top rack. Let nipples and rings dry until cool.

When they've cooled, tear one sac from the roll at the perforation and fold it lengthwise. Grasp it at the tabs and insert the sac in the bottle holder. Next, pull the tabs apart and slide them over the top of the holder. Pull down on the tabs (with an even motion) until they cover the retaining ring and come to rest as far down on the holder as possible (see specific instructions, page 155).

Tear off the tabs and dispose of them. Now you have a complete unit. Add sterilized water, cover with a nipple and cap, and add the formula when ready for use. Heating will not be necessary. Or pour formula into bottles and store in the refrigerator until needed.

BOTTLE PREPARATION METHODS

Prepare a bottle of formula as you need it or a day's supply at one time. Formula and equipment are usually sterilized to kill harmful bacteria; the most popular methods are shown here. Prepared formula always should be stored in the refrigerator

DISPOSABLE BOTTLES

To prepare formula with disposable bottles, sterilize nipples, rings, and caps by boiling five minutes in pan.

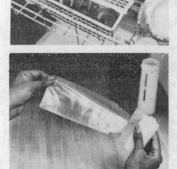

Nipples, rings, and caps also may be sterilized in dishwasher. Place in covered basket on top rack.

Remove single formula sac from roll, tearing at perforation. Don't touch the inside of the sac.

Slide the disposable bottle liner into holder by folding lengthwise. Hold liner by tabs only.

Separate tabs by sliding between fingers; pull over rim at top of holder. Tear off tabs; dispose.

Fill with formula; snap on nipple and cap. Or use sterilized water; add formula when ready to use.

SIMPLE METHOD

Simple method of preparing bottles kills bacteria with hot water from the dishwasher.

Sterilize nipples in saucepan or dishwasher, then store in a jar until ready for use.

Fill with correct amount of tap water, cap with nipple, then add formula at feeding time.

TERMINAL METHOD

Terminal method is traditional way to sterilize. First, wash bottles and nipples in sudsy water.

Drain bottles on cloth or paper towel; be sure to clean all caked milk from nipple openings.

Clean top of formula can with boiling water; use a sterilized punch opener to open the can.

Measure the prescribed amount of warm water from the tap into a graduated pitcher that holds one quart of liquid.

To the water, add the concentrated formula or powder according to the directions, and stir with a long-handled spoon.

Pour the proper amount of liquid into each bottle. Be sure to use a funnel to prevent spilling the mixture.

Put nipples, rings, and caps on bottles. Make sure the rings remain loose so steam can escape from the bottles.

To sterilize the bottles, place them on a rack in the sterilizer. Add three inches of water. Boil gently for 25 minutes.

Remove the bottles from heat, and allow them to cool gradually for about two hours. Tighten caps. Store in refrigerator.

KEEP THE NIPPLES FLOWING

Nipple holes must be the right diameter to let the baby feed easily. If they're not large enough, the baby has to work too hard and therefore may tire of sucking too early and demand another feeding ahead of schedule. If the holes are too large, the formula streams out too fast. The baby may gag or be filled up before the sucking instinct has been satisfied.

To test the nipple, hold the bottle upside down and shake it. The formula should drip fairly rapidly, about one to three drops per second. If it drips in a steady stream, the hole is too large and the nipple should be replaced. If it is slower, you must enlarge the hole. To do this, push a red-hot needle through the nipple from the outside. It's easiest if you insert the blunt end of the needle in a cork, then heat the sharp end with a match or lighter. Enlarge the hole gradually, testing the rate of flow after each insertion until the proper diameter has been reached.

Clean nipples after each use. Butterfat in the milk causes rubber nipples to deteriorate. Wash them in warm, sudsy water, using a small nipple brush. Silicone nipples used with disposable bottles may be turned inside out for easier washing. Be sure to squeeze water through the holes. If formula has caked in the nipples or scum has formed, boil the nipples in water for five minutes to remove it.

TIME FOR A BURP

Both bottle- and breast-fed babies swallow air while feeding. A breast-fed child ordinarily swallows less, because the baby usually sits up to eat, allowing air to escape naturally. But either method may make a child uncomfortable if too much air is swallowed. To relieve the discomfort, the baby must be burped or bubbled.

There are various ways to get rid of the accumulated air. The most popular is to hold the baby upright, with head over your shoulder, which makes for a vertical airway. Pat or rub the back gently until you hear a release of air. Or place the baby, stomach down, on your lap or on a mattress, turning head to the side and supporting it with your hand while you rub the back with the other hand. Another method is to hold the baby in a sitting position, leaning slightly forward, with your hands propping head and back. Often, simply moving the baby into that position will bring up the air.

Two burps during the feeding and one afterward are usually enough, unless the baby still seems distressed. Some nursing mothers automatically burp the baby when they switch breasts. Don't interrupt the feeding to burp the baby. Wait until there's a pause in the nursing.

Although most babies burp two to three times during and after feedings, it's not unusual for babies *not* to burp as expected. Don't worry. Give up your burping efforts after one to two minutes if unsuccessful.

After burping, place the baby in bed on the stomach. That allows for release of any additional air, and if the baby should happen to spit up, milk or mucus won't get into the lungs. If the baby doesn't like the stomach position, place him or her on the side and prop the head with a pillow or blanket.

SPITTING UP

Spitting up during burping or after feeding is common. It isn't significant if the baby is gaining weight. Spitting up after feeding is seldom like the projectile vomiting of illness. Milk just seems to trickle from the mouth and usually contains a few undigested curds.

For unknown reasons, some babies seem to spit up more than others. It may indicate the baby has swallowed too much air during

Three ways to burp the baby: newborns burp best on stomach, in your lap. Pat or rub the baby's back.

An older baby may be held upright, with its head nestling against your shoulder. Pat back gently.

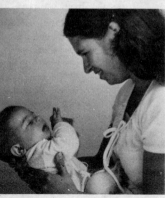

Some babies burp best when placed in a sitting position. Support head and back, then pat.

feeding. If spitting up persists, try burping the baby longer. More time in an inclined chair may help, too.

Some babies continue to spit up persistently despite these measures. The explanation then may be not swallowed air but immaturity of the muscles controlling the passage between the esophagus and stomach. This theory is supported by the fact that spitting up gradually lessens as the child grows older.

Vomiting with force should be reported to the doctor, especially if it occurs after several feedings or continues for several days. Repeated vomiting may dehydrate the baby and may indicate illness.

BOWEL MOVEMENTS

The baby's first bowel movements usually are greenish-black. The dark color indicates the presence of meconium, a substance in fetal wastes that continues to appear during the transition to independent life. The odorless, tarry stools last only about three to four days. Afterward, bowel movements may vary according to whether the baby is breast- or bottle-fed.

Breast-fed babies commonly have loose, watery, diarrhea-like stools during the first month. There may be as many as six to nine a day, perhaps one after each feeding. Some may be little more than a stain on the diaper. The looseness is normal and isn't true diarrhea, which is usually signaled by an abrupt change in frequency or consistency of stools.

On the average, breast-fed babies have more frequent, looser bowel movements, but this is by no means an inflexible rule; in both breast- and bottle-fed babies, the consistency and frequency can be highly variable. The range may vary all the way from no movements to nine or ten a day. The stools may be almost completely liquid, or appear as firm pellets. The color is most commonly yellow and pasty, but movements may be brown, orange, green, or black. None of these variations in color, consistency, or frequency—or even a change in these qualities—is cause for alarm if the baby seems well otherwise.

"Diarrhea" and "constipation" can be difficult to define with this much normal variation. In general, "diarrhea" is suspected if there is an abrupt increase in frequency and looseness, especially if there are other signs of illness such as decreased appetite, irritability, and vomit.

Many babies strain heartily, groan, and turn beet-red while having a bowel movement, but this does not represent constipation, especially if the movements are of normal consistency when they do appear. The baby usually is considered constipated if the stools are both hard and difficult to pass. Sometimes such movements may cause cracks around the anus, and flecks of blood may appear in the stool. If hard stools are a problem, offer the baby water between feedings, or ask your doctor for other suggestions. In general, constipation in the adult sense seldom is a problem in young babies.

CHANGING DIAPERS

Change the baby's diapers after every bowel movement and as often as practical after urination. Put on a fresh diaper after a bath and after a feeding. That usually adds up to about 12 changes a day.

A wet diaper isn't an emergency, however. Don't wake the baby to change a diaper; babies wake if they feel uncomfortable. If the baby is warm otherwise, he or she won't be chilled even if a diaper is soaked.

After a bowel movement, wipe the diaper area with soft toilet tissues that can be flushed away afterward. Cleanse the skin with a soft damp cloth or with moistened cotton balls. Pat dry with a soft clean cloth, being sure to dry the creases. It's not necessary to apply powder. Some doctors suggest a hair dryer on a low setting aimed at the diaper area.

To change a diaper, place the baby on his or her back. Unpin the diaper, placing the pins out of the baby's reach. Fold the diaper under as you unpin, and remove. Wash and dry the diaper area. Lift the baby's legs by the ankles and slip a clean diaper under, with the extra thickness in front for a boy, in the rear for a girl. Pin on each side, back overlapping front. Put your finger between diaper and skin to avoid sticking the baby. Keep pins sharp; most pricked fingers are caused by dull pins. Have several sets. Store in soap when not in use.

DIAPER CARE

Whether you launder your own diapers or subscribe to a diaper service, keep a two-gallon covered pail for soiled diapers in the bathroom. A diaper service usually will provide a deodorized pail, along with disposable liners.

After removing a soiled diaper, scrape or shake the stool into the toilet and flush. Rinse the diaper in the clear water until the stain is removed. Wring out and drop the diaper into the pail. Wet diapers may be rinsed under the faucet, wrung out, and placed in the pail.

A diaper service usually will pick up soiled diapers once or

The daily dozen: to change soiled diaper, unpin and place pad under baby to catch moisture.

Wash genital area with warm, damp washcloth, including all creases and folds. Pat the area dry.

twice weekly, along with your baby's other laundry. In some states, the services are licensed and must meet hygiene standards.

Laundering diapers in an automatic washer at home adds up to about one-tenth the price of using a diaper service but is less convenient. Adequate rinsing is critical to remove detergent, which can cause skin irritation. If the baby already has a rash, you may need to soak the diapers in a commercial purifying solution, a process described on page 167. Extra rinsing and pre-soaking also help. With proper care, home laundering achieves sterilization.

In laundering flame-retardant sleepwear, avoid powder soaps. Combined with hard water, soaps leave a film that can itself catch fire after several washings. Instead, use phosphate-based detergent, or, where phosphates are prohibited, a heavy-duty liquid.

DISPOSABLE DIAPERS
Diapers you use only once and throw away are even more convenient. And using disposables also cuts down on skin rash, odor, and irritations. They're available at discount stores, supermarkets, and drugstores. Even if you use cloth diapers ordinarily, you'll want a supply of disposables for emergencies and for traveling.

Disposables have three layers—a porous inner layer next to the baby's skin; a waterproof outer covering; and, sandwiched between, several thicknesses of absorbent material. Moisture penetrates the inner layer and is absorbed by the center layer, keeping wetness from the baby's skin. The outer layer substitutes for plastic

Lift baby by ankles and slide diaper under hips. Bring diaper up between the baby's legs.

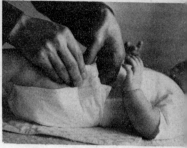

Pin (or tape) diaper on each side. Always keep fingers next to baby to avoid pricking skin.

pants and protects clothing from getting wet. Most disposables are equipped with self-adhesive tapes that replace diaper pins.

DIAPER RASH

Diaper rash isn't a single condition. Instead, the term refers to any skin eruption in the diaper area, where heat and moisture form a natural breeding ground for bacteria. There are several varieties of diaper rash, each of which can make a small baby sore and uncomfortable. All have their own distinctive patterns, which, if recognized, let you treat them quickly and prevent further rashes.

• The most common rash affects the rounded surfaces of the diaper area, such as buttocks and lower abdomen, sparing the folds of skin. It is usually an irritation due to contact with urine. Ammonia formed by the action of bacteria on urine-soaked skin or diaper is considered the major source. Sometimes the rash consists of large red patches, sometimes of rounded, elevated areas of redness and skin breakdown. Most babies have this ammonia-related rash intermittently. It usually responds well to more frequent diaper changes and to letting the baby go without diapers as much as is practical.

• Red, raw places confined to the folds of skin in the diaper area may result from heat and friction, or from the same skin disorder that causes cradle cap. If the rash is caused by heat, remove the baby's plastic pants, because they retain heat and moisture.

• Soreness confined mainly to the rectum and genital area is usually the result of loose stools. Both bottle-fed and breast-fed babies are affected. It may clear without special treatment.

• Sores in the rectal-genital area may result from a yeast infection. These infections tend to cause red patches in the folds of skin, with small red bumps (often with tiny yellow centers) around the periphery. Yeast infections may be treated with an ointment prescribed by your doctor.

• A rash confined to the area of the elastic band in plastic pants at any age is the result of alternate wetting and drying. To prevent it, use diapers, without covering them with plastic pants.

• Tiny blisters and pustules covering the entire diaper area may be heat rash, or prickly heat. The blisters may be found on other parts of the body, too, but are concentrated in the diaper area because of higher temperatures. Fewer clothes will help prevent a recurrence.

• Other rashes, especially those causing large, draining blisters in the diaper area, may indicate more widespread types of skin problems or conditions affecting the entire body. They require a doctor's attention as soon as possible.

To treat all forms of diaper rash, remove diapers as soon as they are wet or soiled. As much as you can, leave the diapers off entirely until the rash heals. To help keep things dry, put two or three layers of diapers and a rubberized pad under the baby in the crib, replacing them as necessary. When you must diaper, use two or three thicknesses of cloth diapers and omit plastic or rubber pants, which may seal in moisture and keep the skin irritated.

In cases of an ammonia-related rash, petroleum jelly or a mild protective ointment may be applied after cleaning and drying, to protect the skin from further contact with urine. Zinc oxide should not be applied while the skin is inflamed but may be used after healing to prevent new inflammation. Avoid powdering with cornstarch, which can be a culture medium for bacteria. If you use baby powder, apply lightly and sparingly, not in large amounts.

An ordinary light bulb, directed toward the exposed area from a few feet away, hastens healing. Cool, wet compresses, soaked in a solution of one teaspoon salt to a pint of water, may be applied intermittently, with "air conditioning" by exposure between applications.

If these simple measures are not successful, a different form of rash may be responsible, or there may be excessive ammonia because diapers have been inadequately sterilized. A strong and persistent smell of ammonia is your first clue. If you launder diapers in an automatic washer at home, several approaches may eliminate ammonia-causing bacteria. Simply adding a cup of chlorine bleach or diaper wash to the laundry may be enough. Or you can soak the soiled diapers in a commercial diaper-soak product or Borax, then wash with mild laundry detergent, repeating the rinse cycle twice. Acidify the washed and rinsed diapers by adding one cup of vinegar to half a washtub of water, soaking the diapers for about 30 minutes and then spinning dry without further washing.

Finally, the simplest but most expensive course is to use a commercial laundry service.

BATHING THE BABY

A bath is an important part of the routine, but you needn't bathe the baby every day. It's strictly an individual and cultural matter. American babies, for instance, are bathed twice as often as European babies, without any difference in the health of either group.

In a warm climate, you may wish to give a bath daily, even sponging the baby off (without soap) every few hours during hot summer months. In winter, you may cut back to a bath every other day or three times a week, because indoor heat lowers humidity and dries out the baby's skin. Frequent bathing increases chafing and itching. The number of baths also should be reduced if the baby has a skin rash. Too much bathing also bothers the baby's delicate skin.

Set a regular place and time for bathing the baby (see Chapter 5 for suggestions). A bath after a feeding is a good idea, because the baby is less restless when less hungry. Many parents prefer a morning bath, so the baby is dressed in a clean wardrobe for the day. After the bath, the baby can be tucked into the crib or bassinet for a morning nap. In many families now, evening is bath time and the father is the bather. That allows him socializing time with the baby, comparable to the mother's intimate periods of nursing.

Almost any place that's warm, free from drafts, and a convenient height is good for bathing. The kitchen sink will do if it's large enough, or baby's own plastic tub may be placed on the kitchen counter. There is no special magic about a bath table except to be sure the height is right for you to bathe the baby without stooping.

Keep baby's bath supplies together in a tray or basket so you won't have to search for them at bath time. You won't need special toiletries. Any good, mild unscented soap will do. A castile-based soap meets these requirements. Liquid soaps are good. Some soaps are less drying than others; trial and error will establish your preference.

Some parents like to apply baby oil, creams, lotions, or powder to the baby after bathing, but none of these is really necessary. If you use any of them, do so sparingly. Oil may clog the baby's pores. Shaking on powder lavishly may infiltrate the baby's lungs.

Until the baby's navel and circumcision are healed, give sponge rather than tub baths. (For instructions on sponge bathing, see page 169.) Afterward, the baby can graduate to a portable bathtub.

Test the temperature of the water on the inside of your wrist; it should be comfortably warm, not hot.

Whether you're giving the baby a sponge or tub bath, use your hands or a soft cloth and gentle soap. Some parents like to start with the face and work in a head-to-toe fashion; others leave the face for last, because some babies don't like face-washing and may protest vigorously. In either case, wash the face carefully, trying not to get soap in the eyes.

Cleanse the baby's head about three times a week, and rinse with clear water at other times. Work from front to back, so that shampoo or soap doesn't get into the eyes. Scrub well, using the tips of the fingers and not the fingernails; rinse thoroughly. Clean only the outer areas of the ears, using a soft cloth or moist cotton. Don't use a cotton-tipped stick and don't wash the inside of either the nose or ears.

Some parents wait to trim fingernails until the child is sleeping. It's possible, though, that the baby will wake suddenly, with a jerking movement. Another way is to hold the baby securely on your lap while the child is awake, holding the hand with each finger extended individually. Cut nails straight across with a blunt scissors; a pointed scissors may poke the baby's delicate skin.

Many babies enjoy their baths immediately. They splash and kick and squeal with delight. But others find bathing traumatic, howling with protest as soon as they're wet. It may take eight or ten baths before they adjust to the water.

Introduce these reluctant bathers to the experience gradually. Soap and wash them on a towel outside the tub; then immerse them in the water for rinsing only. Be careful when you pick up the squirming, soapy infant. Use the "football carry" illustrated on page 169, placing your arm under the baby's head and back, the other hand supporting the head.

Words of warning: Never leave any baby unattended in the bathtub, even for a few seconds. A few inches of water can be dangerous to a newborn; when you turn away to reach soap or powder, always keep one hand firmly on the baby. If the telephone or doorbell rings, wrap the dripping baby in a towel, and take him or her with you when you respond. In a real emergency, put the child on the floor, where the baby can neither fall nor drown.

HOW TO GIVE A SPONGE BATH

Baby's first bath is usually a sponge bath. Tubless cleansing continues for the first three or four weeks, until navel and circumcision are healed. Then the baby is ready for his or her own tub.

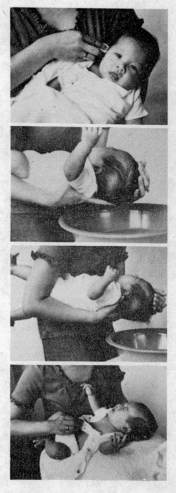

Wash only outer areas of the ears, using soft cloth or cotton. Don't use cotton-tipped stick or swab.

Shampoo scalp three times a week with mild soap. Use fingertips, not fingernails. Rinse well.

Use "football carry": your arm goes under the baby's head and back; your hand holds the head.

Getting prepared for a sponge bath: sit on low chair and undress baby on towel in your lap. Don't remove diaper.

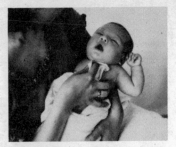

Remove shirt, but keep legs covered. Soap the baby's chest, arms, and hands, including folds and creases in the skin.

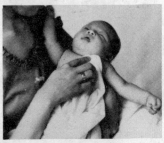

Rinse neck, chest, arms, and hands with clean, warm water. Rinse soap from folds of the skin. Pat the baby dry; don't rub.

Gently, but firmly, support the head, turn the baby on right side to soap, and rinse his or her back and buttocks. Pat dry.

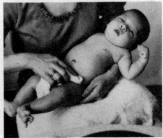

Remove the baby's diaper. Soap and rinse abdomen, genitals, legs, and feet. Wash gently around the navel until the area heals.

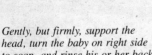

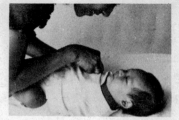

To help keep the baby dry, use powder or cornstarch in the baby's diaper area if you wish. Dress the baby quickly.

HOW TO GIVE A TUB BATH

Bathing a baby isn't a big deal. It may quickly become a highlight of the baby's schedule but needn't be done every day. Three times a week is enough. Have supplies ready before starting.

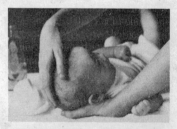

For tub bath, place baby first on soft towel. Wash face with clear water, then shampoo.

Don't forget football carry (page 169) when rinsing the head. Dry face and hair immediately.

Remove shirt and soap the baby's chest and stomach. Keep the diaper unpinned but in place.

With hand under the baby's armpit, turn the baby over. Then soap back and buttocks. Make sure you have a firm grip.

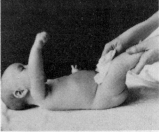

Remove diaper and soap the baby's abdomen, genital area, legs, and feet. Be sure to wash between the baby's toes.

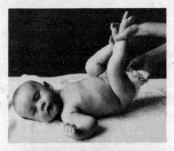

Carefully lift up the baby by the ankles so you can reach and clean all the crevices and creases in the diaper area.

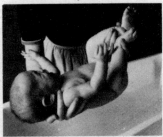

Rinse the baby in clear, warm water. One hand supports the baby's head; the other holds feet and ankles.

While you keep a firm grasp on the head of the sitting infant, rinse the baby quickly, but thoroughly, with a soft washcloth.

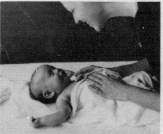

Then, carefully lift the baby out of the tub. Immediately wrap the baby in a large towel, and gently, but thoroughly, pat completely dry.

NAVEL AND CIRCUMCISION

The stump of the umbilical cord usually falls off within ten days after birth, although it may remain for four weeks. Meanwhile, the area must be kept clean and dry. Cleanse it at least once daily, washing with a cotton ball soaked in rubbing alcohol, then drying with a clean cotton ball or soft cloth.

After the cord drops off, there may be secretions from the navel, and a spot or two of blood may appear. The spotting may continue for several days. This is normal; continue to clean the area until oozing stops. If bleeding continues more than a week, notify a doctor.

Circumcision requires no bandage or dressing, either. If the circumcision has been performed by encircling the penis with a plastic ring, the ring will drop off within a week or ten days. If the foreskin has been removed by a different method that does not use a ring, apply petroleum jelly to the healing area after each diaper change to prevent sticking.

SWOLLEN BREASTS

Both boys and girls may have swollen breasts at birth—the result of maternal hormones still in the baby's bloodstream. The swelling eventually will disappear. Milk may drain from the breasts, too. It is not necessary to attempt to extract the remainder of this so-called witches' milk. It is harmless and will disappear within a short time after birth.

A few baby girls may have slight, blood-tinged vaginal discharge, also due to the mother's hormones. The condition is normal and requires no special treatment. It usually stops within a few days.

When a baby girl is bathed or her diaper changed, the vulva should be cleaned with moist cotton. Always work from front to back, so fecal matter does not contaminate the vaginal area. Be sure to dry the fold of the vulva well to prevent rash and irritation.

DRESSING THE BABY

With modern central heating, swaddling the baby isn't necessary. Dress the baby in the amount of clothes that makes you comfortable. If you're not wearing long sleeves, the baby also will be hot in clothes reaching the wrists. If you're cold without a sweater, the baby will also require an outer wrap of some sort.

The baby usually wears two layers of clothing. The layer next to the skin consists of a diaper and undershirt. This first layer is covered by a kimono or gown that ties or snaps in front or back, or a one-piece jumpsuit, with full-length sleeves and built-in booties. In the crib, the baby usually will be wrapped in a lightweight cotton receiving blanket. A heavier blanket should not be necessary except when baby goes outdoors.

When the temperature outdoors exceeds 75 degrees Fahrenheit, you usually can remove the receiving blanket. At 80 degrees, the baby doesn't need the jumpsuit or kimono. On a hot summer day, the baby will be comfortable in nothing more than a diaper.

Of course, during cold weather, you'll want to keep the baby out of drafts, even though there is not firm evidence that drafts cause illness.

Dressing the baby is illustrated at right: Chapter 4 includes a suggested newborn's wardrobe. Always dress the baby in clothes that snap or zip their full length so you can change diapers easily. Change the gown or jumpsuit and undershirt if they are wet. You usually can keep the undershirt dry by turning it back at the waist and leaving a gap between the diaper and shirt. All clothes should be loose enough so they can be removed easily and so they allow the baby sufficient freedom to kick and move.

PUTTING THE BABY TO BED

During the first few days, babies are usually placed on the side to prevent pressure on their healing navels and to reduce the chance of choking on regurgitated stomach contents. Later they can rest in almost any position, but sleeping on the back seems to be safest.

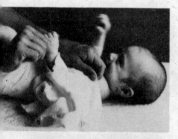

The baby usually wears an undershirt next to the skin. Wrap-around shirts are easier to use than those that pull on over the head.

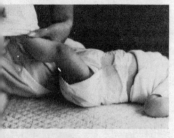

If you're using a jumpsuit, the baby's feet go first. Keep the undershirt dry by turning it back at the waist.

Don't try to place the sleeve over the baby's arm; put your hand inside the sleeve and pull the baby's arm through.

While in bed, the baby should be wrapped in a receiving blanket. A second lightweight blanket may be used but should not be tucked under the mattress. If you lower the heat at night, the baby may need an additional heavier blanket. A blanket made of a synthetic fiber is preferable to one of wool, which may cause a skin rash and is more difficult to launder.

OUT FOR AN AIRING

Babies can be taken outdoors a few days after birth. It's easier in summer, when the baby does not need special clothing. But even a winter baby can go out on a chilly day, provided he or she is dressed appropriately for the weather.

When you dress the baby for an airing, follow the same rules as for indoor wear. To be warm, the baby will need approximately as many layers of clothing as you wear. Indoor wardrobe, a sweater or hooded parka, a lightweight snowsuit or bunting, and a blanket may suffice on cold days. Pick a spot in the sunshine that's well protected from the wind, but be careful about exposing the baby directly to the rays of the sun. Babies get sunburned, too.

At this age, a carriage is best for strolling; if you're just placing the baby on the porch, wheel out the bassinet or portable crib. If you're taking the baby with you while shopping or walking, you may find a canvas baby tote or backpack useful.

WHEN THE BABY SEEMS ILL

Babies are protected against many childhood illnesses, including measles and mumps if their mothers have had these infections, but they get colds and other viral infections like the rest of us. Strict isolation isn't necessary, but you can protect babies to some degree by discouraging visitors, avoiding obviously ill people, and keeping them from crowded places. A cold is most contagious before any symptoms show. And a baby with older brothers and sisters is likely to be exposed to germs carried home from school.

You don't have to be a doctor to recognize when the baby is ill. A normally cheerful baby who cries continuously, fusses, won't eat, or is listless and lethargic probably is coming down with a cold or other viral infection. Such infections are seldom serious and usually clear up in a few days, but consult the doctor if a child seems ill before age six weeks.

Because the baby can't describe symptoms, a useful clue to illness is the rectal temperature. To measure it, you'll need a rectal thermometer—the type with a large round bulb (see page 121). Shake the thermometer until the mercury reads 96 degrees or less.

Then coat the bulb with petroleum jelly. Hold the baby stomach down on your lap or bath table, face turned to one side. Spread the buttocks and insert the lubricated thermometer just beyond the bulb into the rectum. Keep the thermometer in position for two minutes, with the other hand on the baby's back so he or she won't wriggle. Then remove the thermometer and read it. Normal rectal temperatures register higher than the normal oral reading of 98.6°. A rectal reading of more than 100° is considered a fever. After recording the temperature, wipe the thermometer with toilet tissue, wash with warm—not hot—water, and return the thermometer to its case.

It's also possible to take a temperature by holding the thermometer in the baby's armpit. Your pediatrician can show you how this is done. The armpit-axillary method is considered slightly safer since the rectal method may—very rarely—cause an internal injury. A rectal thermometer is used for the axillary technique.

Any fever in an infant under six weeks should be brought to the pediatrician's attention. But fever alone in an older infant, in the absence of other symptoms, isn't necessarily alarming. A child who remains cheery and playful probably isn't seriously ill, regardless of the temperature. A child who is dull and draggy may need medical attention despite a low or normal temperature.

A fever by itself requires little treatment. Give plenty of fluids, remove extra clothing, and sponge the face and body with cool water. If the fever makes the baby uncomfortable, ask the doctor about medicine to reduce it. Acetaminophen, an aspirin substitute, usually is preferred for children under one year. (For more on fever, see page 353.)

Regardless of precautions taken, babies usually have two or three colds their first year—maybe more if they're frequently exposed to other children. Each cold lasts a few days to two weeks. Eyes redden and appetites are lost. Noses run with a clear, watery liquid that later turns thick and sticky. Your baby probably will sniffle a lot, and you can provide relief by sucking out the material with a rubber bulb called a nasal syringe, or aspirator. But no medicine will cure the cold; you and the baby simply have to wait for it to run its course.

VISITING THE DOCTOR
You'll probably return to your obstetrician six weeks after delivery. You'll receive a routine pelvic examination to determine if the uterus and other organs involved in childbirth have returned to normal. The visit will include tests for blood pressure, pulse, and respiratory function; you also may need to give a urine specimen. The

doctor probably will check your weight. If you request it, you'll be given contraceptive advice.

Timing of the baby's first post-hospital checkup will vary with the doctor. The doctor may wish to do a checkup two weeks after birth and again at four or six weeks. The main purpose of these

WHEN TO CALL THE PEDIATRICIAN

To get the maximum benefit when you call your pediatrician, follow these rules:

• Try to call during office hours, when records are available. Some pediatricians have a period reserved for calls and telephone advice. But don't hesitate to phone after office hours if something troubles you. And call regardless of the hour in the event of emergency, including any of the following: serious accident or injury, bleeding that cannot be stopped, unconsciousness, severe breathing difficulties, convulsions, abdominal pains lasting more than two hours, black or bloody bowel movements, or diarrhea in an infant. If you cannot reach your pediatrician in an emergency, take the baby immediately to a hospital.

• If your child seems sick, always take the temperature before calling the pediatrician.

• The person with firsthand knowledge of the child's condition should speak directly to the pediatrician. Don't relay questions or details through another party.

• Write down pertinent information and questions in advance so you don't forget anything important and have details at your fingertips.

• Have a pencil and paper ready to write down the doctor's instructions.

• Give information on the problem to whoever answers the doctor's phone. Sometimes you don't need to speak to the pediatrician directly. The doctor often can relay the answers to your questions through a nurse or aide.

• Be specific in describing problems or symptoms. Instead of saying, "He has a fever," say, "He has a rectal temperature of 102.6." Instead of reporting that the baby has diarrhea, say, "She has had ten large, watery bowel movements in the last six hours." Be ready to tell the age and approximate weight of the child, how long he or she has been sick, what you think is wrong, and what you have done so far. Pinpoint the location of pains as nearly as you can; describe all symptoms, such as headache or vomiting; and, in case of injury, be ready to describe the accident.

early visits with the doctor is for you to ask questions and discuss anything that concerns you. Additionally, of course, the doctor will discuss the baby's feeding and whether he or she is gaining weight satisfactorily, but it is primarily the parents' hour.

To take a rectal temperature, hold the baby in your lap and immobilize the child with a hand on the back.

Here, baby lies faceup. Insert the thermometer just beyond bulb; hold in place for two minutes. Temperatures also may be taken at armpit.

WATCH THE BABY GROW

One of the joys of parenthood is watching your child change from a helpless infant into an active, thinking human being. It's like planting a tree and watching it gradually add leaves and branches and reach for the sky.

But babies don't grow like trees, systematically adding a ring each year. Normal children grow in spurts and leaps and at differing rates. They don't even necessarily develop sequentially, the way a tree puts out branches, which then produce other branches. Many children sit before they can stand, but a perfectly healthy minority progresses directly from a horizontal posture to a vertical one and never learns to sit unsupported until the upright stance has been mastered. The usual order for ambulation is to creep, then crawl, then walk. But some children don't creep or crawl at all.

A wiry, active child may pull to a standing position at six months; a heavier, placid one, at 11 months. It doesn't seem to matter. No one has ever shown that a child who walks or talks early grows into a more intelligent, better adjusted, healthier adult.

In the introductory paragraphs of Chapters 9 through 18, activity lists appear that describe when your child may reach certain milestones of development. The timetables are based on the Denver Developmental Screening Test (DDST) calculations of the chronological age at which 50 percent of normal children can perform a given act. This test will be the basis for noting what most normal babies are able to do at a given age.

It is important to note, however, that an equal number can't yet perform the act—and they are just as normal as the others. The median, too, conceals a wide range. Ten percent of normal children take their first independent step before 11 months. But another 10 percent—who also are normal—aren't walking at 15 months.

Similarly, the number of words a child can speak or understand in the last four months of the first year varies widely. Some eight-month-olds repeat sounds that have meaning for them—"Mama" and "Dada," for example, are spoken clearly and applied regularly and consistently to the baby's parents. Other children, equally normal, will not use words in this way until later in the first year.

You'll have fun watching for your baby's firsts and recording them to be remembered later. But remember that a child's development isn't a foot race. If your child crawls earlier or later than the DDST timetable specifies, if he or she can't crawl and the neighbor's child can, indeed even if your child never crawls at all, don't worry about it. Development, to repeat the point, is strictly an individual matter. Watch your baby—not the calendar.

HEIGHT & WEIGHT
BIRTH TO ONE YEAR

Ancestry, not age, often determines a baby's height and weight. A baby with tall parents will probably be tall; one whose parents are slight may have a slim build. These charts illustrate the range of normal growth for children between birth and one year.

Tall	Heavy
Moderately tall	Moderately heavy
Average	Average
Moderately short	Moderately light
Short	Light

BOYS' HEIGHT & WEIGHT   GIRLS' HEIGHT & WEIGHT

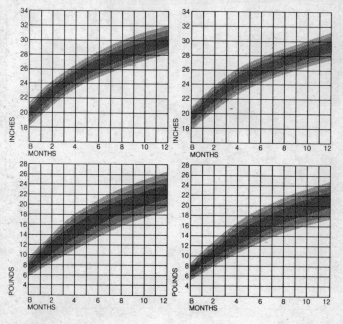

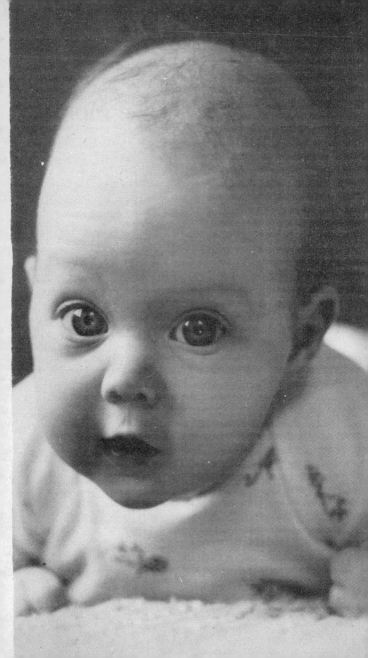

9

Six Weeks to Three Months

HOW THE BABY GROWS

Physically, the average six-week-old probably will weigh ten pounds, having gained three to four pounds since birth and grown to 21½ to 22 inches. The range of size among normal six-week-olds, however, is 7½ to 13½ pounds and 20½ to 24 inches.

The average normal baby, according to the Denver Developmental Screening Test, can achieve the following:

- hold head up at a 45-degree angle when lying on stomach;
- follow an object with eyes for a short distance;
- vocalize with sounds other than crying;
- keep head erect when held in a sitting position;
- smile!

At three months, the average normal baby weighs 13 pounds and measures 24 inches, but normal weight and length may range from 9½ to 16½ pounds and 22 to 25½ inches. Here's what about half of normal babies can do by three months:

- hold head and chest off bed when lying on stomach;
- sit with head steady;
- follow an object moved from one side of head to the other;
- bring hands together in front;
- laugh, squeal, and coo;
- listen to voices and recognize yours;
- smile, socialize, and respond to other people.

THAT FIRST SMILE—AND WHAT IT MEANS

One day during your baby's first two months, you'll gaze into the crib and see a face that suddenly bursts into a bright smile. Maybe the baby will "smile" all over, legs kicking and arms waving like a windmill, wiggling body and head. Your baby—now living up to the legend of a bundle of joy—may even punctuate the smiles with a few gurgles and coos.

That first smile is a marvelous, happy moment for the baby's parents, who until now may have primarily thought of the baby as a hungry mouth to feed and a wet bottom to change. That smile you see and those joyful noises you hear are so spontaneous that at first you may not believe they're genuine.

You'll soon see there's a pattern to the baby's smiles and that they are a definite response to the world, especially to human faces. You'll quickly learn that you can cause a smile by your own behavior. A visit to the crib, a few words, a tickle may cause the baby to grin widely and go into the windmill act.

At first, the smiles that emanate from your baby's crib aren't directed to you. A baby beams at nearly every human face, even a strange or grumpy one. True smiles of recognition don't come until perhaps the fourth month.

Nevertheless, that first smile signals a new and challenging state of development for your fast-changing infant, who now is not only ready for social interaction and stimulation, but needs it as well.

The factors that determine a child's I.Q. are easy to argue about. It *is* known that children who score high on intelligence tests have had (and enjoyed) a great deal of parental stimulation in infancy. Even when they were tiny—too young, seemingly, to understand—their mothers and fathers talked to them, smiled at them, played with them, listened to them, imitated them, responded to them constantly. These babies had many things to look at, listen to, and explore. Even when parents were out of the baby's sight, they chatted, cooed, and sang to the baby. Obviously, these efforts paid off.

Babies are really no different from the rest of us; they too learn from the people around them. Lying helplessly in a crib, a baby offers a smile as an invitation for attention, a way to communicate with you. If that attention is given, the smile is reinforced. The baby smiles again and then moves on to new forms of interaction and learning. If the smile and those that follow are ignored, a baby soon stops smiling—and soon stops reaching out to the world.

YOUR BABY IS AN INDIVIDUAL
A winning smile should remind you that your baby has a unique personality. From the first few days of life, a baby shows a pattern

of individuality, just as adults do. You may find that temperament to be quite different from that of an older brother or sister—or the baby next door. No one knows whether these early characteristics are inherited, or develop in the first days of life. It doesn't really matter. The important thing is to recognize that each baby has an individual style. Parenting will be much easier if you observe, recognize, and adapt to these characteristics.

Here are ways normal babies differ and how the differences may affect your care-taking:

Activity Level. Some babies are active; some, quiet. Yours may wriggle constantly while you change a diaper—or just lie peacefully. Both behaviors are normal. A passive baby isn't dull or retarded; an active one isn't bad or reacting negatively to you. But you may need to be extra vigilant in providing safety precautions for a growing, active baby.

Regularity. Some babies seem to have a built-in clock. They demand to be fed at precise four-hour intervals, sleep exactly so many hours, and almost always eat the same amount. Others are wildly unpredictable. Both types develop normally; but for your own peace of mind, you may need to do a little scheduling. Try to feed an irregular baby before the cries come, and put the child to bed on your timetable, not the baby's.

Adaptability. Your baby may reach eagerly for a new toy and love a bath the first time one is given. Or your baby may take a long time to enjoy anything new, kicking and splashing in terror five or six times before a bath becomes pleasant. The baby who resists change requires more patient teaching, but, once adapted, he or she won't be distracted by every new experience.

"Outgoingness." Some babies are shy and withdraw from new faces or new foods, while others immediately respond to novelty. This characteristic differs from adaptability in that it refers to the baby's reaction on first exposure, not how long it takes the child to become accustomed to a situation. Babies who quickly respond to new faces with smiles will delight relatives and visitors. But these babies may be more difficult to keep out of trouble when they're older.

Sensitivity. Some babies seem oblivious to differences in sound, light, taste, or comfort. They can sleep through the loudest noises, the brightest sunlight, the wettest diapers. Others wake at the slightest noise, crying and blinking when lights go on. A child who is very sensitive to disturbances may make life difficult at first. But noticing small differences seems to help the baby learn faster.

Intensity of Reaction. When your child seems pleased, does he or she laugh and wriggle with absolute delight, or just smile quietly? Does your baby merely frown a little when upset—or bellow with rage? If your baby reacts very strongly, you may later have to teach your child that he or she can get what is wanted without resorting to screaming and crying. Fortunately, the child's unbounded delight when he or she is happy compensates for the angry outbursts.

Distractibility. Does your baby stop feeding when another person enters the room? Or does nothing divert the baby's attention? When the baby is crying because of hunger, does a toy provide a momentary distraction, or does the crying continue? You may have to feed an easily distracted baby in a room away from other stimuli. A baby who can't be distracted from an activity, even briefly, requires persistent firmness when you're teaching him or her to change from one thing to another.

Positive or Negative Mood. Some babies are cheerful more than they are fussy or unpleasant. Any baby has good and bad moods, but, on balance, some babies seem to be in a happier frame of mind quite often, while others cry and fuss more frequently.

A baby's difficult moods certainly aren't easy to live with. But moodiness doesn't mean that your methods of child care are wrong. As parents, you must learn to accept some crying and complaining once you've established that the baby doesn't really need anything—food, dry diapers, etc. Chronic negativism can wear you out, though, and you'll need more time away from the child who seems to have more bad than good days.

Attention Span and Persistence. How long will your baby continue trying to do something—even if it is frustrating or if you try to stop the attempt? Will your baby rivet his or her attention on something near the crib for long periods, or turn elsewhere within a few minutes?

True persistence is neither good nor bad. When a baby persists in activities you like or find entertaining or amusing, you'll be pleased; in activities you don't like, displeased. You'll have to be especially firm and patient in distracting a persistent child, steady and encouraging to a less persistent one.

Some babies acquire these traits in combinations that add up to a difficult or confounding personality. It takes a patient parent to deal with the so-called difficult child, for the task is strictly uphill. You need more help from other members of the family. You must be firm time after time when it might seem easier to give in, and you must learn to continue to be approving and affectionate when the child is cooperative.

Difficult babies, fortunately, can learn to be less difficult, and your devotion to this learning process may prevent trouble for the child later on. Although temperamental differences appear within the first few months of life, they are not unalterably fixed; your actions can modify them. In any case, it's important not to label the baby with a trait ("difficult," "easygoing") that may mark and follow him or her throughout life.

It's best to recognize that these traits arise from within the child, and are not a reaction to "good" or "bad" parenting.

THE SCHEDULE CHANGES

By six weeks, the baby may eat less frequently, giving up one feeding or nursing a day, and stay awake for longer periods. By three months, babies usually are down to four daily feedings—three during the day and one at night. Capacity increases, although the total

The arrival of a newborn will affect the behavior of your other children. Because the baby now has top billing, jealousy is a natural reaction. Assure the older children of your love, but never leave a baby alone with a child under three.

varies from baby to baby. Now the usual daily amount is about a quart of breast milk or formula, about 32 ounces, every 24 hours.

In addition, the three-month-old baby will let you know in short order when bigger servings are called for. Breast-feeding mothers get the message quickly, because either the baby spends more time at the breast or goes at it more eagerly. The bottle-fed baby announces an increased appetite by gulping two or three consecutive bottles down to the very last drop, then crying or gnawing his or her hands afterward and seeming to look for more.

Some parents fear that feeding the baby as much and as often as he or she demands may condition the child to poor eating habits and cause him or her to grow up obese. But there is no scientific support for this fear.

The baby may lie awake a total of eight hours a day, ready to play and socialize. By six weeks, sleep may come in one long stretch of seven to eight hours—fortunate is the parent when it falls between late evening and early morning—and two to four shorter stretches during the day. Some of these rest periods will be only catnaps, but others may last as long as three or four hours.

By three months, the periods of sleep are usually down to three a day, the pattern your baby will follow through most of the first year. After the last feeding of the evening, the baby now may sleep for ten consecutive hours and then take morning and afternoon naps of about two hours each.

SLEEPING POSITIONS

Between six weeks and three months, depending on size and activity, the baby who has been sleeping in a bassinet should be transferred to a crib. And if the baby has been sleeping in the same room with you, now is the time to provide separate sleeping quarters. Newfound and developing senses now enable even a sleeping baby to detect when parents are nearby, and the baby's restlessness and attempts to attract parents' attention may keep everyone awake.

By now, the baby probably prefers one position to another although it's wise to encourage sleeping on the back until six months. Some babies seem unable to sleep until they can press their heads into a corner of the crib or against the top of the crib— some authorities believe that perhaps this position is an imitation of the secure position of the head in the womb.

Even awake, many babies may show a preference for one side of the body over the other. For instance, they may always place the right side of their faces against the mattress when looking out through the crib bars or hold their heads to the right when propped in a sitting position. A few babies carry the favoritism to one side of the body or another so far as to favor nursing at one breast in preference to the other. Sometimes these babies actually turn away or fuss if shifted from one breast to another (although some doctors say the difference may be in the breast, not the baby).

No matter what you've heard, allowing the baby to sleep in one position or another won't cause legs or feet to develop improperly. But constantly lying on one side may cause the baby's head to seem flat and lopsided on that side. However much that may alarm you, it won't last long. The head will round out with age, and, in any case, the pressure will be relieved when the child begins to spend more time sitting.

However, if the seeming reshaping of your child's head bothers you and if you want to do something about it, reverse the baby's crib so that he or she must look the opposite way to see into the room. Or you might try to distract the child this way: Hang an attractive toy in a new direction. Another method is to tilt the mattress by placing towels or a blanket under one side, thus compelling the baby to turn the way you prefer.

TIME FOR THE BABY'S SHOTS

Costing only a few dollars apiece, immunizations are the true medical miracles of the modern age—saving far more lives than $50,000 heart transplants, million dollar computerized scanners, or other technological marvels extolled in the media.

Furthermore, progress in this field has actually increased. Since the mid 1980s, two important new immunizations have entered a baby's shot schedule: against hepatitis B, the most serious of the common forms of hepatitis, and against Hemophilus influenzae type B, the leading cause of infantile meningitis. In addition, studies show that a single measles shot provides inadequate protection, so doctors have added a second.

At two months, your baby begins his or her immunizations. These usually include a hepatitis B and Hemophilus plus a DPT shot, providing combined protection against diphtheria, pertussis (whooping cough), and tetanus (lockjaw). The baby also receives polio vaccine given by mouth.

Hepatitis B continues with doses at four months, then approximately six months after that. The basic DPT series consists of additional shots at four and six months; a second polio vaccine is also given at four months. The baby should receive boosters of both at 18 months and at four to six years. The Hemophilus schedule varies depending on which of the two good vaccines the doctor chooses: two, four, six, and fifteen months versus two, four, and twelve months.

Many babies have a reaction to these shots, especially to the pertussis component of the DPT. Half show redness, swelling, or pain at the injection site; many suffer fever and fussiness for a day or so. Very rarely, the temperature leads to a febrile convulsion (see page 239). Giving liquid acetaminophen at the time of the shot reduces the chance of a febrile reaction.

The fever rarely lasts more than a day. Let the doctor know if this happens. You should also consult the doctor if you think the child is too ill for a scheduled immunization, but don't postpone it for a minor illness such as a cold or mild diarrhea.

Although some former scourges have disappeared (smallpox vaccination, for example, is no longer necessary) and other are far less common than in the past, immunizations remain essential.

IMMUNIZATION RECORD

Child's Name _____ Date of Birth _____

Immunization	Date	Dose	Physician
DPT	____	____	_____
	____	____	_____
	____	____	_____
	____	____	_____
DT booster	____	____	_____
Tetanus booster	____	____	_____
Polio	____	____	_____
	____	____	_____
	____	____	_____
	____	____	_____
Measles	____	____	_____
Rubella	____	____	_____
Mumps	____	____	_____
Tuberculin test	____	____	_____
Others	____	____	_____

Tetanus is a particular hazard in young children; the tetanus germ lives in dirt and dust both indoors and outside. Any injury or animal bite may introduce it into a wound, so keep your child's tetanus shots up to date.

Keeping up to date also eliminates hurried trips to the doctor after minor injuries that you would otherwise handle at home. Note that many laypersons believe that a tetanus injection helps prevent infection, but this is not so. It only prevents tetanus.

Although usually minor illnesses, measles and mumps can lead to permanent brain damage and other complications. Babies are born with their mother's antibodies, but these disappear by one year. Some parents postpone measles immunizations until school age because of worries about a reaction, but this is a foolish risk. Measles is growing more common in the U.S.; most cases occur in preschool children—and measles is so contagious that your child can catch it by passing through a room occupied by a victim earlier that day.

Rubella (German measles) is a mild disease, but it can lead to birth defects if a pregnant woman is affected. Immunization protects the mother and other women of childbearing age from exposure to children with rubella.

Good chickenpox and pneumonia vaccines exist, but so far experts don't recommend them for healthy children. Studies are under way on vaccines against hepatitis A, other forms of meningitis, and several severe viral infections of childhood such as herpes and respiratory synctitial virus. Your doctor will learn quickly when they become part of a child's regular health care.

The following immunization schedule is based on recommendations from an advisory committee of the American Academy of Pediatrics and American Academy of Family Physicians:

- two months—hepatitis, Hemophilus, DPT, oral polio vaccine;
- four months—hepatitis, Hemophilus, DPT, oral polio vaccine;
- six months—DPT;
- six to 18 months—hepatitis B;
- 12 months—tuberculin test;
- 15 to 18 months—measles, mumps, rubella (given as one shot), DPT and polio boosters;
- four to six years—measles, mumps, rubella (given as one shot), DPT and polio boosters.
- Td (tetanus, diphtheria) boosters every 10 years throughout life.

In addition, depending on which form of Hemophilus vaccine the doctor chooses, a child receives boosters either at 12 months or at six and 15 months.

YOUR OWN SHOTS RECORD

Keep a personal record of the baby's immunizations, and have the doctor or nurse enter each shot as it is administered, along with the date. That way, you'll know when the last shots were given and when others are due, without waiting to be reminded by the doctor's office.

Also, if you change doctors or move to another community, it'll be convenient to have your own listing of shots. In the event of injury, the record can be particularly important to determine the most recent tetanus inoculation.

Most states now require that your child have a complete record of immunizations before he or she can be admitted to school—another reason to have a record that is accessible. Your immunization record should look like an enlarged version of the one on page 190.

SITTING UP AND GOING OUT

Now that your baby has become more social, he or she will want to spend more time in sight of you and the rest of the family. An inclined infant seat will enable the baby to sit up and see you. Don't, under any circumstances, prop or place a baby alone and unsecured on a sofa or chair.

Pick a sturdy infant seat. It should be of molded fiberglass,

A stroller may well be the baby's first set of wheels. Lightweight, collapsible models are best. They should have a wide wheelbase and large double-front wheels that turn easily.

slanted so the baby is held in a semisitting position by the force of gravity from which he or she can't pitch forward. It should have a secure strap and sides high enough to prevent slipping to the side, and it should be supported at the rear so it cannot tip over backward.

The best place for the infant seat is on the floor. That way, an active baby won't topple far if his or her gyrations do tip the chair over (and they no doubt will). Always be sure the restraining strap is snugly fastened, but not tight.

Another way many parents keep a small baby close to them is by using a baby tote or backpack. They've been used for centuries to transport babies while parents keep their hands and arms free to work. The baby rides in a canvas or plastic sling strapped over your shoulders and rests on your chest or back. You can talk to and nuzzle the baby while you go about your household or other duties.

A baby who holds his or her head up with little effort also may be ready for a stroller. One of the best investments in baby equipment is a lightweight aluminum, collapsible model. The baby rests in a sling, in a semisitting position, and is secured firmly across the middle.

Buy a stroller that can be opened with one hand and folds compactly. Strollers with turnable—instead of fixed—front wheels are

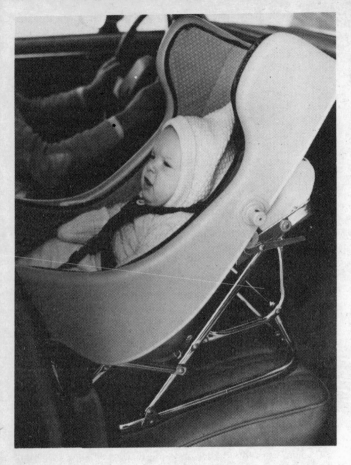

Baby's first car seat faces to the rear and should be mounted in the front passenger seat when only the driver is present. The seat can be moved to the rear when older passengers are in the car. The seat should be labeled "dynamically tested," meaning the baby is protected in event of a crash.

easier to maneuver, especially when you're steering with one hand. When driving with the baby, pack the stroller in the car until you reach your destination.

As for the baby's car seat, if you did not purchase one to transport your newborn home from the hospital, you should do so now.

Under federal standards that took effect on January 1, 1981, all seats manufactured after that date must meet dynamic crash-test standards. They will all hold a child securely in a 30-mph crash and even keep him or her in position in a rollover accident. Child seats must now be marked with the date of manufacture and with the words "dynamically crash tested." Some seats made before 1981 (which you may have inherited or found in a garage sale) give good crash protection but do not necessarily meet current government standards.

The safest model for an infant is a rearward-facing seat resembling an inclined baby rest. The baby rides in a semi-upright position, secured with a harness and surrounded by impact-absorbing materials. A parent alone in the car may install the infant seat in the front passenger seat; otherwise the child is always safest in the rear seat.

You can buy an infant seat that will provide protection until the child is about nine to 12 months old (about 17–20 pounds); or a slightly more expensive convertible model, which is designed to face rearward for an infant, then can be reversed to face forward until the child is about four years old, or weighs about 40 pounds. Although more costly at first, a convertible seat is a better buy in the long run.

Booster seats are used after the child outgrows an infant seat, if you have not purchased a convertible model. They are designed for children from 20 to 65 pounds. Most are used in combination with the car's shoulder-lap belt.

Another type of seat surrounds a slightly older child with a protective fiberglass shield that requires no harness. The padded shield acts as a cushion in the event of a crash. A lap belt circles the shield and holds it in place. However, an active child may climb out of the seat while you are driving.

Some seats for toddlers and preschoolers (and convertible models made before January 1, 1981) require a top anchor strap to meet crash standards. This strap must be fastened to a special anchor plate installed to the rear or clipped to the rear seat lap belts, and must always be pulled tight. Properly used, it provides an extra margin of protection, but may require extra effort and expense to install, especially in hatchbacks and station wagons.

Whichever seat you choose, use it on every auto trip, no matter how short. And use your own seat belt, as an example of the need to buckle up.

ON LONGER TRIPS

Tiny babies usually are ideal traveling companions because they're light, portable, and very adaptable. They sleep a lot, don't get restless, and are easy to carry. Travel with infants is far easier than in the past because you can buy bibs, bottles, diapers, and towels that can be thrown away as they're used—even disposable plastic bags to contain the refuse.

In an automobile, the very young baby should travel in a safety seat, just as on shorter trips. The semi-upright position is all right for naps, too. A slightly older baby can occupy a baby rest or seat restraint. No child should travel unrestrained in a moving car. In some states, transporting a child under four without a restraint is a ticketable offense; older children must wear seat belts.

If you notify the airline in advance (at the time you make reservations, say), you usually can reserve the bulkhead seat with a bassinet that attaches to the wall in front of you. Flight crews on most airlines usually will warm formula for you, and some airlines even provide an emergency supply of disposable diapers.

Bring your collapsible stroller, which will be a godsend for transporting the baby around airports, especially when you have other articles to carry. Most airlines will let you include it in your carry-on luggage. A flight attendant will stow it in the closet as you board.

CRADLE CAP

During the first few weeks, a scaly crust may form in the center of the baby's scalp. So-called cradle cap results from overactivity of the oil glands and resembles adult dandruff. The oil glands are stimulated by the hormone testosterone. The overproduction of testosterone is another by-product of the hormones present in the mother's placenta.

The condition isn't a serious one, although cradle cap can be unsightly. Mild cases can be controlled by washing with a soft cloth and mild soap. In more stubborn cases, rub a small amount of mineral or baby oil into the scalp to loosen the flakes. Rub the oil in well. Allow it to soak, then wash the baby's head with mild soap and a washcloth. Then comb and brush the scalp as thoroughly as possible, making sure to use a brush with medium bristles, until all loose flakes of cradle cap are removed completely. For severe cases or if the child has thick hair, you may have to use a tar or anti-dandruff shampoo.

Cradle cap often persists because parents are afraid to massage or rub the soft spot in the baby's skull. Actually, even vigorous massage with the fingertips won't hurt the baby and is essential to remove all the scales. Usually one or two treatments are all that's necessary, but repeat the treatment if the cradle cap recurs.

TIME FOR PLAY

Babies play almost from birth. Many people are not aware of it, because it's not the organized, purposeful activity an adult considers play. At this point, though, babies begin to play with their hands. The experience of discovering those hands can be as much fun for the observer as it obviously is for the baby. Watch as they hold one hand in front of them, perhaps for minutes on end, bring it to their mouths experimentally, or inspect toys held in their hands. They'll hold up both hands, shift their gaze from one to the other, and move them toward each other, watching the light and shadow. Gradually—often after several unsuccessful tries—they will bring them together until they meet and lock, then squeal with delight.

Your baby's eyes can now focus clearly and follow movement, as the hand play indicates. The baby may gaze for many minutes at a picture on a nearby wall, or at an attractive toy just out of reach, or at your face. He or she may watch as you walk back and forth through the room and follow your shadow as it falls across the bed.

The baby is now ready for toys. Lucky for most parents there's no need to buy expensive toys—because, as the hand exploration shows, enjoyment comes from something as simple as watching fingers move.

You don't need to fill the crib with costly stuffed animals or furry creatures. Instead, suspend a mobile over the crib, where it can be seen as it moves when the bed moves. Soft, lightweight toys, especially if they're easy to grasp, also can be part of the learning process.

SITTERS AND CHILD CARE

How soon you leave the baby for an evening out or a visit to friends is strictly up to you. There's no reason not to leave an infant in the care of a baby-sitter right from birth, if you feel well enough and are secure about it. A baby under three months of age won't notice the difference. But be sure to choose your sitter carefully. Even a relative, friend, or neighbor can be less than fully reliable or responsible. A reliable baby-sitter can only make your evening out more enjoyable.

Even at three months, it's best that the baby be awake when the sitter arrives, so the two of you can be seen together. Invite the sitter to come before your departure to see how you hold, handle, and care for the baby. Even young babies like to be treated in a way that's familiar to them. Show your baby-sitter where things he or she will need are kept, and observe closely as she or he feeds and diapers the baby, so you are sure the sitter knows and cares about the baby.

There are no hard-and-fast rules about when a new mother should return to a full-time or part-time job, and often the question is decided by economics or career commitment. Some specialists in child behavior say there is no substitute for the natural parent in the first two years of an infant's life, although others maintain that a well-loved child can thrive in the care of another if the parents compensate for their absence during periods of reunion. You may want to limit the time you and the child are separated, and strike some balance between your need to work and the child's emotional needs.

Any time you leave your baby, no matter how briefly, make sure the sitter has the following information:
- where you can be reached;
- telephone numbers of the doctor, hospital and emergency room, fire department, and police (keep them posted next to the phone);
- the name and telephone number of a responsible friend, relative, or neighbor who can be called if you can't be reached;
- details about your house—how to regulate heat, how to lock and open the doors;
- what and when to feed the baby;
- when you will return;
- what exactly you expect from the sitter while you're gone.

In any case, the decision is not one to be made offhandedly, but should be planned carefully and agreed to by both parents, even before childbirth. Once reached, however, it is not a decision to feel guilty about.

Unless the father can take over the domestic role, the mother's return to work requires some kind of professional, full-time baby care, either in your own home, in another's home, or in a day-care center. No professional baby care is inexpensive, and all require careful thought before the choice is made. The matter of leaving your child in the care of another is worrisome, too. Ask friends for their recommendations, and explore all possibilities before you choose.

The best and least expensive full-time babysitters often are trusted friends or relatives. You usually know them well enough to have faith in their reliability and responsibility, you know they will have an interest in your child, and you can expect them to care for the baby the way you would do it yourself. Hiring a sitter or housekeeper and training him or her to care for the baby is a more expensive and difficult proposition. You may have to spend long hours teaching and supervising the person (however, the effort is certainly worth it). If you have several children, though, a sitter who can come to your house while you're away is often the best solution.

For a young child, care within a private home often works most satisfactorily. That's because the rhythm of home life is nearer to the child's own experience. Too, your child should get more attention because smaller numbers of children are involved.

Some state agencies license private homes where children are cared and inspect them for safety. Unfortunately, most states have no licensing for personnel.

Commercial day-care centers and those operated by nonprofit or charitable agencies are proliferating. Properly staffed and supervised, they may provide the best care, especially for children above the age of three. They also can be the most economical.

Before choosing a day-care home or center, you'll want to visit and examine it. Have these questions answered:

• Are you welcome to visit the day-care center at any time, and are your suggestions for care of your child welcomed and put to practice? (And if not, are you told why?)

• Does the person or persons caring for the children seem to really care about them, or are those persons impersonal with them?

• Is the home or center clean, safe, airy, and healthful-appearing, with sufficient space for the children to play?

• Is there at least one adult for every four or five older children (or two or three infants), including the person's own children?

• Do the staff and the children seem to be happy and enjoying themselves?

If you find something you don't like about the way your child is cared for, don't hesitate to speak up and demand change. If you are not satisfied, be prepared to make other arrangements. The most important aspect of child care is your confidence that your child is in good hands.

10

Three to Four Months

HOW THE BABY GROWS

Physically, an average normal four-month-old will weigh $14\frac{1}{2}$ pounds and measure $24\frac{1}{2}$ inches, a gain of $1\frac{1}{2}$ pounds and an inch in length from the month before. But weight and length among normal babies will range between 11 and $17\frac{1}{2}$ pounds, and between 23 and 27 inches.

Here's what about half of normal babies can do at four months:

- turn head in all directions and support self on straight arms;
- roll from front to side or back;
- grasp and hold an object; reach for and sometimes grab something offered;
- babble in wordlike syllables; coo, gurgle, chortle, and squeal with pleasure;
- anticipate your approach and become excited;
- look at self in a mirror and smile;
- recognize parents and siblings;
- have crying quieted by a voice or music;
- bear some weight on legs when held in a standing position;
- be pulled to sitting position.

TIME OF CURIOSITY AND COMMUNICATION

In the fourth month of life your baby is no longer helpless and is fun to be around, at least most of the time. The baby likes people, enjoys life, and makes that pleasure evident. Smiles, squeals, chortles, and giggles abound. You'll notice a first attempt to "talk"—a babbling string of sounds that have no translation but are clearly attempts at speech. In the bath, the baby kicks, splashes, and laughs. Sometimes you will hear a baby in the crib, laughing aloud to no one in particular.

Your baby may even develop a "social cough." You'll quickly learn to recognize this put-on, which is just for you. Indeed, you've taught the baby to do it, probably unknowingly. One day in the past the baby coughed. You smiled. The baby liked that and coughed again. You smiled again. Because the baby quickly learned this dry little hack could provoke an enjoyable response, the cycle of cough-smile-cough was reinforced and became a game.

Smiles, laughs, and coughs are only one way a baby reaches out to the world. Your baby is now learning about surrounding events and where he or she fits in. The lesson coming across to the baby is that he or she can cause events and that those events have a somewhat predictable pattern. Watch your baby as you approach the crib and extend your arms. Your baby will wriggle and "windmill" in anticipation, having learned that outstretched arms are a prelude to being picked up. Watch, too, when you dangle an object in front of the child or place it nearby when the baby is lying down. A month ago, the baby merely would have peered at it. But now he or she immediately reaches out. There won't be many direct hits yet, but the baby's aim will keep improving as he or she explores the environment and gets ready to venture out into it. But remember babies differ. Yours may be quieter than others.

TIME FOR SOLID FOODS

How soon to feed the baby foods other than milk is a topic of continuing controversy. Some parents begin to feed their children solids within the first month of life, in the misguided belief that the food will encourage the baby to sleep without interruption through the night. At the other end of the spectrum, some parents believe that an exclusive diet of mother's milk is perfectly adequate until the baby is nine months old or even older.

The recommendation of the American Academy of Pediatrics' Committee on Nutrition is that solid foods not be introduced until sometime between the fourth and sixth month. Prior to that time, that baby's intestinal tract is not mature enough to deal properly with nutrients other than those in breast milk or its equivalent, the committee reported.

Sometime after four months, the committee said, babies begin to develop the neuromuscular mechanisms that enable them to recognize a spoon, chew and swallow nonliquid foods, and appreciate variations in food tastes and colors. Their ability to digest other foods is developing rapidly. In most babies, this ability is quite well advanced by six months.

By this age, too, the baby has advanced beyond simply sucking and thrusting with the tongue, and can lean forward and open the mouth to indicate a desire for food, or turn away to show that he or she has had enough. This ability is sufficiently developed that he or she may demonstrate true likes and dislikes.

A chief reason for continuing to feed the baby breast milk only until late in the first year—protection against disease transferred from mother to child—may be less important in the United States than in less developed countries with higher rates of disease. However, if the baby continues on a sole diet of breast milk, he or she should continue to receive supplements of vitamin D, fluoride, and iron. These substances continue to be important to the child's growth and development.

In any event, the committee declared, there is no need to rush the introduction of solid foods. Babies who eat solids early aren't ahead nutritionally or developmentally. Moreover, the committee said, "pushing" solids may predispose the child to overeating and to a lifetime of obesity. Taking your time introducing solids may be the best course.

START WITH CEREAL

Cereal usually is the baby's first solid food, followed in order by fruits, vegetables, meats, and egg yolks, unless you are advised by your doctor to withhold the latter. The sequence is somewhat arbitrary, depending on your baby's tastes, and can be accelerated if the baby has started solids late. Use plain foods in the beginning, rather than mixtures, and introduce them one at a time.

Precooked, dehydrated cereals, fortified with iron, are available in rice, oatmeal, barley, wheat, and mixed varieties. To prepare, simply add warm milk, formula, or water and stir to the proper consistency. Although they won't be iron-fortified, you can cook your own whole-grain cereals.

Rice is the mildest and most readily digested cereal. Oatmeal and barley may be used interchangeably with rice after the first solid food has been introduced. If there is a family history of food allergies, wheat and mixed cereals may be postponed until after the first year. This is a matter to be discussed with the pediatrician.

MIXING AND FEEDING

Start with a very small amount of cereal. One or two teaspoons is enough. Place the cereal in a clean dish and moisten with warm formula, mother's milk, cow's milk, or water. Stir until the cereal becomes semiliquid. Some babies prefer cereal almost watery; others like a more pasty mixture. Trial and error will identify your baby's preferences.

Some parents mix cereal very thin and feed it from a bottle, using a nipple with an enlarged opening. This often is a means of feeding solids early, because the baby's head can be held erect; it's also less messy for the mother.

A better way is to feed the baby tiny bites from a demitasse or other small spoon. Hold the baby in your lap, nestled in a semi-sitting position in the crook of your elbow or secured in an inclined infant rest. Fill the bowl of the spoon about half full. When you touch the baby's lips, they'll open, allowing you to insert the spoon. The upper lip and gums will guide the food into the baby's mouth.

The first few tries will be messy, so be prepared. Wear an apron and tie a bib on the baby. Because this a new way of doing things, the baby will use the tongue to push this strange stuff right out of the mouth. You'll probably have to scrape food off the baby's chin and bib several times and spoon it back where it belongs. Your baby may even blow or spit out the food until this new type of feeding is mastered.

In the beginning, feed solids just once a day. Many parents choose the morning feeding, although timing actually makes no difference. Start with a breast- or bottle-feeding, then follow with solid food, because a truly hungry baby may balk at this new taste. Later, you can reverse the order so the baby doesn't fill up on milk before the solid food is served.

A baby will let you know enough is enough by turning the head, clamping the jaws shut, or emphatically spitting the food out. Don't try to coax your baby to eat more to finish up or trick the child by spooning a bite in quickly. Feeding problems often begin with these early contests about how much is enough.

ADDING OTHER FOODS

After a week or so of cereal, add solid food at another feeding. A week later, introduce another food. Fruit is the usual choice. Most parents begin with bananas, followed by applesauce, pears, and peaches, but you can choose any order.

By starting foods one at a time and serving them exclusively for a week, you can quickly learn whether they agree with the baby. If the baby suffers diarrhea, constipation, a skin rash, or any other change after the feeding of a particular food, you can identify the culprit and discontinue it.

Fruit furnishes natural sugars, vitamin A, and certain minerals. It usually is served at the same meal as cereal and sometimes replaces it. A baby who rejects cereal may be given fruit first, or fruit may be mixed into the cereal. If you find the baby doesn't like either, stop offering the cereal for a while and try again later.

Vegetables, a chief source of carbohydrates, may be added to the menu about two weeks to a month after fruit. Serve vegetables separately from the other foods, following the same rule of introducing one at a time at regular intervals so you can watch for the baby's reactions. Begin by serving yellow vegetables with a mild flavor—squash or sweet potatoes, for example. Then progress to carrots, beans, peas. Beets and spinach usually come later. Some vegetables may be unpopular, but you should acquaint your baby with all varieties.

Meat comes next, about a month after vegetables. As the baby drinks less and less milk, meat will provide most of the baby's protein, iron, and the vitamin B complex. (Vegetable sources of protein, such as beans, may be substituted for meat, according to the American Academy of Pediatrics' Committee on Nutrition.) The most popular meats are beef and chicken, followed by lamb. Liver and heart have a high iron content.

COMMERCIAL VERSUS HOMEMADE BABY FOOD

Those tiny jars of strained baby food are a great and wonderful convenience, and they allow you a year-round choice of foods for the baby. On the other hand, commercial baby food is about double the price of homemade food—and no more nutritious.

In recent years, manufacturers of baby food have changed the ingredients of many products to make them more "natural." Flavor-enhancers and food additives have been eliminated and salt and sugar content reduced. The supermarket shelf now carries jars marked "No salt added" and "No sugar added." Fruits containing tapioca, used as a sweetener and extender, are plainly marked. Manufacturers acknowledge that in the past many ingredients were added to please the palate of the mother, not the baby, and that today's food is better for the baby.

Preparing your own baby food allows you to capitalize on the freshness of seasonal fruits and vegetables and to control seasonings and additives. And by fixing foods yourself, you can preserve more nutrients while feeding the baby the same food given the rest of the family. However, you'll probably still want to keep a ready supply of commercial foods for convenience and quick use. In addition, you'll find that some foods are difficult to duplicate at home without extraordinary time and effort. Precooked, dehydrated cereal is the best example.

INSTANT FOOD FOR BABY

Your baby doesn't always need specially prepared foods, commercial or homemade. Thanks to modern appliances and good refrigeration, you can feed your five-month-old some of the foods you feed the rest of the family. With two minutes and the proper equipment, you can convert the family dinner of steak and peas into strained, liquefied dishes for the baby.

Of course, to prepare some foods for a baby, all you really need is a fork. Just peel and mash a banana and add a little milk for a more liquid consistency. Egg yolk, if the baby can eat it, is equally simple. After boiling the eggs, remove the shell and the white, mash the yoke with a fork, and add apple juice for moisture.

Here are some other fruits that also can be prepared quickly and easily. Peel an apple and scrape the flesh, then blend with apple juice to a liquid consistency. The result is a kind of instant applesauce. You can do the same with pears or peaches.

A blender or food processor simplifies preparation of other foods for the baby. When preparing vegetables for the rest of the family, simply scoop off a few spoonfuls before you add seasoning, place the baby's portion in the blender, set it at high speed, or puree setting, and presto! Fresh dinner for the baby. You can also make instant cereals for the baby from those you buy off the shelf. Some babies at five months of age are also ready for zwieback, arrowroot biscuits, or soft crackers, and they may eat custards or puddings.

Observe a few safety rules when preparing adult foods for babies, however. Always remove all strings and chunks from foods: they might cause the baby to gag. Avoid berries, nuts, raisins, popcorn, corn, whole peas, or other foods with small morsels, because they may become lodged in the baby's windpipe.

When offering the baby table food, it's usually best to use fresh fruits and vegetables. Frozen and canned or processed foods defeat the purpose of controlling the ingredients yourself. Always prepare the food as simply as possible, omitting seasonings and flavorings that are more suited to adult tastes. And prepare the baby's dishes separately.

Serve meat and vegetables as individual dishes. Later, after the baby has become accustomed to meat, mix it with vegetables to produce a kind of stew, which often will greatly improve the baby's appetite for meat. Later you also can add noodles or spaghetti to the baby's pureed meat to provide a nutritious and tasteful dinner almost any baby will enjoy.

HOW TO PREPARE YOUR OWN BABY FOOD

When fruits and vegetables are in season, prepare homemade foods for the baby. Wash fruits and vegetables well; omit all seasonings. Here are some suggestions for preparing fruits and vegetables:

Fruit.

Apples: Peel, core, and slice. Puree in blender, mixing with

To prepare baby foods at home, make sure your kitchen equipment and hands are clean and all food ingredients are fresh.

Start baby meats by cutting beef chuck, lamb, chicken, or liver into cubes. Trim all the fat. Add one cup of stock per cup of meat.

On the stove, bring the meat and stock to a boil over high heat, then reduce the heat and simmer until the meat is tender.

*Cool, then drain, reserving liquid.
Measure meat. In blender, place
1/2 cup cooking liquid for each cup
of meat. Add the meat; blend.*

*Spoon the pureed meat into
ice-cube trays, cover, and place it
into a freezer or the freezing
compartment of the refrigerator.*

*When frozen, remove the cubes
from the trays, and store in plastic
bags for use as needed. Heat in
saucepan until the meat is warm.*

apple juice. Serve immediately. Or cook in a little boiling water 20
to 30 minutes, then puree into applesauce. Freeze (cooked only).

Pears: Just before serving, peel, slice, and puree pear in a
blender.

Peaches: Peel and remove pit. If the fruit is very fresh and
ripe, puree in a blender. If not, steam first.

Vegetables.

Acorn squash or sweet potato: Bake in 425-degree oven for 45
minutes. Allow to cool, then remove seeds and scoop out pulp.
Mash or puree in blender. Add apple juice for better consistency.

Peas and green beans: Remove stems and strings of beans. Cook in a little boiling water 20 to 30 minutes; puree, adding a little milk.

White potato: Bake in skin for 45 minutes; scoop out potato, mash with fork, and add milk for thin consistency. Heat as desired. Mix with cooked, pureed carrots.

Spinach: Cook in water and puree, adding some of the water in which the vegetable was cooked.

A CHANGE IN BOWEL MOVEMENTS

The introduction of solid food usually also will bring about a change in the baby's bowel movements. The consistency may become either pastier or thinner, depending on the food given, and may retain the food color. Carrots often produce a yellow-orange movement; peas, a greenish one. A red bowel movement following a meal of beets results from the vegetable—welcome words of reassurance to parents who sometimes think the baby is bleeding internally.

Some new foods may cause diarrhea, constipation, or skin rash. Watch the baby's bowel movements for a few days after each new food is tried. If there is a reaction, discontinue the food for a month and try it again.

Don't force a baby to eat a certain food. If your child refuses to eat it at first, try again the following day. If the food is still refused, put it aside for a time and try at a later date.

None of the baby's reactions to new food is a matter for concern, but of course any problem that persists should be discussed with your pediatrician. The introduction of solid foods may then be postponed until the problem is evaluated.

YOUR BABY IS MORE ACTIVE

Muscles are growing stronger and larger, and your baby now is able to twist and squirm around—no longer satisfied to lie in the crib or bassinet or even to sit and watch you contentedly from the infant seat.

A clean, carpeted floor is a safe place, if you're nearby to watch. Be sure the baby is out of traffic and won't be stepped on, and clear the surrounding area of furnishings that might be pulled or knocked over. Remove small objects that might wind up in a curious baby's mouth. The baby can't move very freely at this point, but it's difficult to predict what he or she might do, so don't leave the child alone.

At this age, you also can improvise a play space by fencing the

baby into a corner with furniture and boxes. Better yet, invest now
in a playpen, which the baby will use for a year or more as play
space and a place for naps. A lightweight collapsible model with
mesh sides is the most useful, because it can be folded easily and
moved from room to room or even outdoors in pleasant weather.
The playpen should have a raised floor to keep the baby above
drafts and damp ground. It also should have a moisture-proof pad
for the pen's floor. If buying a secondhand model, be sure the
catches are still strong and the sides won't collapse.

Confining the baby to a playpen early makes the idea more
comfortable; he or she isn't likely to rebel when restricted later. It
also keeps the baby safe while you leave the room or occupy yourself with other duties. And it enables the baby to enjoy the company
of the family without someone constantly watching him or her.

ADD MORE TOYS
Continue to stimulate the baby with interesting and eye-catching
objects. A baby's curiosity is boundless and needs to be fed constantly. Toys for babies at this age don't necessarily have to be
something you buy—any safe and attractive object serves the purpose. A box, pie tins, and brightly colored blocks are all good
choices. Because your baby now can reach for and often grasp toys,
a rattle or other noisemaker will be especially enjoyed.

When you do buy toys, choose them carefully. Every year,
infants are hurt by toys that seem "cute" or harmless to adults.
Don't give the baby any toys with sharp corners or edges that might
cut, or anything brittle that might shatter and cause injury. No toys
with small parts, either—they might lodge in the nose, throat, or
ears, or be swallowed or aspirated into the lungs.

Soft toys are fine, and appeal both to babies and their parents.
But avoid those with strings or ribbons, which easily can become
wound around the baby's neck. A mobile hung above the child's
crib captures the attention as it moves with the air currents or the
motion of the bed. But be sure it is hung high enough that it cannot
be reached—even by a climbing child.

You may want to purchase a toy chest at this time. Choose one
without a lid that might fall suddenly on a child's fingers or hand,
and that is free of self-locking devices that might trap a child inside.
The best choice is probably a box without a lid, even if that offends
your sense of order. A toy bin made of fabric is durable and safe.

If you have older children, be sure to keep their toys out of the
baby's reach.

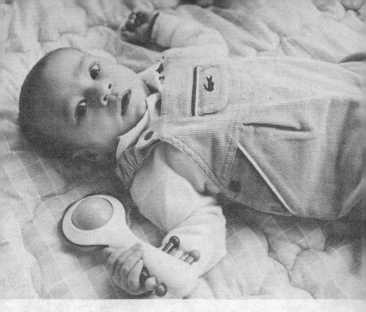

Allowing the baby to lounge in a playpen will make the idea more acceptable later on. It also will keep the child safe and sound—without constant supervision.

A good checklist for purchasing a toy at any age has been issued by the U.S. Consumer Products Safety Commission, as follows:

• Will my child be able to use this toy safely?

• Are there any labels to indicate for which age group the toy is intended?

• Does the toy have points on either the outside or inside that can puncture if the toy is broken?

• Does the toy have sharp edges that can cut?

• If the toy is make of plastic, is the plastic durable enough to survive rough play?

• Are there small parts that can be swallowed or inhaled?

• Does the toy involve shooting or throwing objects that can injure eyes?

• Does the toy make sharp, loud noises that could damage a child's hearing?

11

Four to Five Months

HOW THE BABY GROWS

Physically, an average, normal five-month-old boy will weigh about 16½ pounds and measure 26 inches; a girl, 14½ pounds and 25¼ inches. These figures probably are more than double birth weight and six inches more than the length at birth. Ninety percent of normal babies, however, range from 11½ to 20 pounds and 24 to 27½ inches. An average, normal five-month-old will probably be able to:

- sit up well with back supported;
- pull to a sitting position with head held erect;
- reach for objects and often grasp them;
- shift objects from hand to hand; may drop one deliberately to pick up another;
- "talk" to themselves and others;
- react to their name;
- anticipate a whole object by seeing part of it; recognize familiar objects;
- show emotions, including anger and frustration; may protest—loudly—when something is taken away;
- raise arms to be picked up;
- hold bottle with one or two hands; pat bottle or breast.

WHAT IS THE CHILD SAYING?

Your baby now may begin to babble a good bit of the day. Long strings of sounds are formed with lips and tongue—"baba" and "mama" and "dada," which, often to a mother's dismay, usually comes first. You can interpret them as the baby's first words or not, as you choose. Usually, when the baby says "dada," he or she doesn't mean "father," but is just vocalizing. But a quick smile from daddy reinforces the association, and the baby will try it again and again.

Thus speech begins. Though not actually trying to communicate a message, a baby definitely is enchanted with the sound of his or her own voice. It's important for you to encourage these efforts wholeheartedly. You must "talk" back to the baby, smile, laugh, and help show the child that speech is the most important way people communicate.

It's perfectly all right to use baby talk, repeating the baby's own sounds. Some people say baby talk only confuses children who believe they're saying what adults are saying. There's little evidence this is true. Cultures the world over have the equivalent of baby talk. Eventually, children learn to refine their speech, making it conform to consistently normal patterns.

The baby may now—or soon—recognize a very few words. The baby begins to develop a passive vocabulary—words that are understood but can't yet be used.

The baby's conversation is so social at times that you, in fact, may have to squelch it. When you have a visitor while holding the baby in your lap, a stream of loud babble and gab from the eager child may drown out the adult voices in the room. It may be necessary to place the baby in a playpen or crib in order to be able to continue with your visit.

THE ENCOURAGING PARENT

The baby is learning quickly now, and you'll be surprised at how much he or she masters without formal instruction from you. Most of the new lessons come from diligent observation and trial-and-error mimicry. Some parents try to "teach" the baby to eat with a spoon or drink from a cup, holding the child's hand and moving it from plate to mouth "so he'll get the idea." Not much results from these efforts except frustration. When a baby has the coordination (and most of all, motivation) to try drinking from a cup, he or she will try it, with or without lessons.

That doesn't mean that the parent's role in a child's development is strictly passive. No child learns to use a cup or spoon unless a cup or spoon is available. You provide the opportunities and equipment for learning, and resist the temptation to step in quickly to show the child "the right way" if his or her own efforts fail.

The first smile and the first attempts at speech are a wonderful time for parents. You needn't push the baby to learn—parents are more model than instructor in the early months.

Similarly, you want to praise and applaud the baby's tries, successful or not. Even a six-month-old recognizes the pleased tone of compliments, and will try the task again to win that delighted smile once more.

Keeping hands off is easier said than done, of course. Some parents like to prod a child a bit by helping with eating or standing, and there's no real harm in that. But don't feel guilty if you haven't "taught" the baby every step of the way, and don't try to push. When you grasp a six-month-old's hands, he or she may pull erect and put weight on the balls of the feet. That doesn't mean that the baby is ready either to stand independently or walk alone. Just wait.

A FASCINATING TIME

For a parent, this period of the child's development is an undeniably wonderful and fascinating time. Your child is discovering there is more to the world than just baby—or, indeed, baby and mother and father.

The concepts of time, space, cause and effect are being learned. When the baby's hand comes from outside the normal field of vision to an object within that field, it's a clear example of learning that things exist outside the baby's own small environment. When the child pushes a toy over the edge of a chair and watches it fall, it's a lesson in cause and effect. The baby sees your hand come around the edge of the doorway and squirms with anticipation, having learned that the part is a portion of the whole, and that soon a face—then a whole body—will appear.

If one or both parents work outside the home, socialization is particularly important for the baby—and for the parents and other children as well. Allow plenty of time and opportunity for everyone in the family to get to know each other, which is the best form of learning, anyway. The breast-feeding mother will get her share of closeness with the infant during the nursing period; many families schedule the baby's bath for evening, so that father gets his turn at being close to the child, too. A living-room romp with the older children, or just a time when the family is together, also is an important, if informal, kind of learning for the baby.

CHANGING MILK FORMULAS

Bottle-fed babies usually switch from commercial formula to dairy milk shortly after they begin eating solid foods. Most babies now are given homogenized milk. Low-fat or fat-free milk is not recommended until after the first year. Some parents misguidedly give skim or fat-free milk in the belief that this will protect against obesity later, but the American Academy of Pediatrics' Committee on Nutrition has opposed the practice. Infants fed defatted milk may lack dietary iron and may deplete their stores of body fat, resulting in slower weight gain and development, the committee said.

Having the baby drink the same milk as the rest of the family is a convenience and probably saves money, but, nutritionally, there's no need to rush the change. The daily regimen of baby food furnishes plenty of carbohydrates and sugar and the baby will thrive quite nicely on a diet of solid food and formula. Formula and bottled milk have the same caloric value.

The change in milk, whenever is occurs, may alter the baby's bowel habits. Constipation is a common result. Dairy milk contains less sugar and carbohydrates than prepared formula does, and its protein forms a harder curd. The combination often produces a firmer stool.

To make the bowel movements less hard, feed the baby more fruit—or introduce fruit into the diet if you haven't done so. Prunes are traditionally the best remedy for constipation. Peaches and apricots also soften the stools.

If the baby develops cramps, colic (see page 143), or digestive problems, a previously undetected allergy to milk may be the cause. Because most commercial formulas are based on cow's milk, the allergy to milk and milk products usually is discovered much earlier, but occasionally, the condition does not appear until the child first encounters dairy milk. In this case, dairy milk must be withdrawn from the diet, and a nonallergenic milk, usually a "milk" made from soybeans, must be substituted for cow's milk.

WEANING, IF YOU WISH

When to wean a breast-fed baby is strictly a matter of the mother's own enjoyment and convenience, just like the initial decision of whether to breast-feed at all. There is no scientific proof that the baby will be less healthy if you discontinue nursing. On the other hand, there is no reason to stop at one year or even two years.

Some mothers wean at about the time the baby is introduced to solid foods, at four to six months, which also may be the time when those who have not already done so return to jobs outside the home. Many of them continue to nurse at home while providing a bottle during the day to be fed by the care-provider.

Regardless of whether you wean sooner or later, it should be done gradually, not abruptly, for the sake of mother and baby. You can wean a baby in a week, of course, because your milk production immediately lags as soon as the demand drops. The emotional wrench for both mother and baby can be severe as each gives up a loving—as well as nourishing—event.

It's easier to adjust when you drop one daily feeding at a time. When the baby begins to show a lack of interest and the time seems appropriate for weaning, eliminate that feeding the following day. Usually, the noon feeding is easiest for the baby to give up, which may also fit in with your schedule. Express breast milk to relieve the discomfort caused by breast fullness.

Weaning can usually be completed in two to four weeks, depending on how quickly you wish to wean the baby. Mothers' opinions are divided on whether to eliminate the morning or evening feeding second. Many mothers like to cling to the morning feeding because they enjoy the cozy feeling of nuzzling with the baby in bed, undistracted by household noises and other daily disturbances. On the other hand, many feel that the evening feeding, when the baby is tired, helps the infant to sleep well during the night.

There are probably as many methods of weaning as there are mothers. If you start to wean a baby at five months, you probably will want to shift from breast to a bottle of dairy milk, then wean from bottle to cup later. If you do not wean until later, the intermediate step can be dropped.

Gradual weaning shouldn't cause engorgement of the breasts or discomfort for more than a few days, because your milk supply quickly adjusts to the reduced demand. But if your breasts feel painful and full, wearing a tight-fitting brassiere that does not press on the nipples should help. If, for some reason, it becomes necessary to discontinue nursing abruptly, you can hand-express milk until the supply stops.

A NEW TIMETABLE

Solid food may change the baby to a more grown-up schedule of three meals a day; with solids morning, noon, and evening; a bottle- or breast-feeding following each meal; and the final bottle- or breast-feeding at bedtime. By the end of the fifth month, your baby may eat about four ounces of baby food a day and drink about 24 ounces of milk.

The baby's sleeping schedule will remain about the same, with a 10-hour sleep at night and morning and afternoon naps of about two hours each (although a few lively babies may sleep only eight hours, total). But the baby will spend much less time lying half-awake in bed. Once those eyes open, an active baby will be anxious to be up learning about the world and exploring it as completely as possible.

In fact, this wakefulness may become quite a problem. At the first crack of light, your baby may no longer lie chewing hands or fussing restlessly but may call and cry out for companionship: "Someone come and visit me!" As early as 6 a.m., the household may be notified that the day already has begun and that the rest of the family should be awake, too.

It's not easy to alter this inconvenient schedule, because it goes against the baby's burgeoning curiosity and interest. You can try keeping the baby up later at night so he or she awakes later in the morning. Or you can wake the child after a few hours and offer another bottle of formula or water. Exercise before bedtime, a "rough-and-tumble" with parents or brothers and sisters, or simply time to wiggle and squirm on the floor may tire the baby enough to lengthen sleeping hours sufficiently so he or she doesn't wake and call out quite so early the following morning.

It actually may be necessary to move your baby farther from the rest of the family until this period of early wakefulness ends. Such a move can be beneficial to everyone, allowing you and the others in the family more rest and giving the baby a chance to be independent awhile longer. A mobile carefully placed over the crib (see page 210) will give the youngster something to look at when he or she first awakens and may keep him or her occupied for at least a short time.

HERE COME THE TEETH

Your baby's first tooth may appear anytime from the third to the twelfth month. The fifth or sixth month is the most common time, but don't be alarmed if teething occurs later (or earlier). Teething seems to be influenced by family background. If one child in the family teethes at four months, the others probably will do so, too.

The first tooth is usually a lower central incisor, one of the two in the middle of the mouth. The matching lower central incisor follow quickly. Then come the four incisors above, followed by the two remaining incisors in the lower jaw. All eight usually are in place four to six months after the first appears.

The first clue that your baby is teething may be a sudden, tiny glimmer of white—or a sudden, unexpected bite. Some babies get their first teeth before parents are even aware of them. Drooling often is thought of as a prelude to teething, but may begin several months before the first tooth appears through the gum.

Teething can make babies uncomfortable, fussy, and irritable; they'll cry continually and push away the breast or bottle no matter how hungry they are.

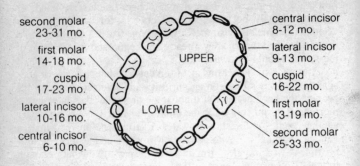

second molar
23-31 mo.

first molar
14-18 mo.

cuspid
17-23 mo.

lateral incisor
10-16 mo.

central incisor
6-10 mo.

UPPER

LOWER

central incisor
8-12 mo.

lateral incisor
9-13 mo.

cuspid
16-22 mo.

first molar
13-19 mo.

second molar
25-33 mo.

You can relieve the discomfort by rubbing the baby's gums with your finger or offering a clean, cool teething ring. A piece of toast to chew on may help. You also can buy a fluid-filled plastic ring that can be frozen to provide cool relief.

Many illnesses are blamed on teething, but, in fact, the process is natural and does not make the baby sick. A high fever or rash that accompanies teething probably stems from some other cause. If your child seems to be sick while teething, look for another explanation. If you can't find one, call your pediatrician.

Remember that as soon as teeth appear, tooth decay can begin. If you breast-feed or use formula with a fluoridated water supply, decay isn't much of a concern. The American Dental Association, however, warns that many parents use sweetened drinks—sugar water, sweetened gelatin, or soft drinks—as a kind of pacifier for an infant, and that the sugar in these liquids can promote decay even in the very young. The ADA suggests that the baby never be put to bed with a bottle containing a sweetened liquid, and that parents wipe off budding teeth and gums with a damp cloth after each feeding. If you do give a bottle as a pacifier, the dentists' group says, it is better to fill it with cool water.

DRINKING FROM A CUP
Central to weaning from breast or bottle is learning to drink from a cup. Start with a small cup that fits the baby's mouth. Some have a lip, a small straw, or a narrow opening that cuts down on leaks and spills. A cup with two handles is easier for a baby to use. And don't forget a bib—that's a necessity.

That first tooth usually will pop through when the baby is six months old, often appearing as a small gleam of white in the lower jaw. Teething may make the child uncomfortable and irritable, but it does not cause illness.

Offer only a little liquid in the bottom of the cup at first, and go slowly; a beginning drinker can take only a tiny sip at a time. Feed the baby with the cup first, to illustrate that the container holds liquid. Encourage the baby to try it unaided as soon as possible, and increase the amount as the infant becomes more dexterous.

If your baby takes a bottle, you'll probably find that he or she already pats or holds the bottle with one or both hands at feeding time. Continue to hold the child in your arms while feeding, but encourage the baby to manipulate the bottle. The sooner a baby learns independence, the better for both of you.

NEW FURNITURE, NEW CLOTHES
As the child grows stronger, better coordinated, and more energetic, the time will come to move him or her out of the immobile inclined infant seat. At about five months, you may want to make the transfer to a walker, a wheeled contrivance of ancient origin that allows a child to sit in a sling, put weight on the feet and move about via a combination of feet and wheels. Most come with a tray for baby's toys and a crotch strap to prevent baby from slipping through. Be sure to buy one with wide-set wheels to prevent sliding or tipping and remember that a mobile baby requires added safety precautions.

Until now, the basic wardrobe has been shirt; diaper; and kimono, sacque, or jumpsuit. These were fine so long as the baby spent most of the day lying in a crib. But as he or she sits up more and becomes more active, your baby requires different clothing. Overalls and coveralls with padded knees will enable boys and girls to creep and wriggle on the floor or in the playpen without their legs becoming uncovered. Be *sure* to buy the types that unsnap at the crotch for easier diaper changing. To make dressing a simpler task, use small pullover shirts that unbutton at the baby's shoulder or neck. At night, a five-month-old is active enough to kick off blankets and coverings; bundle the baby in a sleeper bag. The baby is not yet ready for shoes and won't be for a few months.

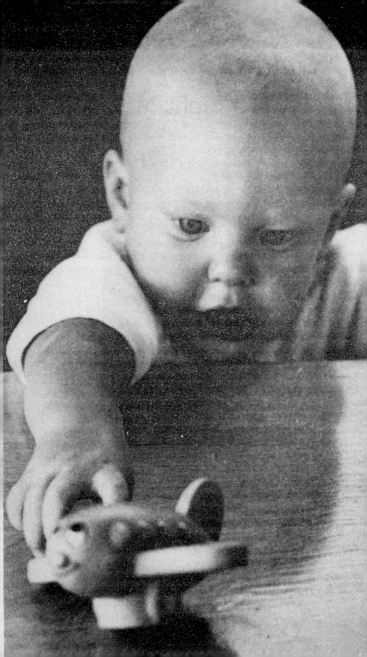

12

Five to Eight Months

HOW THE BABY GROWS

Between five and six months, the average normal baby weighs $16\frac{1}{4}$ to $17\frac{1}{4}$ pounds and measures 26 to 27 inches. But your baby may weigh as little as $12\frac{1}{2}$ pounds or as much as $19\frac{1}{2}$ and measure 24 to $28\frac{1}{2}$ inches and still be considered within the normal range of weights and lengths.

Here are some things about half of average normal babies can do between five and six months:

- sit well with support;
- try for toy that is out of reach;
- bear some weight on legs;
- pull on a toy when you pull;
- turn toward a voice;
- attempt to locate an object that falls nearby;
- recognize a familiar face.

By eight months, the average normal baby weighs $19\frac{1}{2}$ pounds and is 28 inches long, but weight between 16 and 23 pounds is within the normal range. Normal length ranges from 26 to 30 inches.

Here are some things about half of average normal babies can do at eight months:

- grasp objects with thumb and finger;
- play peekaboo;
- say "dada" and "mama";
- sit without support; get self into a sitting position;
- stand well while holding your hands;

- creep on stomach;
- be shy with strangers;
- hold a block in each hand and bang them together.

YOUR CHANGING BABY

The baby who starts this period at rest and is content to remain stationary is vastly different from the increasingly mobile baby who completes it. The time between five and eight months is marked by a tremendous spurt of physical development, highlighted by growing control of the large muscles that ultimately will transform the child's world from a lying-down to a standing-up one. At five months, the baby depends on you for transportation. At eight months, he or she can scramble about independently.

Change can come so fast during these 120 days that it is often difficult to remember what the child was doing last week. Yet at no time are the differences in pace and order of growth more apparent. Active Alice at eight months may be standing erect, clinging precariously to furniture or her playpen for support, whereas Placid Paul is content to sit for an hour in his walker, playing with toys and making little effort to move about on his own.

Physical and mental development go hand in hand. An important milestone occurs when the child can reach a sitting position without help. About half of the infants can do so by the eighth month. Plopped on the buttocks, the baby can hold an object in either hand, drop one and reach for another, touch, feel, and inspect. When sitting is combined with creeping and crawling, he or she can spot an interesting object, advance on that object, reach it, then sit down and study it at a leisurely pace.

You may be surprised, though, at the number of things the baby can do easily *without* learning to sit.

As the baby gains greater independence, your own role changes. The emphasis now is on vigilance and support. With any opportunity, the baby is literally into everything. You should allow plenty of room for the baby to explore and test budding wings, while keeping your child free from potential injury or harm. And as the baby gains greater control over his or her body, twists, rolls, and quick, darting movements are commonplace. Merely changing a diaper becomes a wrestling match in which you keep offering toys to keep the writhing child's attention until the task is accomplished.

THE BABY'S DIET CHANGES

By now, you probably have introduced most simple fruits, vegetables, and meats to the diet. You can add mixtures and combinations—"baby dinners," meat-and-vegetable stews, mixed cereals, noodle dishes, simple soups. Desserts based on gelatin or milk also may be included.

Commercial baby foods offer a convenient variety of combinations for the baby's every taste, but if time permits, you may want to make your own specialties. Those baby foods you buy in a store are usually expensive for the nourishment they contain, and meat-and-noodle or meat-and-vegetable combinations may have little meat in proportion to the amount of vegetable. If you do use them, they should not substitute for a daily serving of meat.

With a blender or food processor and a little ingenuity, you can prepare your own tasty foods, such as these two suggested by a pediatric nutritionist:

Chicken and Rice Stew
1 whole chicken breast
3/4 cup water
1/4 cup rice
1/4 cup diced carrots or cut green beans
1/2 cup milk

In a saucepan, cook chicken breast in the water, covered, until it is tender. Take chicken from broth. Remove chicken from bones and dice the meat. To the broth, add the remaining ingredients. Cover and cook until rice and vegetables are tender. Puree mixture in blender or food processor. Serve warm or freeze and store according to instructions on pages 208.

Potato-Celery Soup
3 potatoes, peeled and quartered
1 rib celery, chopped
1/2 cup chicken broth or stock
1/2 cup milk

Put the vegetables in a saucepan with enough liquid to cover them, and boil until tender (20 minutes). Drain, but reserve the liquid. Place vegetables in blender or food processor with a little of the liquid until they have reached a thick consistency. Return this paste to the saucepan, add stock and milk, and stir over low heat. You also may wish to include a small, chopped onion with the vegetables; eliminate it if your baby does not like the taste.

The baby's inborn iron supply has disappeared by the sixth month, so be sure to include iron in the daily diet. Iron-fortified cereal is the best source. Meat also is a good source, as are certain leafy vegetables, including spinach. A balanced diet usually will provide the essential daily vitamins, although some doctors continue prescribing vitamin supplements. If your local water supply is not fluoridated, continue using a fluoride supplement.

There's no such thing as a set menu for a baby during this period, because individual appetites and tastes are so different. The most important rule is that the diet be balanced, although not every food group needs to be represented at every meal or even every day. Here is one suggested day's menu:

- morning—egg yolk and cereal.
- noon—vegetables and pudding or fruit.
- evening—meat and fruit or vegetables.

Breast milk, formula, or bottled milk should accompany each meal. The baby may drink some milk from a cup, but continue breast- or bottle-feedings until the baby can handle the cup without spilling much.

ADDING FINGER FOODS

With increasing dexterity, the baby is ready for self-feeding. He or she usually is accomplished enough with thumb and fingers to pick up bits of food at seven months, although some children will do so earlier and some later. The first finger foods may be bits of dry cereal, soft toast, zwieback, arrowroot biscuits, or graham crackers, and tidbits of soft fruit—bananas, for instance. As feeding skills improve, add small pieces of cooked carrot or potato, scraped apple, scrambled egg, soft meats such as hamburger, scraps of cheese, or small pieces of soft bread spread with liverwurst.

Because the baby has at most only a few front teeth, be sure to pick foods of a texture that can be successfully gummed or chomped into a liquid before swallowing. Avoid chunks of uncooked fruit or vegetables. Give the baby only one or two bits of food at a time, so he or she doesn't cram them all into the mouth at once and choke. Keep the pieces small enough so even the food that is swallowed whole won't become lodged in the throat.

Sensitivity to the gag reflex—which causes adults as well as babies to gag or even vomit when the back of the throat is tickled—varies among babies, and yours may react when the first finger foods are offered. If this happens, wait a few weeks and try again.

Remember that nourishment isn't the sole purpose of self-feeding. It's also a learning process, in which the baby gets an opportunity to investigate the food for texture, feel, and softness before subjecting it to the ultimate taste test. You may see your child sit for minutes on end, peering intently at each hand as he or she squeezes a morsel of food in it or—to your dismay—flattening and pounding it on the tray before eating. Table manners probably will differ greatly from those described in books of etiquette—and that's all right for now. Probably the baby will simply smash and stuff the food into the mouth with an open hand. When finished, there may be more food on face and floor than inside!

Self-feeding also is a lesson in independence, of a kind important to both babies and parents. By restraining your impulse to be neat or to see that the baby "eats enough," you're providing an opportunity for your offspring to follow his or her own appetite and pace. At the same time, you're freeing yourself for other duties while the baby eats.

DOWN WITH MILK

As the desire for solid foods increases, the appetite for breast milk or formula usually declines. The amount of intake varies from baby to baby but at seven months stabilizes at about 20 to 24 ounces. The baby's slowing growth rate is one reason for the drop. Birth weight doubles in most babies during the first three or four months of life, but the upward curve begins to taper off in the last half of the first year, and by 12 months, birth weight, on the average, has only tripled.

In addition, solids now provide much of the energy and body-building materials the baby formerly received from milk. Meat is the main source of protein; vegetables and fruits furnish the necessary carbohydrates and sugars, as well as many minerals. Meat and eggs provide iron and other nutrients.

Actually, the baby doesn't need too much milk at this point. Pediatric nutritionists say that a daily pint—16 ounces—of milk is sufficient for a seven-month-old, and some of that may be obtained from foods containing milk. Some of the liquid that used to come from milk will now come from water and fruit juices.

And unlike the earlier period when appetite was relatively consistent, the amount of milk drunk may vary considerably from interval to interval. That baby may take only an ounce or two at morning and noon feedings, then eagerly gulp three times that amount in the evening. A baby may even go one or two days with substantially lower intake. These fluctuations are normal and not a matter of concern if the baby is healthy and thriving.

FEEDING WITHOUT PAIN

Many parents fret about the amount their babies eat and try to keep the baby filled up by coaxing, wheedling, and prodding. These not-so-subtle pressures turn mealtime into a battleground. You need to remember that when left to their own devices, babies usually eat more than enough. As growth slows, only 15 percent of their intake goes into body development. It's hard to believe, yet true, that a baby can thrive even though an occasional extreme meal may consist of no more than a few Cheerios, a cracker, and a few swallows of juice!

Moreover, overfeeding at this time may lead to bad eating habits—and potential health problems—that will last for a lifetime. Force-feeding a baby often has counterproductive results—as many a parent discovers when suddenly splattered by a spray of strained carrots.

Unfortunately, an active and curious baby also is readily distracted at mealtime. There's just too much to be observed and learned to concentrate on something so ordinary as food. This is a good time to introduce finger foods, which will focus the baby's attention while you spoon-feed the more liquid items. Or let the child hold a cup or spoon while being fed.

Just as the baby's appetite for milk may wax and wane now, so does the desire for solid food. Infant appetites now begin to resemble those of adults. At some meals, your baby may eagerly gobble up a half-jar of vegetables and look around for more. At another meal, he or she may take only a tentative nibble of the very same food, then firmly turn away and refuse another bit. These ups and downs, though frustrating to parents, are of little consequence if the baby appears healthy and in good spirits.

Now, your baby will begin to show likes and dislikes. Spinach usually is on the disliked list; fruits are usually a favorite. Many babies seem unable to abide the taste of meat. Providing a balanced diet is sometimes difficult under such circumstances, but you can circumvent finicky tastes by mixing a disliked food (meat, for example) with a favorite vegetable, or by spreading it on bread to form a finger food. Sometimes the baby can be persuaded to eat a disliked food by alternating spoonfuls with a popular one.

Introduce new foods at the beginning of the meal, while the baby is hungry. (But if he or she is really ravenous, the strange taste may be rejected. In that case, switch to a familiar food until the baby is satisfied, then return to the new one.) As before, try only a few spoonfuls of the new food at the first serving, then increase the amount at subsequent meals. Follow it with a food you know the baby likes.

Usually it's wise to offer milk at the end of the meal rather than the beginning, because some babies fill up on fluids and are too satisfied to eat solid foods. This order is particularly important now because the baby's store of iron needs regular replenishment; if he or she concentrates on milk, an iron-deficient food, a condition called milk anemia may result.

DINNER WITH THE FAMILY

Usually you'll feed the baby alone, before the rest of the family sits down to begin the meal. That's because it's a slow and sometimes frustratingly messy process, and the baby's schedule is somewhat less flexible than that of adults or older children. But you may still include the family's youngest member in the dinnertime circle, if you wish. If the baby is old enough to sit unsupported, he or she may be placed in a high chair or feeding table near the family table and be given a few finger foods to toy with while other family members eat their meals. If the baby can't yet sit in a high chair, he or she can inhabit a playpen not far from the dinner table, so parents and siblings can see and respond to the baby while they eat.

If the baby can sit alone well enough, it's certainly time for a high chair or feeding table. The baby chair and swing will still be the most popular places for the baby to sit, but chairs more like those adults customarily use are better suited for the time the baby takes up eating at the dinner table.

If you buy a high chair for the baby, choose a sturdy model with a wide base that won't tip when the baby is older and more active. The type with a removable tray is probably the best choice, because it's easier to keep clean. Make sure the tray has a strong clasp that won't be dislodged if the baby leans against it. The chair also requires a crotch strap to prevent the baby from sliding under the tray or from climbing out when your back is turned. Pick a model with a tray wide enough to hold a baby dish, with a lip that will prevent inevitable spills from leaking onto the floor. If you choose a painted wooden high chair, make sure a lead-free paint has been used to cover it.

Many parents prefer to use a feeding table. A model with a seat in the center surrounds the baby with the surface of a table, thus cutting down on spills and providing a sizable area for eating and playing. As the high chair does, the table requires a strap to keep the baby from slipping or climbing out. Be sure to keep the high chair or feeding table away from stoves, electrical fixtures, the family table, appliances, or electric cords.

THUMBS AND PACIFIERS

Photographs of babies in the womb show them sucking their thumbs; a few are actually born with calluses as a result. Sucking is a natural instinct that helps the baby locate and consume food. Almost all babies suck their thumbs, chew on their fingers, or gnaw their fists when fussy or hungry. One study of 70 normal babies showed that 61 were thumb-suckers at such periods.

Parents often worry that teeth will be damaged, but there is little basis for the fear, especially in the early months of life. According to the American Dental Association (ADA), it is natural for an infant to suck his or her thumb up to the age of two. This probably is not a matter of concern even if it persists until the child is three or four, unless done often or with heavy pressure on the jaws.

After the age of four, constant thumb-sucking may alter the position of the permanent teeth and change the shape of the jaws, squeezing the upper teeth together, the ADA says. One result may be a need for expensive orthodontic work (braces) later.

If regular thumb-sucking isn't present at birth, it usually begins at six weeks and increases in frequency as the number of feedings decreases. The peak usually is reached at about seven months, when many babies seem (to their despairing parents) to have a thumb plunked in their mouths at all times. Incidentally, the peak of thumb-sucking comes as the baby becomes more mobile, and some specialists in child behavior see it as a good rather than a bad sign. As new adventures become more and more frequent and available, the baby is ambivalent about leaving behind an earlier, more secure way of living. The ever-ready thumb provides comfort.

As the child grows more confident, the amount of thumb-sucking will probably decrease, but the thumb probably will find its way back to the mouth for several years during upset, fatigue, or stress. Even a child of six years or older may revert to the comforting thumb when tired or when the demands of the world seem momentarily overwhelming.

Probably the worst course of action is to nag the child about thumb-sucking, yank the offending thumb from the mouth, or otherwise show displeasure. Any of these is likely to upset the baby further and perhaps ingrain the habit even more deeply. Most children give up the thumb—except in times of stress—by 18 months to two years; with those who don't it should be a matter of concern only if it is a persistent part of a larger fabric of obvious psychological upset.

Pacifiers are another of those topics in child care with vehement opinion split into two camps. Some parents argue that the thumb is inexpensive and more convenient, is the proper shape, never gets lost or falls on the floor, and doesn't make the baby's mouth look like a corked bottle. Proponents of the pacifier say the device, especially new models shaped to prevent pressure on the upper jawline, is less likely to damage the teeth and jaws. And because it's removable, a pacifier is easier to get rid of when the time comes to wean the baby from it. As with thumbs, using pacifiers

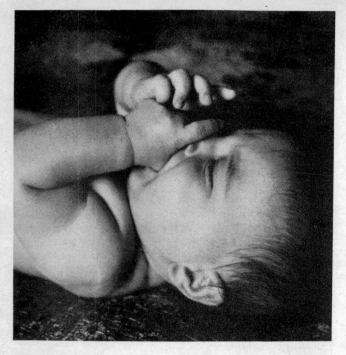

Thumb-sucking comes naturally to most babies; it's a comfortable way to deal with a rapidly expanding world. Don't bother the child about it—it's not the dental problem once feared.

usually begins at or shortly after birth (some are even used in hospital nurseries to placate the baby's sucking instinct), reaches a peak about the middle of the first year, declines thereafter, and generally is voluntarily discarded sometime around the second birthday. There is no dental harm even if the baby clings to the pacifier for another year or two.

SOME SPECIAL HABITS

Comic strips have added the words "security blanket" to the language, but most parents didn't need to be told that many children become inseparably attached to a special blanket, stuffed toy, or other cuddly object. Indeed, the often disreputable-appearing fabric becomes—to the parents' dismay—the baby's most cherished possession and chief source of solace, preferred over mother or father in times of stress or upset. Let the parent try to wrest the object away (even to wash it) and a tearful, poignant tug-of-war takes place.

Actually, like thumb-sucking, blanket-carrying is an important step in the baby's march to independence. Prior to about six months of age, the child depends fully on mother and father for emotional comfort and security. The older child tries to strike out alone yet still needs security and love. The blanket serves as a bridge between the total dependency of infancy and the independence of adulthood.

Some babies develop an elaborate ritual involving the treasured blanket, entwining it between the fingers or clutching it against the cheek, while sucking a thumb in just a certain way. Often the baby will maintain this posture for a half hour before bedtime, will resist being deflected from it, and will be unable to sleep until the arrangement is resumed in bed.

Despite parental worries, blanket-carrying, too, is harmless in early infancy. Although the blanket collects its own colony of germs when the baby refuses to allow laundering, no evidence exists that illness can result. After the baby is about two years old, the blanket may lose its favored position, although it still may be reserved for bedtime and as a refuge in moments of stress. Eventually, a child gives up the security blanket voluntarily; although even if it persists as a bedtime solace throughout childhood, no harm is done. Blanket-carrying requires attention only if it is accompanied by other signs of emotional upset.

Another habit that may appear at about the same time is rhythmic rocking. This usually begins when the child is able to support the body weight on all fours. Crouched in this position, he or she rocks rhythmically forward and backward, often for as long as a half hour. The tick-tock motion actually can propel a crib across an uncarpeted floor, distressing parents considerably when it collides with a wall or other furniture. Except for wear and tear on the furniture and parental nerves, consequences are minor. Specialists in child behavior theorize that the rocking soothes the baby before bedtime or that perhaps it helps prepare the child for crawling and walking. Fortunately, the habit usually disappears within a few months. Apart from moving the furniture or equipping the crib with rubber bumpers or the legs with rubber coasters, little can be done to stop the rocking.

A more disturbing habit—which also, to parental relief, is usually short-lived—is head-banging. In an all-fours position, the baby rhythmically whacks the crown of his or her head against the side of the crib—sometimes using the head of the bed as the target, sometimes the side rails. The banging may continue for ten minutes or more. Parents are naturally worried and try to stop the child, only to have the practice resume as soon as the baby is returned to the crib. Fortunately, the banging somehow doesn't seem to hurt the baby; on the contrary, the rhythm seems to be soothing. Head-banging seldom persists more than a few weeks, and no lasting effects have been recorded. For your own peace of mind, however, pad the crib.

A few other normal babies cultivate other, different rhythmic patterns upsetting to their parents. Some, for example, will sit in a chair and wag the head back and forth like a metronome for as long as 15 minutes at a stretch. Others bow from the waist in the same measured, to-and-fro motion. The reasons for these rhythmic activities are not fully known but seem to serve some inner need. The erratic behavior seldom lasts more than a few weeks.

BABY ON THE MOVE

With greater control over their large muscles, babies as young as seven months begin to fashion their own ways of getting about. Some techniques are remarkably ingenious. Until your baby can support himself or herself on all fours, he or she may scoot along on the stomach, steering with the arms. Often the baby creeps backward first (the muscles controlling forward movement develop more slowly), and this reverse direction may last a month before the baby masters the head-first techinique.

Babies who learn to move from a prone to a sitting position often work out another method of locomotion. Propelling themselves with a hand behind them, while pulling forward with an extended foot, these "sitters" are able to bounce along on their bottoms. They often can attain a remarkable speed, however clumsy they look. Some babies, too, learn to pull with their arms before their bent legs can support them, and they inch along on their elbows and follow with their legs in a kind of modified hop. Finally, truly adventuresome sorts may bypass all these methods, pull to an erect stance by reaching overhead from a lying position, and then daringly lunge from one piece of furniture to another in a more or less upright position.

Crawling usually follows creeping—but not always. Some children creep, then stand, then drop to all fours. Usually, crawling begins during the eighth month, when the arms and legs are sturdy enough to support the baby's weight. The baby frequently will spend a week posing on hands and knees before working out the rather sophisticated and coordinated technique of making arms and legs work together. As with creeping, the baby may crawl backward first. Several weeks may pass before he or she learns to move forward. Once mastered, however, crawling will be the baby's main means of progress for six months or more. Even after learning to teeter about in an upright position, crawling may be the baby's choice when it's necessary to get somewhere in a hurry.

NEW SAFETY PRECAUTIONS

Capable of quick movement and with new powers of locomotion, a seven-month-old boy or girl can reach and grab many places and objects that once seemed out of range. Additional precautions are necessary to keep the baby safe from accidents.

Here is a safety checklist for the five- to eight-month-old child:

- Install gates on all stairways, top and bottom.
- Cover all unused electrical outlets (especially those near the floor) with safety caps or tape.
- Keep electrical cords out of baby's reach; unplug lamps or appliances when the baby is on the floor.
- Keep cans, bottles, sprays, and boxes of cleaners, detergents, pesticides, laundry bleaches, liquors, medicine, and cosmetics out of low cabinets—under the kitchen sink, for instance.
- Remove matches, cigarette butts, ashtrays, small objects capable of being swallowed, sharp objects, and breakables from any room where the baby might play on the floor. Remove lamps and tables that might be pulled over.
- Keep high chair, table, or playpen away from stove, work counters, heaters, and furnaces.

TIME FOR FUN AND GAMES

As the baby quickly develops skills and coordination, he or she also is becoming more playful. After reaching six months of age, the baby quickly works up a repertoire of games, punctuated by laughter and excited movement.

"Peekaboo" is one of the first the baby will enjoy playing. It needs almost no explanation. Facing the baby, a parent covers eyes, uncovers them, and shouts, "Peekaboo!" The baby quickly gets the idea and imitates; he or she covers the eyes, waits for you to call, "Where is Kim?" then uncovers his or her eyes to cries of "There he (she) is!" and squeals with delight. Before long, the baby has devised all kinds of enthusiastic variations for this popular game—covering the eyes with a diaper, screwing eyes up tight, turning away and turning back.

"How big is baby?" is another six-month-old's game played over and over again. When a parent says, "How big are you?" the baby extends arms directly overhead, in a movement similar to the signal a football referee gives for a touchdown or field goal. "So big!" cries the parent, and the baby giggles with glee.

A much less popular game with parents is "I-drop-it-you-pick-it-up." Sitting in a high chair, the baby shoves a toy off the tray, shuts the eyes in anticipation of the loud crash, then waits expectantly for the parent to retrieve the toy (or cries until the parent does so). Once the toy has been returned, the baby promptly drops it again, and again, and again.

Actually, all three games are important stages in the baby's development, stages that indicate the child is constantly making progress. "Peekaboo" demonstrates the baby's confidence that you and the other elements of the world are fixtures, that they're here to stay and will not disappear simply by closing the eyes. "How big is baby?" helps with the lesson of spatial relationships and with verbal cues. When objects are dropped over the edge of table or chair, the delay before the expected noise shows the baby has learned about timing—that an interval passes before the crash occurs. And all three games clearly show that your child is developing a ready sense of humor, one that will stand him or her in good stead in the coming months and years.

THE SLEEP SCHEDULE CHANGES

Most babies will continue to take two daily naps, morning and afternoon, but the total time may shorten. The morning nap may be reduced to an hour or less. A rare eight-month-old will give up one nap—the morning nap, although longer, usually is abandoned first—but most retain the pattern of taking two naps a day until after their first birthday.

Like nearly everything else, the need for sleep varies widely among children. When the baby begins to stay awake longer or sleeps less than a sibling or a neighbor's child, parents sometimes worry that he or she isn't getting enough rest. That's unlikely. But if your child seems tired, grouchy, or out of sorts, don't hesitate to enforce a nap regardless of what the clock says.

A strict bedtime is another matter. Most children, even at five to eight months, don't like to be put to bed, especially if there are other children in the family who remain awake. It's simply a matter you have to be firm about. Put the baby in the crib, talk quietly for a few minutes, and then make your exit, closing the door with finality. At this age, many babies will begin to call out and cry for you to return. One such return is probably all right, if for no other reason than to convince yourself the baby isn't ill, but after that, the cries should be ignored. Otherwise, the baby will keep you trotting back and forth, back and forth, for an hour or more, until both of you are exhausted and cranky.

The baby also may wake during the night and cry or call out. Some parents believe this is because the child is hungry (the practice often coincides with a decrease in milk intake), but that is rarely the case. A much more plausible explanation is simply that the child wakes to a darkened room in a silent house and cries out to be reassured that you are still nearby. The baby usually will calm down if you go to the cribside, lift him or her, and speak a few words reassuringly in soft, loving tones. Be sure that you don't give the baby a bottle to take to bed; if you want to offer a few extra ounces of milk, hold the child in your arms for the feeding. Rocking, walking the floor, or taking the baby to bed with you should be avoided.

MORE TIME FOR PLAY

Play is the baby's education, and the mobile child needs both more time and more space for it. A five- to eight-month-old may spend an hour at a time in the playpen but needs a regular unfettered period on the floor or outdoors on a grassy lawn where he or she can explore and investigate. It might be wise to invest in an expandable outdoor corral that can be formed into a circle large enough for the baby's outdoor explorations and experiments.

Toys also must keep pace with development. When the baby can sit unsupported or get about by creeping or crawling, he or she needs toys that can be pulled and pushed and that will move just as the baby does. The baby is ready for a music box, too. By now, he or she can distinguish and locate sound, and nothing holds the attention as music does. Add a ball, too. A five- to eight-month-old delights in pushing it, watching it roll away, and then scooting after it—or in having you return it.

Toys needn't be expensive nor even labeled "toys." The baby is entranced by the ability to make noise—a handful of clattering pie tins can provide play for a half hour.

All the world is a plaything for the growing baby, who needs both a regular time and space to explore it. Toys don't have to be expensive items bought in a store; everyday utensils can keep a child enthralled for hours.

FEAR CREEPS IN

Combined with the baby's new spirit of adventure will be some new fears. Actually, the moments of fright, too, are landmarks in development—indications that the baby has become aware of the consequences of some actions or that he or she is now conscious of differences and details that once were obscure.

Sudden loud noises, even the kind the baby has heard before, may trigger howls. Water running in the bathtub, the noise of a vacuum cleaner, a clap of thunder may bring tears and shrieks. The baby who has splashed delightedly in the bath for months may now cry as he or she watches the water run down the drain.

Be reassuring. If the noisy sweeper distresses the baby, pick up the child and talk quietly, while moving the sweeper back and forth to associate the noise and reassurance. During a thunderstorm, hold the child, and with a few words, make the point that the frightening moment is over and you are still at hand.

At this same time, shyness with people outside the immediate family may develop. Whereas once the baby "make up" to virtually every adult, now he or she may become wary perhaps even of grandparents, neighbors, or the doctor whom the baby has visited many times. The baby's tears and fears may upset the grandparents who have previously been welcomed so avidly, but they only need to be reminded that the phase is temporary.

You also may find the shyness applies to baby-sitters, to day-care providers, and to visits to other homes or unfamiliar places. With sitters or day-care center employees you may be obliged to spend a longer time with the baby before leaving him or her. (Even babies can be great actors, and the sitter will usually confirm that the baby didn't cry for long after you left.) When you visit a strange place, be sure to stay with the child and reassure him or her of your presence throughout the visit.

13

Eight to Twelve Months

HOW THE BABY GROWS

By the age of ten months, the average normal baby boy weighs 21 1/4 pounds and measures 29 inches; the average normal girl, 20 pounds and 28 1/2 inches. Ninety percent of normal babies are between 17 1/4 and 25 pounds and 27 1/4 and 31 inches.

Here are some things half of normal babies learn to do by ten months:

- play pattycake;
- hold a block in each hand and bang them together;
- identify "mama" and "dada" and call them by name;
- pull to a standing position;
- stand without support for a few seconds;
- walk or sidestep, holding onto playpen or furniture;
- wave bye-bye.

The average normal boy weighs 22 1/2 pounds and measures 30 inches on his first birthday; the average normal girl, 21 1/4 pounds and 29 1/4 inches. Normal weight ranges between 18 1/2 and 26 1/2 pounds and normal height between 28 1/4 and 32 inches.

Here's what half of normal one-year-olds can do:

- stop a rolling ball when you push it, then try to roll it back;
- indicate wants without crying;
- drink from a cup, spilling only a little;
- take a few steps;
- stand alone, stoop, and return to a standing position;
- understand many words;
- say two to three words in addition to "mama" and "dada";
- say "no" and mean it.

YOUR BABY IS DIFFERENT

It's almost impossible to generalize about the "average" baby between eight and 12 months old. Children simply develop in too many directions at once. Statistically, half of one-year-olds can take a few steps, speak a few recognizable words, and make an effort to feed themselves. Yet year-old Johnny may have been walking since nine months—and not say his first word until 15 months. Susan, on the other hand, may gabble a blue streak while remaining contentedly fixed in a sitting position. The range of accomplishments is truly astonishing.

Unfortunately, walking and talking bring out parental competitive urges. Mothers and fathers like to boast about how early a child walked or talked, especially if their child walked or talked before a friend's child. Parents of children who take the slow-but-sure route to transportation and communication may become frustrated and anxious. They may worry that their baby's development has been delayed and subtly try to push the baby along. Equally bad, a child's supposed slowness may make parents feel they are doing something wrong.

In children's growth, as in the Bible, there is a season to all things. Studies repeatedly show there is always an appropriate moment in development when all systems are ready for the next step forward. When a child's bones, nerves, muscles, coordination, and, most of all, ambition have matured sufficiently, the child walks; when the brain centers and the vocal muscles are ready, the child talks. Apart from providing opportunity and encouragement, you can't do much to hasten the process. If your child seems ready to walk but is wary of trying, you might try to stimulate him or her by placing a toy just out of reach as a motive to do so. But a mother who holds her nine-month-old's hands and "practices" walking may find she has gained nothing for her efforts but a sore back.

In any case, a seemingly slow child quickly makes up for lost time. The infant who walks at nine months may spend the next three months refining the movements. The child who walks later may master crawling, walking, and sitting in a week's time and two weeks later have overtaken and even surpassed the early riser.

DIFFERENCES BETWEEN THE SEXES

Apart from the obvious, boys and girls aren't terribly different. An average baby boy weighs about a half pound more and is an inch longer at birth than a baby girl, and some difference in size and weight usually persists into adulthood. But the differences in size among individual members of either sex are far greater than the differences between the sexes as a whole, either in infancy or maturity.

Temperamentally, boys and girls may seem different. Boys are thought to more rough-and-tumble, more curious, and more outgoing, whereas girls are considered verbal, gentle, and reserved. But no one knows if these differences are actually inborn or are the product of conditioning. Films and audio recordings of parents with newborns have shown that mothers and fathers talk and behave differently toward girls than boys right from birth. A father may soften his voice and coo to his daughter and adopt a gruff, see-here-old-man tone with his son.

In any case, temperamental differences vary widely within a single sex, just as physical sizes do. You can't necessarily expect a little girl to be more talkative and a little boy to be more active. A rambunctious girl who is into everything is just as normal as her subdued sister, and a slow-moving male just as much of a boy as a brother bent on raising the roof.

Some parents like to reinforce the presumed feminine qualities in little girls and the masculine ones in boys; others feel the child's behavior should be allowed to develop by itself without attempts to mold it into stereotypes. This is a matter of family style. More important than the approach is to be aware of your attitudes and their influence on the child. Here are some points you may wish to consider:

• Do you have different standards for boys and girls? Is your son's boisterousness considered normal behavior, your daughter's self-assertion abnormal?

• Do you push your child toward stereotyped activity? Do you buy athletic equipment for a boy, even in infancy, dolls and dishes for a girl? Do you roughhouse with your son but not with your daughter?

• Do you allow both sexes equal emotional expression? When your son cries, do you tell him that's sissy stuff but tolerate crying and emotional displays in a daughter? Are you equally affectionate with both sons and daughters?

• Do you expect neatness from a girl, even a toddler, but excuse disorder in a boy?

• Do you pair the family by sexes? Is the father expected to have a different attitude and responsibility for a son's upbringing than a mother has for her daughter?

Most of us have qualities that we admire in children and those we don't. We reinforce those we like and ignore or criticize those we disapprove. Even in infancy, your child quickly learns to recognize which behavior is rewarded; when the reward is withheld, he or she tries to live up to your expectations.

Most parents treat their children somewhat differently, according to the child's sex. It is a perfectly human trait.

STANDING AND WALKING, STEP BY STEP

Any time after seven months, your child may enter the vertical world of grown-ups. Sitting on the floor of a playpen with legs extended, your baby may reach above his or her head, grab onto the playpen, strain sufficiently—and there, the buttocks are off the floor. The next time, a slight kink of the knees and downward pressure with the heels will elevate the baby a little higher. Another try may bring a bit more height. At last, the baby will grasp the top rail, flex the knees, tug laboriously, and finally stand triumphant and upright like the other members of the family.

Unfortunately, at first your baby won't know how to get back down. Amid terrified bleats and howls, he or she may cling to the playpen rail until little legs cave in from exhaustion and the baby drops back with an abrupt plop! If you rush to the rescue and ease the baby down gently, you may be greeted by a new protest of displeasure. No sooner is the baby sitting than he or she emphatically yanks back up again to savor some more of this newfound perspective on the big, wide world!

After a few days, the baby will be going up and down with relative ease—lowering those well-padded buttocks gently until the last few inches of free fall. Next may come a new step—actually, a sideways shuffle. Crunching toys, crackers, blankets, and bottles underfoot, the baby may sidestep around the confines of the playpen while holding onto the top rail. Released from the pen, the baby will cautiously apply the same principles to circumnavigate the furniture.

Soon the baby will learn to stand without holding. This lesson is usually accidental. One day the baby may be standing at the playpen rail, holding a toy in one hand and the rail in the other. Almost absentmindedly, he or she will relax the grip yet remain upright without being aware of the accomplishment. Balance may be maintained from a few seconds to a minute or more. Before long, the baby will be able to repeat the act deliberately, and the periods of independent stance will steadily lengthen. This, too, will quickly become routine as the baby learns new tricks, like stooping to pick up a toy and then returning to a standing position.

All these preliminaries to walking may take place within a few weeks or be spread over several months. There is no fixed date when a baby sets sail alone. Most babies (90 percent) walk by the age of 15 months, but another 10 percent, equally normal, are still sedentary at that age, either because they lack the confidence or ambition to walk or simply because they have more important things to do, like crawling.

Regardless of when they come, your baby's first independent steps are a milestone you're not likely to forget. Some babies accidentally achieve the goal themselves. Perambulating about the living room, the baby may let go of a sofa, lunge toward an inviting chair—and "walk" without knowing it. Sometimes parents try to "help," which may not actually help, but can be fun. When the baby seems to be standing well and shows good balance in stooping and sidestepping, sit on the floor a short distance from where the baby is standing, stretch out your hands, and urge him or her to "come to me." You may have to ask several times before he or she makes the initial attempt without aid. But finally, whether you're there or not, leaning forward, the baby will venture forth. It'll be only one to two quick steps at first—almost falling—but the milestone will have been reached.

The next days, weeks, and months are fun to watch. Some babies, once started, may be hard to stop—in more ways than one. A new walker often can't get enough of this novel new form of locomotion and may literally exhaust both self and parents by lurching around the living room to refine newfound skills. Heedless of consequences, he or she may keep going like a windup toy until something brings the adventure to a halt. Another child may take those few steps, then sit down for a few days or even weeks before trying again, as though considering whether the effort is really worthwhile. And still another may seem to concentrate on each individual move, going slowly and methodically at his or her own pace, regardless of encouragement from parents.

In the jumbled sequence of development, not every child fits any of these models. Some learn to stand or sidestep well, then remain at this stage for several months. A few babies learn to walk backward before they can walk forward. Difficult as this seems for an adult, the baby's sequence of motor development makes it easier to do.

Meanwhile, for most babies, walking is just for fun. Crawling is for important business. Even after mastering walking, a one-year-old often will drop to all fours when the idea is to *get* somewhere. This crawling ability—often combined with climbing—can propel the baby into dangerous situations and hazardous places, requiring increased parental vigilance.

SAYING A FEW WORDS

By now the baby is firmly established in the world of verbal communication. The exact number of words a child can speak or understand at this age varies widely. Each child develops speech in a unique pattern. But even the baby who has not said a word knows that vocal sounds are the way humans express their ideas and wishes and is beginning to test the notion.

Up to now, the baby has strung together repetitive sounds in a meaningless but imitative babble: "mamama" and "dadada." Sometime during the last few months of the first year, the sounds begin to take on meaning for most babies. "Mama" and "dada" (or the baby's version thereof) are applied regularly and consistently to the baby's parents. New words follow over the next few months. "No" is (to parents' dismay) an early addition. "Bye-bye" is another. "See?" accompanied by outstretched toy, dish, or bottle to be observed, also arrives early. So do names of brothers and sisters, usually with the baby's own unique pronunciation.

Baby's first word is a landmark—but you may not be aware of it. Some babies speak their first word clearly, spontaneously, and unmistakably, as though they had been silently rehearsing it for weeks. More often, the baby's first attempts at speech are only partially recognizable or even completely unrecognizable to adults. Only after the baby repeatedly has used the same sound for an object or person will adults catch on that the baby has something to say and is making an effort to say it.

In addition to speech, the baby's passive vocabulary—the words he or she understands but can't repeat—expand rapidly during the last part of the first year. By their first birthday, most babies recognize their own names, and some carry out simple commands like, "Give me the bottle," and respond to simple questions like, "Where is the airplane?" by pointing upward or looking toward the sky. Months may pass, however, before these words and simple sentences enter the baby's spoken vocabulary.

The baby understands nonverbal communication at this stage, too. Your moods of anger, frustration, uncertainty, or fatigue are unfailingly more clear than words.

SELF-FEEDING TIME

By now, self-feeding may be the order of the day. In fact, the baby may insist on it. You'll still have to feed the soupier, mushier fruits and vegetables, but the baby will get a lot of nourishment from finger foods and "lumps."

Much of the food will be the same as the rest of the family is

Your baby may spill a few times, but practice and more practice make perfect. Real skill at using a cup and other utensils may not be apparent for another year or so. Encourage the baby's efforts—and keep paper towels handy.

eating. As the baby develops more teeth and gets the hang of chewing, he or she can eat more and more adult foods. You no longer have to strain foods; simply mash them or cut them into small and manageable pieces. By their first birthdays, most babies have anywhere from two to eight teeth, so they can pulverize most foods you serve them. Molars don't arrive until the age of one year, however, so babies can't do much grinding. That means chunks of food—raw carrots or meat that requires chewing, for example—are still off the menu. Stick to ground meat, soft lunch meat, cheese, and soft or cooked vegetables and fruits.

Definite likes and dislikes continue to show themselves and appetite may slacken. Yet babies are surprisingly skilled at working out a balanced diet for themselves, taking in enough food for growth. In one historic experiment, babies barely old enough for finger foods were allowed to choose their own diet from a smorgasbord of choices. Although they sometimes ate only one food at a meal and ignored all others, over the period of observation their selections balanced out to include all the essential nutrients.

But the baby still isn't ready for fancy dishes. Confine the menu to simple foods and combinations. Restrict seasonings, and limit salt and sugar. When preparing adult food for the baby's meals, serve the baby first, and then season it for the rest of the family.

SPOON AND CUP TIME

Let the baby practice with spoon and cup. Real skill may not come for another year, but the baby gets the idea of manipulating them and gradually cuts down on the spills. Some babies can raise a cup at the proper angle to drink as early as ten months, but most aren't quite so precocious. Eighteen months is a more likely date for that achievement. If messiness at the table disturbs you, let the baby experiment with drinking from a cup in the bathtub—even if a little bathwater is swallowed in the process.

The baby's appetite for milk may continue to decline, then stabilize at around 20 ounces. So long as the baby is healthy, the reduction is no cause for concern. Indeed, some babies may develop a real distaste for milk by this time. If yours is one, don't worry about it. By 18 months, most essential nutrients—protein, carbohydrates, sugars—can be obtained without milk.

SIBLING RIVALRY AGAIN

The baby's walking, talking, and cute antics may draw so much attention that competitive feelings are rekindled (see page 138) among older brothers and sisters. The rivalry may become so intense that you actually have to protect the baby, especially if the other children are younger than three or four years old.

The competition usually takes one of several forms. When the baby sets out walking on unsteady legs, the older child may "jokingly" nudge, bump, or crowd so the baby is upended. Such thumps are likely to make him or her wary and uneasy about walking and actually delay mastery of the skill. Or when the baby tries to converse with you, a sister or brother may talk louder to outshout the little rival. You also may find the older brother feeding the baby a diet of cigarette butts or paper clips or giving him or her dangerous toys to play with. And when a parent returns from work at the end of the day, the crawling baby who hurries to the door may be "accidentally" trampled by equally eager siblings.

Competing with an attractive one-year-old isn't any more fun than competing with a newborn, and you'll have to be patient with the older children. It's also true that competition isn't strictly a one-way street, and sometimes you'll have to champion the older child's rights against the younger. That means making sure the older child gets enough attention and is not constantly compelled to give in to a younger sibling. The older child's toys, for instance, should belong to him or her and be kept from the inquisitive and inadvertently destructive hands of the baby.

Older brothers and sisters are an important part of a baby's life, too. The baby can learn as much from them as from you and may actually prefer the loud and romping company of brothers and sisters. Under your watchful eye, allow them to play together and stimulate each other. Caution the older children to be careful, but remember it also is important for the baby to learn the concept of self-protection. Try to keep your interference to a minimum.

If yours is an only child, you may find that he or she shows an increasing interest in other babies. A ten-month-old may spend long minutes studying the face of another baby in a magazine. Or, being pushed around the supermarket in a stroller, your offspring may greet and reach out to other small passersby.

Babies this age, of course, don't really play together. At most, they may play side-by-side or investigate each other by looking, poking, prodding, or passing possessions back and forth. But the company of other children can stimulate a child's development. Specialists in education during early childhood have found that children develop faster socially if they are repeatedly exposed to their peers and can watch and imitate them. Your one-year-old child may not be ready for a regular play group yet, but frequent outings in the park, visits to neighbors, and time in other children's homes may be valuable.

SKILL AT PLAY
The thumb-and-finger grasp is mastered between 8 and 12 months. Soon after that, the baby can form a neat pincers with thumb and forefinger, so that he or she can deftly scoop up objects as small as a raisin.

By now, the baby can differentiate the use of hands, carrying a bottle, for example, in the left hand while pushing a ball with the other. "Handedness," however, hasn't developed yet. The baby uses hands interchangeably and won't begin to favor one over the other until after 18 months of age.

The baby's style of play changes to complement this new skill. Now, a favorite pastime becomes skillfully retrieving dropped objects, stuffing them one by one into a can or bottle, then dumping them out again. Helped by the pincers, the baby can select one toy from many, turn the pages of a book (although he or she may do this more often with the palm of the hand), lift blocks, and even pile one on another. The baby also may be able to hold a crayon and stab marks on a piece of paper.

SEEING AND REMEMBERING
Now you may be aware that your baby takes in whole events and scenes and remembers them later. To your surprise, he or she knows the proper place for every bit of furniture in a familiar room and quickly recognizes when you've added a new chair or changed the position of another. A quick jab or gesture with the forefinger toward the misplaced object lets you know what the baby has seen and remembered.

Memory for time and events sharpens, too. Elaborating on peekaboo and drop-the-cup-and-listen-for-the-delicious-crash, the baby now recalls that last night you dangled him or her on your knee. He or she crawls up, ready to play the new game again. Hide-and-seek, infant style, played with brothers and sisters, replaces covering the eyes with the hand and playing "Guess who?" or "Peekaboo." A rudimentary game of tag can be another favorite, but just running and scampering about with a parent in pursuit can become a popular routine.

Now the baby will set down a toy and remember where it was stored. If it is placed out of the line of sight, he or she will confidently reach for it and expect it to be there. Once upon a time, each encounter with a toy was a new experience. Now the baby knows the stuffed calico dog is the same, whether found in the playpen, on the high chair, or behind the sofa.

An airplane roars overhead, or a car whizzes by. The baby looks up or hurries to the window, having learned from experience to link the sound and sight. When the door opens at day's end, signaling a parent's return, the baby gleefully stampedes to the door or turns in that direction, recognizing the cue and its meaning. Taking a coat from the closet may be associated with an auto ride.

All these developments help your child assemble a picture of the world and a place in it. Lessons are learned that some objects are fixed and some change, that people come and go, that there is a time and order to events. Most of all, they show the child that he or she can affect these events and that they they can affect the child.

SET UP A PLAY SPACE

A child needs a place to play. Not just a playpen but the baby's own area with space to use toys and with low storage shelves.

A play area needn't be elaborate. A corner of a room will do, if it's out of the traffic pattern. The best choice is near the living area of the house, where the baby will play more contentedly because the parents or other family members are in sight. If the play area is to be in a bedroom or nursery at the other end of the house, always leave the door open so the baby will know you're there. You can install a gate in the doorway if you want to confine the baby.

Simple equipment is enough. Durable wall-to-wall carpeting, linoleum, or tile is better than waxed floors or scatter rugs, which are hazardous footing for a novice walker. Make your own shelves or buy unpainted ones. Finish them in bright colors with a durable paint. Even boxes turned on their sides will serve for toy storage. Avoid toy chests with lids, which may slam down on little fingers. The baby needs to spend some time in the play space every day but also needs some time to explore and experiment in the rest of the house.

LEARNING TO SAY NO

An early entry in the baby's active vocabulary is the word "no" and the mood that goes with it. Some time before the first birthday a spunky baby will pronounce the negative with emphasis.

When the baby isn't hungry and you try to spoon in a few vegetables, you may be admonished with a firm, "No." Take away a fragile object the baby is clutching and the child will insist, "No!" with accompanying tears. Bedtime may bring a shower of negatives—"no, no, no!"—and vigorous shakes of the head.

Being negative is just another sign the baby is growing. The message is that he or she is no longer malleable, able to be shifted about as parents choose, without a murmur of protest. As the months go on, you'll hear the word more and more as the baby makes it clear that his or her wishes are to be included in any household decision. You may find yourself longing for the days before speech, and you may have to think up some clever ruses to circumvent the negative response.

"No" is an important addition to the child's vocabulary. As an active baby gets into everything, you'll be using it more and more. "No" spoken quickly and forcefully keeps a baby out of trouble. "That's a no-no" is a catchphrase that teaches what is permissible and what is not.

Use your "no's" judiciously, however. If the house has too many "no-no's" and too many fun things are forbidden, the word will lose its meaning; worse yet, it becomes a challenge.

AND THEN THERE'S MISCHIEF
Once your baby has an inkling of which actions are approved and which forbidden, mischief comes to the fore.

One favorite trick is to tease you into attentiveness. The baby will scuttle toward some temptation that's definitely a no-no, then pause until you're aware of where he or she is traveling. Once you've noticed, the baby churns into action, heading full steam for the target, only to squeal with delight on being intercepted. Or the baby may gain your attention, then move toward something that's known to be dangerous, confident that you'll be there to step in if anything goes wrong.

Around the age of a year or a little later, you may see the baby bearing down on a vase or keepsake that's known to be forbidden, repeating "No, no, no" all the while. Odd as it may seem to you, that's a very sophisticated concept. It's the beginning of self-control, an ability that later will help the child to realize what's approved and what's disapproved.

CHANGING MOODS
The idea of "No" arrives not quite simultaneously with the idea of "Yes." Seeking your approval or hoping to avoid your disapproval are two new moods you may detect in a baby around the first birthday. Now, actions are no longer governed exclusively by the child's own obvious desires but by the reaction they may provoke in you.

Whereas crying and smiling were once the gamut of emotions,

KEEPING BABY SAFE

By now, the baby is so active and, often, so surprisingly strong that a new set of precautions is needed, which must strike a balance between containment for safety's sake and freedom to explore for the benefit of the baby's own development. Parents of an eight-month- to one-year-old child must be extra vigilant because changes come so fast. The time when a parent says, "Oh, he can't do that," is just the time when the baby does it.

In the supermarket, a baby this age is leaning out of the stroller, trying to snatch cans from the shelves, and bending almost double in an effort to scoop papers or objects off the floor. He or she may even climb out of the stroller if left unattended. At home, the baby can climb quickly to dangerous heights, scale the stairs, or scoot outdoors if a door is temporarily left ajar. He or she probably can open drawers, closets, bottles, and packages.

Review all earlier precautions, and then add these:

• Baby-proof all closets or drawers that you think the baby can reach and some others you think he or she can't. Empty them of all small or sharp objects; possible poisons; breakables; plastic bags; and beans, peanuts, or other small bits of food that might cause the baby to choke.

• Install baby-proof catches on all drawers and doors to prevent baby from opening them. Lock those areas from which you cannot remove contents.

• Do not store cleaners, cleaning fluids,

detergents, or other cleaning materials where the baby can reach them.

• When cooking, always turn pot handles away from the front of the stove so the baby can't reach them and pull over the contents. Keep hot foods and items away from the baby's high chair during meals.

• Don't use dangling tablecloths. A one-year-old can pull down the cloth—dishes and all.

• Keep medicines and household products under lock and key. The ban extends to medicines like aspirin, which can harm a baby if swallowed in quantity. Be especially careful when someone is ill and medicines are out of their usual place.

• Never leave the baby alone in a bathtub or wading pool. He or she can drown in a few inches of water.

• If you have a backyard pool, make sure it is fenced and has a gate that latches firmly.

now your baby may appear sad, hurt, euphoric, tearful. When you leave, he or she may burst into tears. Chided for committing a no-no, the little transgressor may don an expression that would break the hardest heart.

Just as the baby has learned that dropping a cup from a high chair causes a noise moments later, so he or she has learned that a given action may win a smile or frown. That doesn't mean every action is taken with the idea of manipulating you—although a one-year-old is capable of manipulation, too. It does mean that many actions are performed after carefully weighing the consequences.

A baby now can tire in a few minutes of a toy that once would have riveted concentration far longer. The baby performs more, too, playing for your applause in his or her accomplishments hour after hour. (But your pride and joy probably will refuse to repeat them in front of company.)

You'll also see the baby express tenderness. A doll, stuffed animal, or toy will be cuddled, loved, and carefully tended. This kind of "mothering" is the beginning of adult love—which begins with you, then is transferred to an object beyond you, and finally to persons beyond the object.

Dealing with the baby's changing moods isn't easy for many parents. Up to now, parents have seen their baby almost as an extension of themselves, to be handled or maneuvered according to their own schedule or convenience. When the baby looks hurt, some parents melt. When a child cuts loose with anger, the parent overreacts with adult anger. For parents, the end of a child's first year also is a difficult period of growth. Now you must recognize that your offspring is not merely a helpless being to be acknowledged at your will but a personality to be dealt with in his or her own right.

14

Twelve to Eighteen Months

HOW THE BABY GROWS

By age 15 months, the average normal baby weighs 24 pounds and measures 31 inches. The range for normal babies is 20 to 28 pounds and 29½ to 33½ inches.

Here are some things your baby may learn to do between 12 and 15 months:

- use a spoon and spill only a little;
- imitate a parent doing housework;
- build a tower with two cubes;
- scribble with a crayon;
- walk backward as well as forward.

The average normal baby grows an inch and gains a pound and a half during the next three months. At 18 months, normal weight is 25½ pounds; normal height, 32 inches. The range for normal babies is 21½ to 29½ pounds and 30½ to 34½ inches.

Here are some of the things normal babies achieve by the age of 18 months:

- remove some or all of their clothes;
- build a four-cube tower;
- walk up steps, holding rail or using wall as support;
- point to a baby's picture in a book or magazine;
- use name when referring to themselves.

A BLUR OF MOTION

At this age, you'll quickly learn the meaning of that expression, "the patter of tiny feet." Quick little legs and rapidly improving coordination will carry your son or daughter just about anywhere he or she wants to go. And go the tireless baby will—upstairs, downstairs, outdoors when there's an opportunity, and into every corner of the house. Once the art of walking is mastered, your baby may be on the move from morning to night—leading you on a merry chase.

At first, the pace may be hesitant and wobbly. But by the middle of the second year, your baby's steps will become quick and sure; he or she may even be able to run a little. Stairs no longer may be an obstacle. A one-year-old may be able to walk downstairs while holding your hand but only crawl upstairs. Six months later, the toddler may walk upstairs under his or her own steam, using a rail or the wall for support. Coming down is an all-fours, stern-first proposition. And watch out! Your toddler now can climb. The baby not only learns how to scale chairs, shelves, and tables, but also how to rearrange furniture to reach a tempting object.

Of course, toddlers' temperaments differ: some children are more content to sit and study their surroundings with their eyes; others prefer to investigate with fingers or feet. Regardless of the approach your child takes, childish curiosity now reaches its zenith. Free at last from many of the physical limitations of the first 12 months of his or her life, the baby throws all the inexhaustible energy of childhood into learning just what it is that makes the world tick.

And it's fun for you to observe this boundless drive to learn. Watch closely when you give your child something for the first time—a cookie, for instance. First there's an exploratory taste—more in the name of research than hunger. Then the baby may pound the cookie, squeeze it, hold it up to the light and eye it speculatively, trace its perimeter with a finger, roll it, set it down to inspect from various angles, rub with the palm of the hand, crumble it, and feel the texture of each crumb. Finally, having discovered every important detail about this fascinating object, the baby may actually eat what's left of the cookie—or, bored with the whole thing, abandon it.

TRYING TIMES FOR PARENTS
Another side of a one-year-old's independence is a growing sense of self. The child wants to do what he or she wants to do when he or she want to do it and protests and resists any attempt on your part to interfere or divert attention from the goal at hand. Quickly, this tenacious me-first attitude puts little Jason or Jennifer on an unwavering collision course with the world.

Naturally, you want to give your child freedom to explore and learn to the fullest—but without danger and without trampling the rights of others. Because children at this age are frequently oblivious to danger and haven't the slightest idea what rights are, clashes are bound to occur. The important thing to realize, though, is that your one-year-old isn't being defiant, disobedient, or "bad." The concepts of right and wrong simply haven't penetrated yet and won't for several more years. When a one-year-old deliberately and carefully drops the sugar bowl on the floor after you've told him not to, it's because he wants to see what happens when it hits, not because he's a "bad boy."

Moreover, a toddler—unlike most adults—doesn't absorb a lesson in a single teaching. You may have to retrieve your young dynamo from the top shelf of the bookcase or stop him or her from stuffing towels into the toilet five or six (or more) times before the message begins to take hold clearly.

You'll never eliminate all the power struggles that may crop up at this age. But you can reduce them by diminishing the possible sources of conflict. Controlling the baby's environment is as much for the child's benefit as it is for yours. The fewer times you have to interfere, the less frazzled your nerves will be at the end of the day and the better your relationship with the baby.

First, review and reinforce the safety precautions described in earlier chapters. Try to stay one or two steps ahead of the baby; if he or she is now tall enough to reach the doorknob, assume that it will only be a matter of time until the knob is turned and your baby is toddling out the door. Install a bolt the child cannot operate.

Second, keep temptations and "no-nos" away from curious little fingers. If your child's favorite pastime is rummaging through drawers, remove valuables and replace them with toys, pans, or other harmless substitutes.

Third, don't rely on verbal warnings to check a child's disapproved behavior. If possible, take the forbidden object from the child, saying "No!" while you do it. If the child is playing with the television set, which can't be moved, take the child to another part of the house and offer him or her another toy to play with. Some determined children will quickly resume the taboo behavior, but fortunately most children have a short attention span and become absorbed by a new toy or less bothersome activity.

Of course, a slap on errant hands or whack on a diapered bottom will momentarily distract a child. But in spite of the resulting howls, a lasting lesson seldom is learned. Linking deed to punishment is still too vague an association for most toddlers to make:

What the child really learns may be that parents are unpredictable and sometimes hurt you. In any case, you'll have to repeat the lesson again and again. A spontaneous vocal outburst by a terrified parent whose child has just entered a danger zone, like climbing onto the sill of an open window, can be an effective teaching tool. On the other hand, such obvious excitement on the part of Mom or Dad may so overwhelmingly fascinate the baby that he or she will repeat the action just to see the reaction one more time.

Even the most serene baby can leave parents exhausted by evening. The simplest, most routine act becomes a terrific and tiring tussle; you may have to learn to change diapers on the run because the baby won't lie down even for 30 seconds. The parent who provides child care during the day will need plenty of support and assistance.

AT THE SAME TIME, DEPENDENCE

You'll see it happen frequently. Striking out on some adventure of his or her own, your child will suddenly turn to look at you or even trot back to make sure you're still there. Or, off in another room out of your sight, the baby will repeatedly call out to you as a means of ensuring your continuing presence. For all the baby's bravery, he or she will cling tightly, whine, stubbornly refuse to let go of you.

You can understand the emotional conflict. It's like dangling from a tree branch and maintaining your grip until at last you feel the ground under you. To your little adventurer, you represent safety, stability, reliability, familiarity; he or she is eager to discover the world beyond, but who knows what tigers lie out there? Should he or she give up the known to challenge the unknown? The child needs to know that if he or she ventures too far, you will still be there as a refuge and retreat.

The fear of strange places, new situations, and different people, which may have begun earlier, may continue. Where once the child cheerfully remained with any baby-sitter, he or she may now shriek and cry uncontrollably at any indication that you are leaving. If you take the child to a friend's house for a visit, the normally curious youngster may refuse to leave your lap. If the child has been cared for in a day-care center, you may now find that he or she refuses to enter the center or acknowledge the sitter. On the other hand, the baby-sitter may be accepted, but all others, even a favorite aunt, uncle, or grandmother, are shut out completely.

Dealing with this kind of anxiety calls for patience—both from you and from the "strangers." Your child is still grappling with the concept of time; at 18 months or less, the baby is just beginning to learn that farewell doesn't mean forever. If he or she seems anxious about you at home, reassure the child by repeatedly calling to him or her when out of sight. Keep talking as you move about the house, even if you feel as if you're talking to yourself. If you're going out, sit with the child before leaving and reassure him or her that you'll be coming home soon.

Pick a sitter carefully. During this period, you want one who will pay attention to the child's needs and make the transition easier, not simply a custodian who will watch television while the child sleeps. Pay the sitter for an extra hour to spend with the child while you're present, so the child won't feel abandoned when you do leave.

THE CHANGING APPETITE

In the first year of life, your baby gained about 16 pounds. In the second year, the gain will be only about five. Some children continue to be good eaters; but many have a more or less dramatic decline in appetite, and some become unbelievably picky eaters.

Because a one-year-old usually is less hungry, he or she will pick and choose which food to eat. Some days, almost nothing will be eaten at any of the three meals; the hunger strike may even continue for several days. Then the baby will suddenly gobble every scrap and ask for more. Relieved, you may offer bigger servings at the next meal, only to have it rejected again.

The baby may go in binges, confining consumption to mashed potatoes or scrambled eggs or peanut butter and firmly refusing all other foods. Vegetables, for example, may be absolutely out. After a week of this, he or she may just as firmly refuse the favored food and go on to another specialty. The situation may be further complicated by the baby's inexhaustible energy and overwhelming curiosity. In the interests of science, he or she may mix all the foods together—then refuse to eat the unholy mess. Or the baby simply won't sit still long enough for what you consider a proper meal.

This is an exasperating time for parents, who become convinced the baby will starve to death if they don't kill the child first. The objective quickly becomes to force food down the baby's throat at any price. The baby balks, the parent becomes convinced the baby is simply being disobedient, and the battle is on. In this way, many a lasting eating problem has begun.

The basic fact is that the year-old baby simply needs fewer calories than the six-month-old child. That may be hard for you to believe at the rate he or she is burning them off, but studies have repeatedly shown that a baby's consumption, despite the ups and downs, evens off. Even a baby who won't eat vegetables obtains, over a period of time, the necessary vitamins, minerals, and fiber from fruit and other food. Obviously, you should worry if the baby seems not to gain weight or is clearly losing it. But most 12- to 18-month-olds thrive despite what parents consider birdlike appetites.

THE BABY'S MENU

By now, baby can eat just about anything you eat and will feed him-or herself. Eating with a spoon will still be a somewhat messy business, and you'll have to look the other way sometimes. For the sake of convenience, you'll probably continue to offer commercially prepared baby foods on occasion. Now, most babies' milk intake probably will be down to about a pint every 24 hours or so.

One reason the baby's menu can be expanded is because more teeth have appeared. The ages when children cut primary, or "baby," teeth vary extremely, but the average child gets his or her first molars, or grinding teeth, shortly after the first birthday and by midyear may have as many as 16 teeth—eight front incisors, four cuspids (or canine teeth), and four molars. Thus equipped, an 18-month-old can deal with many adult foods.

Among the foods on your 18-month-old's list of favorites are the following:
- Chopped hamburger • Bananas • Jelly
- Lunch meats • Mashed potatoes
- Chicken, diced or chopped • Cottage cheese
- Meat loaf, lightly seasoned • Plain cookies
- Puddings • Scrambled eggs
- Smooth peanut butter • Applesauce
- Sliced orange • Cooked or canned fruits
- Macaroni and spaghetti • Bread
- Crackers • Chopped or mashed vegetables

A few foods are still off limits, primarily those that are not easily chewed and may become lodged in the throat. The list includes peanuts, popcorn, chunks of raw fruits or vegetable, fruits containing seeds or stones, and fruits with thick skins, unless the skins have been removed beforehand. Meat (including Vienna sausage or hot dogs) should be given only if it is soft or cut into very fine pieces. Whole-kernel corn usually is withheld from babies because, unless it is well chewed, corn passes through the digestive system unchanged.

Most one-year-olds resist spicy or strongly flavored foods, in-

At this age, the baby tries for a mouthful in any way that's handy. Disregard the sloppiness and spilled food during dinnertime; they will disappear as soon as the baby learns more efficient ways to get the job done.

cluding corned beef, dried beef, and such vegetables as radishes, parsnips, broccoli, and cauliflower.

In the interests of better health and sounder teeth, you may want to postpone giving the baby sugared foods or sweets. It probably is unrealistic to believe that you can keep a child away from candy or cookies forever, because he or she may encounter them in another home. Study after study has shown that even very young children prefer sweet tastes to other tastes. At the very least, you can postpone offering desserts, puddings, and other sweet foods until the end of the meal.

Basically, a toddler will eat (or at least sit down to eat) three major meals a day, with a break for crackers and juice at midmorning and midafternoon. At each major meal, the baby's menu might consist of one filling dish, such as cereal, eggs, potato, macaroni, or spaghetti, plus a fruit or vegetable. Meat or another high-protein food may be offered once a day. The filling food may be a small sandwich, although babies 18 months or younger are likely to tear apart the sandwich, ignore the bread, and eat the filling.

MORE WAKING HOURS

The baby's sleeping habits will change between 12 and 18 months—and you'll probably think the change is for the worse. By this age, many children have eliminated one nap a day (usually the morning one) and sleep fewer hours at night. Despite the tremendous output of energy during the day, a 12- to 18-month-old fights being put to bed and may call and cry and thrash for an hour before dropping off to sleep. Worst of all, the baby may wake during the night and rouse the entire household with cries to be freed and permitted to resume the day's activities.

One reason for a baby's sleeplessness is "separation anxiety," that fear of being away from you even for a brief period. Another reason is simple excitement. After a day in which one thrilling discovery followed another, it takes time for the baby to unwind, just as it does for you to relax after a particularly triumphant day. A baby just can't wait to get back to the business of learning, which stimulates early rising and waking during the night.

Parents may feel that babies don't need two naps a day—but Mother and Dad do! You needn't worry about the baby getting enough sleep; that takes care of itself. But you'll have to take firm steps to see that *you* do. Here's how:

At naptime, place the baby in the crib, however loud the protests, and make sure he or she remains there at least an hour. Leave the bedroom door open so he or she can hear you and is aware of your presence. At night, set a regular bedtime and be relatively consistent about it. Develop a nighttime ritual that clearly means bedtime has arrived. The ritual will vary according to the baby's (and your) temperament; in some families, it may be roughhousing followed by a quiet interlude. In others, the baby may nuzzle on your lap for a time while you talk soothingly. Or you might look at a picture book together, sing, or listen to music. This is also the time when a thumb-sucker or blanket-twister performs whatever ritual puts him or her into a sleepy mood. Regardless of the method, the message is to tell the child the curfew has arrived. When sleep seems near or the designated period has elasped, take the baby directly to the crib, tell him or her goodnight, and leave.

You'll undoubtedly hear a few protests, cries, and squalls. You may want to return to the baby's room once, just to satisfy yourself the cries really don't signal a problem. Then you have to disentangle yourself, leave the room, and, if the cries continue, grit your teeth and ignore them—as hard as it may be to do so.

Allowing a baby to cry into sleep is easier said than done, especially if you live in cramped quarters or if the cries may disturb neighbors in an apartment. It may be necessary to put some distance between you and the baby; sleep on the sofa for a night or two, or keep the bedroom door closed until the baby is asleep.

Crying in the middle of the night can be even more distressing. Again, once you've satisfied yourself there's nothing wrong with the baby, one course of action is just to ride it out. If that's not practical, one parent may have to stay awake until the child becomes sleepy again.

THE INEVITABLE TEMPER TANTRUM

Even the sunniest, best-behaved baby may throw a temper tantrum during the first flush of independence. These outbursts usually begin around the first birthday and may continue intermittently until the child is three years old.

Temper tantrums result from frustration. Armed with that new independence, the child wants something or wants to do something, and the desire is thwarted. It may be a simple thing, like wanting a cookie or snack you won't permit between meals.

To adults, the fireworks that follow are far out of proportion to the cause. The child falls to the floor, screams, kicks, pounds with the fists—any physical activity to vent the rage. The ear-splitting, nerve-racking performance can continue for minutes on end and is particularly embarrassing when it happens in such places as the supermarket or on a downtown sidewalk.

The simple explanation for tantrums is that one-year-olds have very few ways to express emotion. They can't curse or shout as an adult can; they can't go for a soothing walk around the block; they can't even argue with the parent who has refused the cookie. They aren't yet clear on the notions of time and the future, either, and haven't mastered the adult concept of delayed gratification. To them, "no" means "never."

Tantrums often occur late in the day when the child and the parent are tired; sometimes they seem to be triggered by over-

Temper tantrums are a normal response to an occasionally frustrating world. If the outburst occurs in public, you may want to take the child from the scene. Otherwise, don't fuss, and don't give in to the baby's demands.

stimulation. The cause really isn't important. The outbursts are normal and don't reflect on your performance as a parent. The treatment is to be as matter-of-fact about them as your nerves will allow.

When a tantrum occurs, you'll probably want to scoop the child out of a public place as quickly as possible, just for your own peace of mind. Otherwise, make sure the child won't be injured if he or she collides with furniture, knocks over lamps, or breaks things during the tantrum. You might place the child in a crib or playpen until the tantrum subsides, a location that will keep him or her safe and also isolated, thus conveying your disapproval of the behavior.

Make as little fuss as possible. Don't argue, plead, or reason with the child, and don't give in to the demands, even if you can recognize what they are. Surrendering only teaches the child that tantrums are an effective means to an end. Just walking away from the child may be the most graceful way of handling a tantrum. Many children require an audience for their performance.

Some diehards continue the din up to half an hour; others begin to wind down after ten minutes or so. Loud cries will give way to whimpers; the child may look for forgiveness. Be matter-of-fact here, too. Hold the child in your lap, make comforting noises and gestures, and don't scold or lecture. A simple hug is better than showering the child with affection.

Of course, not everyone can be calm in the face of such an eruption each time it happens. Parents of a normally placid child have a particularly difficult time because the tempest seems to be out of character. The startled parent is sure he or she must have done something terribly wrong to provoke such an unusual reaction and out of guilt may give in to the child's demands. A temper tantrum is seldom directed at you or anything you've done; it's a first step toward learning how to express emotion.

THE BEGINNINGS OF DISCIPLINE

No one is born with a knowledge of the rules of society or respect for the rights of others. Part of a parent's role is making clear to a child just how far he or she can go. The word for this is discipline, which most parents associate with punishment. In fact, discipline refers to teaching the child the limits of accepted behavior, the boundaries of permissible action.

Give your child plenty of freedom to develop and grow independently. But don't give in to every whim, or the child will be ill-prepared for the world outside the home where restrictions do exist.

On the other hand, don't inhibit the child with restrictions or interfere in everything he or she tries to do; allow for a degree of self-education. Make a stand when it seems necessary, but don't restrict a child with too many "don'ts."

Remember that the other members of the household have rights, too. Older children are entitled to privacy from their younger brother or sister; they should have possessions of their own and time to themselves, free from the baby's demands. The exhausted parents need relief, too. The demanding child who keeps a parent shuttling back and forth to cribside must learn that parents need time for themselves.

Amazingly, repeated studies show that the most obedient child is the one who is least frequently bossed. When a rare command is given, the child understands, even at an early age, that it is important and must be followed. Children whose lives consist of an endless stream of orders and directives quickly learn to ignore them.

THE HELPFUL BABY

Helpfulness is another side to the baby nearing the middle of the second year. Although still spunkily independent, the baby also seeks your approval and looks for ways to please you. One way to is "help" around the house. The baby will begin to mimic your motions in sweeping, dusting, and cleaning.

Sometimes, you'll wish he or she weren't so helpful—as, for instance, in cleaning up after a meal by ostentatiously sweeping the crumbs and debris onto the floor. But these situations are good times to teach basic lessons. The first step toward getting a child to pick up his or her own toys begins by making a game of it—"Let's put the dolls to bed for the night" or "Let's put the cars into the garage." The game will enlist the baby's cooperation.

It's far too early, however, for the baby to be expected to do this alone or to understand the need for order.

DRESSING AND UNDRESSING

At one year to 18 months, the baby also takes the first steps toward dressing independently. As with many accomplishments, however, he or she starts backward. A one-year-old hasn't the necessary control of small muscles to fit buttons into buttonholes, snap fasteners, or close zippers. But he or she can *un*do these things and undress completely.

It'll be six months or more before the child really gets the hang of dressing. Meanwhile, you'll come into the nursery and find the baby stripped to the skin, having discovered not only how to unfas-

The baby now begins to take a part in dressing independently. But you'll find that undressing is much easier and will occur at any time of the day or night. If possible, buy clothes that are hard to remove.

ten clothes but how to remove them, including diapers. During the day, pants, shirts, and shoes may be discarded quickly. You may have considerable picking up to do for a few days—or even weeks—and it may be difficult to keep the baby in clothes, especially at night. If possible, dress him or her in clothes that can't be removed easily, such as nightclothes that snap in the back or shirts that pull over the head. Trousers or coveralls that button to shirts also are discarded less easily.

Trying as this period will be, capitalize on it by teaching the baby to cooperate. With a little encouragement, an 18-month-old will raise his or her arms for a pullover shirt or sweater and will learn to help put on trousers or jackets. A child's clothes mostly consist of a pullover shirt and trousers or coveralls.

BABY'S FIRST SHOES

The baby doesn't really need shoes until he or she begins to walk outdoors. In fact, walking barefoot strengthens the arches and the leg muscles, and a baby's feet are just as warm as the hands. Shoes are needed only to protect against rough floors or splinters.

When shoes do become necessary, nothing elaborate is required. Sneakers—canvas shoes with rubber soles—are said by many pediatricians to be adequate. They're also inexpensive. During this period, shoes are outgrown at the rate of about a pair every six weeks. Make sure the new shoes fit well. The toes should not be cramped, but the shoes should not slip off. The distance between the baby's toes and the end of the shoe, with full weight on the foot, should be about the thickness of your thumb. When the distance is less, discard the shoes, even though they're not worn out.

Make sure the baby's socks fit, too. They should be large enough so the toes don't curl under but not so large as to cause folds that might produce a blister. Socks that stretch to fit the baby's foot are the best buy.

Should shoes be low-cut or ankle-high? Traditionally, a baby's first shoes have been white leather high-tops, but they confer no special advantage in walking. The extra height does *not* give additional support to the ankle. However, high shoes are more difficult for the baby to remove, so you may prefer them.

NEW TOYS FOR THE BABY

Toys are the baby's learning tools, but you needn't invest in high-priced playthings labeled "educational." The baby can learn just as well from toys you make or improvise—or simply from household objects and utensils.

HEIGHT & WEIGHT
ONE THROUGH SIX YEARS

The growth range widens as children grow older. One two-year-old may be ten pounds lighter and half a head shorter than another—both are perfectly normal. And children don't grow as evenly as the chart's graceful curves indicate. Spurts and bursts are a normal part of growing up.

Tall — Heavy
Moderately tall — Moderately heavy
Average — Average
Moderately short — Moderately light
Short — Light

BOYS' HEIGHT & WEIGHT   GIRLS' HEIGHT & WEIGHT

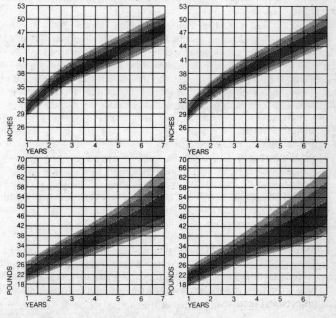

Some of the baby's favorite pastimes at this age are building, throwing, and putting objects into containers and pouring them out again. Given paper and a crayon, he or she will scribble spontaneously; you can hope this activity won't carry over to walls or furniture. As the child approaches 18 months, he or she also can look at pictures in books and magazines, especially likenesses of other children.

Other favorite toys are blocks, large dolls or stuffed toys, balls easily rolled or thrown, and wagons or other wheeled toys that can be pulled or pushed. The baby also may like play dishes, cooking utensils, and a mallet and board for pounding. Be careful about toys small enough to be swallowed, however; any toy with parts under an inch and one-half in diameter should be kept from one-year-olds.

You also can make very simple toys. A cardboard box into which he or she can pile blocks and pour them out again is a good example. Pots and pans or canned goods that can be dragged out of kitchen cupboards, piled up or clanged together, and then returned will be used as often as the most expensive toy. You may find, to your chagrin, that the child prefers treasures of the garbage can to anything you buy.

Supervised water play is also fun for children under two years of age. In warm weather, put the baby in a washtub or small plastic pool in the backyard. Allow extra time in the bathroom during the winter, and let the child play with unbreakable bottles and glasses, toys and rubber boats, and animals. Remember that most children this age like to do things themselves, rather than watch a toy in action. But even at this age, never leave a youngster unattended in the tub or pool.

A FEW MORE WORDS

Although the number of words the baby understands grows rapidly, the number he or she can pronounce grows less quickly. At 18 months, a child's vocabulary may include names for parents, siblings, pets, and perhaps even for him- or herself. Usually, there are special versions of certain everyday words, including "bottle" or "blanket" or "truck." Not all these words will be understood by an outsider, but family members usually can translate them.

If your baby hasn't such an extensive command of words, don't worry about it. Speech comes slowly for some babies, but most make up for the delay. Continue to speak to the baby in short, simple sentences. If he or she seems to understand your meaning, it will not be long until the sound is imitated.

You can help broaden your baby's vocabulary by encouraging him or her to ask for things by name, rather than point to them. You shouldn't be in too much of a hurry to satisfy your child's wants. When the baby does begin to say words in his or her own special way, don't be overly corrective; pronounce the word correctly once or twice, but let the baby get the idea.

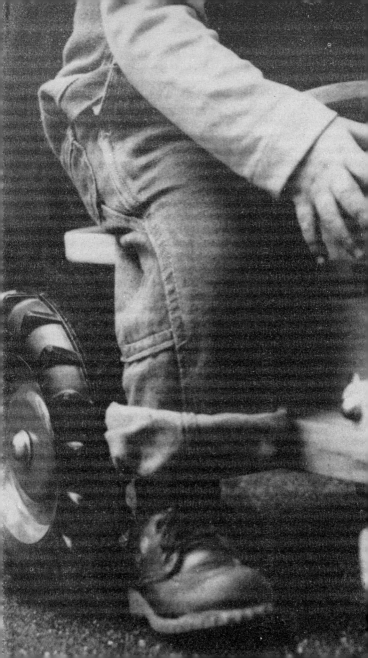

15

Eighteen Months to Two Years

HOW THE BABY GROWS

The growth rate slows considerably during the last half of the baby's second year. The average normal two-year-old weighs 28 pounds and is $34\frac{1}{2}$ inches tall. The range for normal babies is $23\frac{1}{2}$ to $32\frac{1}{2}$ pounds and 32 to $36\frac{1}{2}$ inches.

Here are some things normal babies learn to do between 18 and 24 months:

- use words in combination to make simple statements or questions;
- identify one or more parts of the body;
- follow simple directions—most of the time—if only a single step is involved;
- put on some items of clothing—but try more than succeed;
- wash and dry their hands, with parental supervision;
- identify pictures of animals by name;
- build a tower of eight blocks;
- pedal a tricycle; propel a kiddie car with feet;
- kick a ball forward or throw it overhand, neither with accuracy.

THE ART OF CONVERSATION

A two-year-old's communication is no longer limited to a few semi-intelligible words, noises, grunts, and gestures. Vocabulary increases, pronunciation improves, and the patterns of adult speech begin. The number of words—and ideas—the baby comprehends grows dramatically.

The baby may begin to speak in sentences (although many normal babies do not combine words for another year). They're not complex, adult statements and questions: just two words put together to express basic wants and thoughts. At first, sentences will consist of just a noun and a verb, without much respect for the niceties of grammar: "Fred eat," "Mommy stay," "Go bye-bye." There will be simple questions, too: "Where Doggie?" "Who that?" But in a surprisingly short time, your son or daughter will be stringing together three or even four words into an understandable combination.

Meanwhile, as many parents are amazed (and pleased) to learn, the baby "understands everything you say!" "Passive" vocabulary grows so greatly that you can now communicate ideas that a few weeks or months ago were totally over the child's head. "Let's go in the car," you'll say, and Rachel or Ted will dash for the door—obvious proof the message has been understood. You can give simple commands or directions, confident they will be carried out: "It's time for lunch," and the baby will head for the high chair or eating table. You may even find yourself in a parent-to-child dialogue complete with statements and responses:

"Who toy?" "That's Jennifer's toy." "Where J'fer?"

"Want cookie." "No cookies until lunch." "Want cookie!"

Of course, developmental rates are erratic. Children vary in how quickly they master communication skills. Some shy, quiet children don't add words so quickly or roll them off the tongue so glibly as more outgoing, energetic personalities (although temperaments aren't always a key to verbal ability). Even the most verbally precocious may develop vocabulary in a spurt, slow down for a few weeks or months, then take another great leap forward. Girls are thought to be more fluent than boys the same age. Children in some families are more verbal than children in other families, but even children in the same family may not master speech at the same rate.

You'll find the baby has quite a storehouse of knowledge. An average 21-month-old can correctly identify one or more parts of the body. Ask, "Where is Adam's nose?" "Where is Adam's hand?" and a stubby finger may accurately point to the named part, perhaps accompanied by the emphatic declaration, "Nose!" "Hand!" or even "Adam hand!" A child nearing his or her second birthday may be able to point to the baby, horse, or dog in a book. Most children this age can tell you their names. Family members now are all identified by name, usually with a highly personal pronunciation.

Now that the child's speech has improved, you may find that

behavior and disposition improve, too. There may be fewer tantrums and temperamental outbursts when your son or daughter is able to tell you what he or she wants. You may even be able to reason with the child when things don't seem to go the right way. And the baby will now have a say in the family's affairs, not simply be a passive listener.

You can help your child develop language at this stage just by talking to him or her. In fact, you'll probably find yourself doing so almost unconsciously, just to watch the responses. "Time for lunch," you'll say, and plop him or her into the high chair. Your comments and conversations help the child to learn new words, as well as the purposes of oral communication. When you give commands or directions to a child, try to see they are carried out to strengthen the concept that words have meaning.

TIME FOR OUTDOOR PLAY

Your offspring is now ready for more play outdoors. Depending on where you live and the size of your purse, you may wish to establish his or her own area in the yard or on the porch. If a parent is home during the day, the best location is directly outside a window where you can keep an eye on the child and he or she can be aware of your presence.

The play area need not be large. A space 15 by 20 feet allows plenty of room to roam. The play area should be completely enclosed, with a gate latch that resists little fingers or is beyond their reach, so you can feel free to leave the child alone.

For play equipment, a small sandbox complete with pails, shovels, spoons, and other digging implements is basic. If the baby can climb, a small slide is inexpensive fun. Swings will come a little later, although you may wish to install an entire "outdoor gym" at once. You can sometimes find these at garage sales or secondhand stores, although you should check them carefully for safety features. For almost no money, you can equip the area with boxes, cubes, discarded tires, and even old tree stumps for the child to climb on, crawl over, or tunnel through. Falls will be frequent, so a grassy surface or sand is best.

Your son or daughter also is ready for more advanced toys. A few two-year-olds can pedal a tricycle or miniature auto; younger children can manipulate a kiddie car or other vehicle propelled with the feet. Indoors, a rocking horse can provide hours of fun, and building blocks become an important part of the toy chest.

If you live in an apartment or haven't room for your own play area, take the child to a park or playground often: Space to run freely is important at this age. Neighborhood parks usually have a fenced toddlers' area with special equipment. Occasional supervised visits to a wading pool, lake, or seashore also are fun. But don't let the child play on the sidewalk or in an unconfined area outside the house.

TIME FOR PLAYMATES

More and more, your child will enjoy playing with children the same age. Children under two still don't really play together, but just watching each other is half the fun. Put a pair of two-year-olds side-by-side in a sandbox, and each will dig his or her own hole, fill his or her own bucket, and push his or her own truck, but there will be a good deal of pausing, observing, mimicking, and imitating. Also, toys will be grabbed, snatched, and passed back and forth. Pushing and shoving are part of the routine.

Not much time will be wasted by two-year-olds on the niceties of language, but you'll be surprised at how effectively the two youngsters manage to communicate with each other.

Some children plunge right into social situations and enjoy them; others take time to warm up. Your child may not feel comfortable with more than one playmate at a time; playground noise may be frightening. A shy, quiet child may hang back and cling to parents or be much more content to play alone within sight of the others, gradually working into the group. Other children may use the bull-in-a-china-shop approach. They may hit, poke, bite, or grab toys without giving them back. Such encounters between two-year-olds often are accompanied by a great deal of crying and complaining.

Within the limits of safety, you should try to keep hands off and let the children work things out for themselves; the tussles aren't really arguments. If one child pushes another, the second is likely to push back: the message is conveyed in a primitive way that pushing is unpopular and should be stopped. If you move in to end things too quickly and retaliation isn't allowed to take place, the aggressor doesn't have a chance to learn the consequences of aggressive behavior. In fact, your child may actually be encouraged to hit because you are inadvertently protecting him or her.

If one child continues to act aggressively and the other doesn't strike back but runs away or cries and whimpers, you may be obliged to step in. If your child is the aggressor, speak firmly and sharply in disapproving tones. If the other child is the fighter, first you may have to negotiate with the child's parents. It may be necessary to separate the children.

Relationships between children often are more difficult for the parents than for the youngsters themselves. If another child repeatedly bullies your child, you may have to bring up the matter tactfully with the other parent. Parental standards differ, and it is sometimes hard for a child who has had clear, precise training to deal with a child who has not. In fact, you'll often find the other parent is giving the child a double message, vicariously enjoying the youthful aggression, while ostensibly disapproving. If so, you may have to soft-pedal the relationship with the other parent, rather than continually subject your child to a relationship that he or she is not able to handle.

LEARNING TO DRESS

The first step in dressing takes place when the child learns to name the items of clothing and the parts of the body they cover. The process of putting on clothes is usually too much for an 18-month-old, but you can begin the educational process now. Start by naming each garment as you put it on, and then send the child to get it from the drawer or closet.

Next, enlist the child's cooperation. Teach him or her how to poke feet into trousers or hold hands in the air so a sweater can be pulled over the head. You can make a game of it: "Where is Susan?" as the shirt goes over the head; "There she is!" Finally, as your child approaches two years of age, he or she can begin to put on certain items of clothing under your supervision.

At first, it's really play; the child is just imitating adult behavior. Not much is accomplished beyond pulling on socks or shoes or worming into a jacket. You'll have to show how things go on or they'll wind up backward, upside down, sideways or twisted, with shoes on the wrong feet. You'll also do the fastening. Buttons and zippers are still too much for little fingers; the small muscles haven't matured enough to allow that kind of dexterity. Even so, the child will be delighted with the dressing accomplishment.

Don't expect too much of the child at this point. The objective is really to let him or her play at the idea of dressing and learn about clothes at the same time. Patiently let the child fumble with buttons or tug at shorts; don't step in too speedily to help. Eventually, of course, you'll have to do it, after allowing a brief, tolerable period for the child's education. But be sure to praise the child's efforts.

Patient supervision applies to more lessons than dressing. You'll have to show restraint in many things as your child grows older, so he or she can learn independently.

A SENSE OF ORDER

Because the child likes to imitate grown-ups, it's now easy for you to begin helping him or her acquire a sense of order. As you work about the house, get the baby to help you with the less complicated projects at hand. At first, of course, it's only play for the baby and may be a little extra for you, but the lesson will carry over into taking care of the child's own possessions.

When you teach in this way, simplify the child's needs. Install low hooks and hangers in closets and bedrooms so clothing can be reached easily. Assign specific places for jackets, shoes, and rain gear. At first, the child will be able to do little more than retrieve the garment from the hook when you ask for it. But once the notion is clear that clothes go in a specific place, it will be easier to teach him or her to hang them or put them away later.

At this age, children don't really play together. But they do react to their companions. Watch closely and you'll see each observing the actions of the other and then trying them on for size.

The child's play area should have its own storage spaces—drawers, boxes, and shelves—to hold toys. Make a nightly ritual of helping the child put the toys away for the next day's play. Of course, he or she can't do it independently at this age, but you're building a solid foundation for later behavior.

Teach the child to wash and dry hands, too. Again, training comes fairly easily because a child under two likes to imitate grown-ups. Buy a low stool or box so he or she can reach the faucet, and give him or her a personal towel, hung at an appropriately low height. Children usually prefer cool water, and you shouldn't expect a high standard of cleanliness at this point. Right now, the basic lesson is just to show how the procedure works. Teach the child to wash and dry hands before each meal—but you should expect to remind him or her for the next two or three years.

TAKING CARE OF THE TEETH

With 16 to 20 teeth, the two-year-old is more than ready for a toothbrush and a program of dental hygiene. Again, natural mimicry helps to establish good habits. Buy a small brush for the child and his or her own toothpaste and cup. At first you must hold the brush to demonstrate how it's done. The child will quickly get the idea and want to take over. Allow him or her to do so under your supervision. Of course, a child this age can't brush adequately, and you'll have to finish up after he or she has fun with the brush.

It's true the so-called baby teeth will be lost and replaced by permanent teeth, but that doesn't mean their care should be neglected. The American Dental Association (ADA) recommends the child's first dental checkup be conducted as soon as 16 baby teeth have appeared, or by the age of three, when the child can cooperate with the dentist. The ADA points out that cavities in the baby teeth or the loss of them can cause the child's permanent teeth to be pushed out of alignment. Orthodontia or other corrective measures may be necessary later. The ADA suggests a regular checkup each year after the child's first one and that dental work be done, if necessary.

Prevention, of course, is the most important ingredient of good dental care. Cavities now are recognized to be of bacterial origin; bacteria in the mouth combine with sugars, remaining on or between the teeth to produce an acid that destroys tooth enamel and eats into the heart of the tooth. Although some families seem to be more cavity-prone than others, limiting the amount of sugar can reduce cavities in many children. For better teeth, restrict chewing gum, cookies, ice cream, and sweet desserts. When sweets are eaten, the teeth should be brushed immediately, if possible, to remove the sugars that cause decay. When brushing is not convenient, the mouth should at least be rinsed with water. At the very least, the child who has eaten sweets should have his or her teeth brushed before going to bed and should not be allowed food in the crib.

The practice of letting the baby go to bed with a bottle can be potentially harmful to cavity-prone youngsters, especially if the baby keeps the bottle in the mouth throughout the night or sucks on it periodically. Sugars in formula, milk, or juice, not normally damaging, thus bathe the teeth constantly and promote tooth decay. No harm seems to result when the baby drinks for a short period and the bottle is discarded or removed by parents.

If the water supply in your community is not fluoridated, your doctor or dentist may prescribe fluoride supplements for the child's teeth. These are recommended by both the ADA and the American Academy of Pediatrics.

Although not so effective as fluoridated water in preventing decay, these treatments include using chewable fluoride tablets, allowing the dentist to paint the teeth with fluoride, and brushing with fluoridated toothpaste.

EATING PROBLEMS

The picky appetite continues. There are two related reasons: the child eats less because the rate of growth has slowed and less food is needed; and the body slims as the supply of baby fat is used up, so that contours begin to resemble those of an adult. Mother and father observe and conclude the child isn't eating enough. Result: they try to push more food on the child, the child resists, and each meal increasingly resembles a power struggle.

The most sensible and straightforward rule for feeding at this stage is simple: observe how much the child ordinarily eats; serve approximately that quantity or a bit more; try to balance out the nutrients over a period of time (but not necessarily at one meal or even in one day); offer three main meals a day, with a cracker or cookie in midmorning and midafternoon.

At mealtimes, let the child decide how much is enough. When he or she seems to have lost interest, try offering one more bite. If it's not accepted, take the food away and let the child leave the high chair or table.

Given a choice, most children prefer sweets to other foods, so you'll have to work hard to keep him or her from concentrating on sweet desserts while neglecting other foods. There's probably no way to avoid sugar completely, but do your best to limit the child's intake of refined sugar to protect the teeth. Perhaps you can restrict it to plain cookies or simple desserts. An occasional treat, of course, is fine. Good ice cream is a nourishing food readily eaten by young children.

READY FOR TOILET TRAINING

There's no set schedule for toilet training. Most parents expect to begin when their youngster is about 18 months of age, but the child, not the calendar, tells you when the time is right. Logically, there is little point in trying until the child recognizes that he or she is having a bowel movement and can communicate that fact to you. There's wide variation as to when recognition and communication occur; even when they do, many children simply aren't interested in bowel training—they have better things to do! Studies show that four out of five normal children are daytime-trained by 2½ years, but some haven't mastered the technique by the age of four.

Of course, some parents boast of a child who was bowel-trained at a year of age, or even earlier. What this usually means, however, is that the *parent* was trained. Having observed that the child had a bowel movement at a regular time each day, the alert mother or father placed the baby on the potty at the appropriate hour and "caught" the movement. The mystified child usually had no idea what he or she was doing.

When you feel your child is nearly ready for training, buy a small potty chair for the child to use. A freestanding chair with removable potty is usually better than a seat that fits the standard toilet, because it's closer to the ground and the child won't be afraid of falling or of the flushing noise. Also, you can move the potty chair to where you are, instead of isolating the child in the bathroom.

Every family has its own words for the need to urinate or defecate. It's important for a child to use these words to tell you (or if you ask) when it's time to use the toilet.

Long before the child does, you'll probably notice the bowel movements follow a pattern. That's not true of all children: some are wildly irregular and may have a movement only every few days, making training more difficult. But most children have a daily movement; a common time is just after breakfast, apparently because the reflexive movements within the intestines resume their normal daytime pace. A few children have two or more movements a day.

Once you've discovered the appropriate time, place the baby on the potty chair for a short period as that hour approaches. Don't make the stay too long, and don't, by any means, strap the child in place. If the child produces a movement, be sure to praise the effort, so the message is clear the purpose of sitting has been fulfilled. If nothing happens, allow the child to leave the chair when he or she wants to.

Some children will sit for a time without results, then have a movement immediately after standing up. The association is clear; the timing is off. In cleaning up, try to be as mater-of-fact as you can. Remembering the child's growing vocabulary, explain that movements are to be made in the potty and that being clean is nicer than being soiled. Repeat the message when it's time to change soiled diapers. Suggest the child tell you if he or she wishes to use the potty.

READY FOR URINE TRAINING

Bowel training may be accomplished within a few days or weeks, but some months will pass before the child is reliable and motivated to use the toilet. Urine training takes even longer and may be marked by long efforts without success. Urine training usually follows bowel training by up to six months. At first, sitting down is usually the appropriate posture for urination—for boys as well as girls.

The first clue that it's time for urine training comes when you notice the child's diapers remain dry for longer periods during the day, perhaps for two hours or more at a time. This usually happens some time after 18 months of age. That's because the bladder has grown and has a larger storage capacity. It also indicates the beginning of control over the bladder.

Another clue comes from the child. He or she may come to you after urinating and complain of wet diapers. The child may even hold the crotch or tug at the diaper, either before or after urinating. Again, the child's timing is off, but there's a clear association between wet diapers and the act of urinating. It also indicates the child is beginning to feel uncomfortable when wet, a fact you can take advantage of when urging him or her to urinate in the potty.

Once you're aware of these indications, begin placing the child on the potty at approximately two-hour intervals. Before and after naps, at mealtimes, and at bedtime are appropriate moments. You'll have to set the schedule for a while. The child isn't likely to be aware that he or she is ready to urinate until the last minute. As

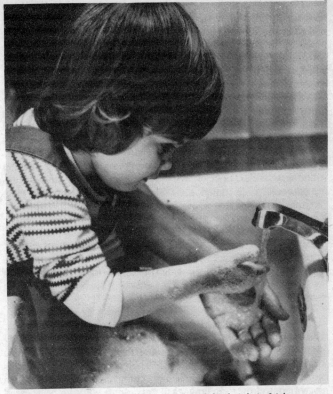

Teaching a child under two how to wash and dry hands is fairly easy. Though your son or daughter won't become proficient at it right away, the basic procedure—to be followed before and after meals—is the important lesson.

with bowel movements, the child will often urinate after leaving the potty.

Complete control of the bladder takes time to develop; once a child's bladder is full, he or she may not be able to wait even another minute to empty it. Also, boys in particular may have a more difficult time retaining urine. Some boys can't hold back urine for more than two hours until age three.

Remember, you'll also have to teach the child the proper words to tell you when he or she needs to urinate.

Training pants instead of diapers are helpful, once the baby can stay dry for two or more hours. They're not only simpler to put on and take off, but they have the psychological advantage of being "grown-up." Some doctors believe that babies feel free to urinate in diapers, whereas they exercise greater control while wearing training pants.

KEEPING THINGS CASUAL

Although many people regard it otherwise, toilet training needn't be a big deal. Like other aspects of child-rearing, training isn't a competition, and years from now, it'll make little difference that you had to launder diapers for six more months than the parents next door. Patience on your part is as important to the baby's toilet training as bladder control. You may experience a long stretch without success, even though the child clearly understands the task; nothing is so annoying to parents as when they ask, "Do you have to wee-wee?" and the child solemnly denies it, while the puddle grows around his or her feet. Exasperating as the drawn-out procedure may be, scolding, shaming, or demanding immediate and perfect results doesn't help to keep diapers dry. In any case, the baby has the ultimate weapon. Nothing you can do or say will cause him or her to urinate or defecate (or withhold it) if he or she doesn't want to.

ACCIDENTS AND BREAKDOWNS

Even after the child is reasonably well trained, accidents will happen. Stress or excitement may cause the baby to urinate; some babies can't urinate on an unfamiliar potty and will wet their pants instead. Accidental urination is more common in cold weather than in warm weather. In any case, accidents should be treated routinely—but not ignored. Mention to the child that he or she would be more comfortable with clean and dry clothing.

With some children, toilet training seems to go fine for a while, then collapses. The child will return to earlier habits; you may even feel compelled to use diapers again. Often, there's an obvious reason: when a new child enters the household, for instance, an older child may revert to babyish practices. Sometimes, though, no reason can be discerned.

When that happens, treat the setback as calmly as possible. You may even drop toilet training for a time, return the child to diapers, and wait. Usually, the child will independently disclose a new readiness for further training. If the child simply balks at using the toilet at the times or places you suggest, let him or her pick the times. Sometimes, the child simply hasn't achieved full muscular control. He or she may be unable to relax while sitting on the toilet but may be able to relax while standing. But, if possible, avoid making toilet training an issue. It's a battle no parent can win.

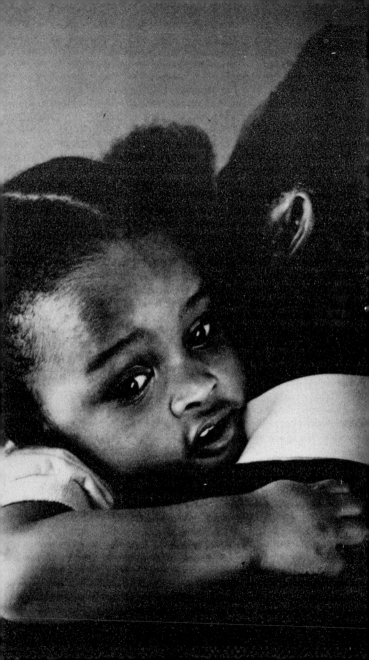

SECTION
3

Two to Six Years

Your child is a baby no more.
For two to six, he or she
advances rapidly toward independence. Looking back four
years from now, you'll wonder
where the baby went. Your own
role changes just as quickly.
You'll need new answers, new
strengths, new skills. Just one
thing will never change. These
early years will strengthen the
bond that unites parents
and child for a lifetime.

CHAPTER
16

Two to Three Years

HOW THE CHILD GROWS

Between the second and third birthdays, the average normal child gains four pounds and grows $3\frac{1}{2}$ inches. Average weight for a three-year-old boy is $32\frac{1}{2}$ pounds; average height, 38 inches; for girls, 31 pounds and 37 inches. The range for normal children is $25\frac{1}{2}$ to 38 pounds and 35 to $40\frac{1}{2}$ inches.

Here are some things half of the normal children learn to do between the ages of two and three:
- dress with supervision and button some buttons;
- play interactive games, such as hide-and-seek;
- tell their own first and last names;
- use plurals, pronouns, and prepositions in speech;
- copy a circle with a crayon;
- understand such words as "cold," "tired," and "hungry;"
- know where things belong and help to put them there;
- follow simple directions;
- feed themselves almost completely;
- be toilet-trained during the day and remain dry all night some of the time;
- recognize and identify some colors.

INCREASING SELF-RELIANCE

Day by day through the third year of life, children grow more self-reliant. Each new adventure makes them more conscious of their own individuality, their own control over their minds and bodies. Independence increases. They learn to do many things for themselves—after a fashion, at least—and, indeed, insist on it. The statement "Me do it" is familiar to any parent.

Feeding will be strictly a "do-it-myself" project, as it should be. The child's style of eating will still lack finesse, and at the completion of a meal, the table may resemble San Francisco after the earthquake. Watery soups and runny puddings will still defeat the novice eater; sandwiches will continue to be dissected before they're digested. But he or she is much better coordinated than a year ago. And with a full complement of teeth, the child can now eat firmer foods that previously were withheld, such as breadsticks.

Skill in dressing will improve steadily. As any parent can tell you, at first a two-year-old's attempts to put on clothes are little more than play, humorous imitations of what grown-ups do. Most of the actual routine of dressing a child falls to the parents. But as the months pass, your child will become more adept at wriggling into a playsuit or pulling on socks. A three-year-old may even laboriously manage a few buttons, even if the correct button doesn't match the proper buttonhole. Ironically, as mastery improves, the child loses interest in what is no longer a hill to climb—but a tedious chore.

You'll continue to establish the child's routine of eating, sleeping, and playing, but the child will want some voice in it. He or she will want to play when he or she wants to play and may stubbornly state the case with emphatic words and gestures. For your own convenience and the child's welfare, you may have to be firm.

Increasingly, your role becomes more that of model than nurse. You demonstrate, the child imitates, you correct and help. Some of the imitations are just for fun at first. But you may be astonished at the amount of time and concentration your child will devote to mastering some simple task, like pedaling a kiddie car, as he or she continues to seek new worlds.

THE LITTLE MONARCH
The two-year-old is a creature of moods, too. One of them is a kind of haughty, regal manner that is insistingly self-indulgent. With all the imperiousness of Napoleon or Catherine the Great, the two-year-old monarch will boss everybody—parents, siblings, domestic animals—and insist on having his or her own way. Nothing short of a palace revolt will overturn the royal dictum, "Gimme cookie!"

Two is also the traditional age of disobedience—although it may merely be the parents' label for the child's tendency to do as he

To a two-year-old, the whole world is a private kingdom where all wishes automatically come true. Parents, siblings, and small kittens will be wrapped up by the child's desire to have it "my way."

or she pleases. It's not so much defiance; the child resents restrictions, resents limits, and doesn't want to be told what to do. "No" will be another mainstay of the vocabulary, although you'll usually hear it as "NO!" You may find yourself enforcing a number of rules with "friendly muscle" instead of "sweet reasonableness." It won't be enough to tell the child to stop doing something; you may have to physically call a halt.

Actually, you'll find a two-year-old's behavior shot full of contradictions. One day your son or daughter will be balky, contrary, cantankerous; anything you suggest will be rejected, even if it is something that delighted him or her only yesterday. Just wait: to-morrow will bring sunshine, cooperation, and agreeableness. Ann or Andrew will be a pleasure to be with. These behavioral zigzags can be exasperating to parents, who often wail, "He was so nice yesterday and so terrible today!" Consistency is simply not in the cards yet. It'll be at least a year until he or she is predictable—and closer to four before he or she obeys consistently.

All this is just another phase of growing up. The child is now learning the art of the possible—discovering the limits of behavior, what is permissible and what isn't. Still self-centered, he or she hasn't learned to distinguish between what he or she wishes would happen and what can *actually* happen. The two-year-old operates in the here and now and can't always fit present attitudes into a pattern of behavior, as an adult usually can. And many a two-year-old's attitudes really don't mean much; they're just tests. Even using the word "no" is just another way of learning what happens after say-ing it.

A FAVORITE PARENT
Part of a two-year-old's inconsistency may be attachment to one parent or the other. Some children cling to mother or father and openly dismiss the other. Boys usually attach themselves to fathers and girls to mothers; later, the preference may be for the parent of the opposite sex.

This, too, is just a phase and won't last. The best policy—for both parents—is to ignore this phase and ride it out.

That may be easier said than done: The rejected parent feels hurt; the favorite, defensive and guilty. Sometimes the rejected par-ent also tries to make up to the child and win back him or her. If so, the child may learn to play one parent against the other. Parents should stand together, unified in their approach to children; they shouldn't be sensitive about presumed shows of favoritism.

THOSE MADDENING RITUALS
With growing powers of observation and memory, a two-year-old knows and remembers where everything in the house belongs and how every act of daily routine is performed. Amazingly, he or she will even remember exactly where you're supposed to turn the car on the way to grandmother's house or which aisle you usually visit first in the supermarket. And, often to your dismay, you'll have to do everything in precisely the same manner and keep everything just as it was yesterday, the day before, and the day before that.

Lunch must always be served on the same plate. The teddy

bear must always be propped in the southwest corner of the crib—moving it to the northeast will bring squalls of protest. The bedtime ritual must follow exactly the same sequence—story, drink, toilet, drink, toilet, "Night-night." Change the order, omit one step, even substitute "So long" for "Night-night," and you'll hear about it. The objections will be loud and tiringly sustained.

At age two, the world is an avalanche of novel experiences and situations slightly altered from the day before. Naturally, a young learner wants some things to count on—some things to remain reliably cemented in time while he or she moves on to new, exciting matters. From your point of view, maddening though these rituals may be, they should be accepted without complaint unless they become too long, too complicated, or too intrusive on family life.

NIGHTMARES AND NIGHT FEARS

Nightmares often begin when the child is between two and three years old. But Bobby or Barbara doesn't know they're nightmares. He or she wakes, shouting in fright, to tell you that there are monsters in the room. So far as he or she is concerned, there *are* monsters lurking over behind the dresser. To a child unable to divorce fantasy from reality, even in daylight, the monsters are real.

If nightmares and night-waking are frequent, occurring every night or two, they may indicate that something else is troubling the child—the arrival of a new baby, a move to a new house, a shift in day-care arrangements. But if they occur only occasionally, then simple reassurance is enough to deal with them. Don't reason with the frightened child, explaining there are no monsters; don't turn on the light to show him or her, because he or she knows better. On the other hand, don't support the fantasy by chasing the monsters out.

Instead, distract the child as quickly as possible. Hold and soothe him or her with reassuring words until the tears stop. Then point out the familiar surroundings to ease the fears: "There's your own pillow right here"; "There's your teddy bear. Let's put him right here beside you"; "I will be in the next room and I can hear you."

Don't fuss too much about the incident (attention to it only reinforces the impression), don't remain with the child so long that he or she awakens fully, and don't transfer the child to your bed; the switch may be the beginning of a pattern of nightly awakenings. If the child recalls the incident the following night and expresses fears about staying in the room, you may wish to install a night-light for reassurance.

PLAYMATES AND PLAY GROUPS

The company of peers is no longer just a casual part of childish life. If your son or daughter is not already mingling with contemporaries in a day-care center, you should arrange for regular companionship and stimulation of others the same age.

Two-year-olds still play individually, rather than together, but cooperation and interaction—still sprinkled with shoving, pushing, and grabbing—steadily increase as the third birthday approaches. It's fun for parents to watch this stage, for three-year-olds' play is heavily laced with imagination and fantasy.

Your child may be fortunate enough to have playmates in the neighborhood, even a few steps away. If another two- to three-year-old is next door, the two may be together nearly all day, scampering back and forth between the houses and play areas without adult escort.

In an urban area or a neighborhood with few children, you'll have to schedule playtime. It needn't be an elaborate or formal arrangement, just an exchange of visits with a friend whose child is about the same age.

Or you may wish to set up a scheduled play group, whose members arrive to play at established times and places.

City parents often shepherd their children to a playground at a set time each day, knowing that other children the same age will probably be on hand. Often, the occasion is a social get-together for the parents, as well as a playtime for the children. In suburbs, a kaffeeklatsch may serve the same purpose. You and your friends can set a regular time to assemble with the children and rotate the meeting place.

Another informal arrangement resembles a baby-sitting co-operative. Two or three children gather at John's home one day, Martha's another, and Linda's a third. The designated parent supervises the children that day.

As the children grow a little older, some play groups begin to resemble preschool sessions. One parent is assigned to supervise the children at each gathering and to provide a program. This is usually something simple: a trip to the playground, paints and paper for fingerpainting, clay for modeling.

Charitable, governmental, and commercial organizations also sponsor play groups. These usually are more formal than those at child-care facilities and may be supervised by a certified specialist in early-childhood education. Some are operated in conjunction with an adult-education course in child development. Play groups also are operated (for a fee) in many cities and suburbs.

There aren't many rules to remember when establishing your own play group. Try to choose children of approximately the same age and temperament, children who are likely to stimulate each other and blend well together. The choice of adults is important, too. You want other parents whom you like and in whom you feel confidence. You'll also want to inquire discreetly about the other homes—if there's enough space for two or three boisterous three-year-olds, and whether normal safety precautions are observed.

Two hours a day, two days a week are a good beginning schedule for a play group. Children this age have a short attention span, so there should be plenty of activity to divert them. They need a good balance between physical play and crafts requiring the use of small muscles. The supervising parent may not be called upon to watch the children each minute but will have to look in regularly, referee disputes, and help the youngsters change directions. Three highly energetic three-year-olds are about as many as one parent can handle at a time; two parents can handle six or eight children.

Play groups work well when all children are about the same age, but it's also valuable for your child to have a mix of playmates. Playing occasionally with older children and occasionally with younger ones allows an opportunity both to follow and to lead. Don't segregate the sexes. Three-year-old boys and girls play equally well with each other.

IMAGINARY PLAYMATES

Often, a three-year-old's most devoted and beloved friend is invisible to everyone else. Boys and girls at three years of age often invent an imaginary playmate—human or animal—who in their eyes is very real indeed, someone or something to take into account as the business of the day unfolds. Your son or daughter may conduct actual conversations with "Gerald" or "Sandra," give him or her a personality, and even bring him or her into the family circle. You may have to set an extra place at the dinner table. And watch out! A terrible tragedy may take place when an unknowing visitor ignores or even sits down on the unseen friend.

In the half-magic, half-real world of the child, a friend you can talk to but not see isn't so illogical. After all, adults converse every day with people out of sight on the telephone; on television, they watch the movements and actions of people who aren't really present. The creation of a mythical playmate is one way a child works out the sometimes shifting borders of reality and learns for him- or herself what's real and unreal.

The imaginary playmate also fulfills another role. Your son or daughter didn't spill the milk on the new tablecloth: "Gerald did it." "Sandra," you may be told, "opened the gate," and allowed your three-year-old to escape from the yard. And if you don't buy the story of Gerald as scapegoat, you may hear the child afterward—criticizing Gerald in the same firm tones you used minutes before. Having an imaginary playmate around helps a boy or girl work out his or her own conflicts in a satisfying way. (Sometimes a stuffed toy or the family dog serves the same purpose.)

Because imaginary playmates are normal, parents should not do much about them. If Gerald begins to interfere with family life—if you have to buy an extra ice-cream cone for him, for example—you may have to put your foot down a little and suggest that Gerald come another time. Don't deny that Gerald exists—it's fruitless; his closest friend won't believe it anyway—but don't be caught up in playfully encouraging the fantasy, which will only confuse the child further. As the lyrics suggest in the children's song, *Puff, the Magic Dragon*, one day the playful fantasy will just fade away, and Gerald will disappear from the family circle forever, a welcome visitor for a time whose stay is no longer necessary. You may actually find yourself missing him more than the child does.

STORIES AND STORY TIME

Reading or telling stories to your youngster takes on special significance when he or she is about 2½ and has enough grasp of language to understand more of the tales. The first stories needn't be anything elaborate. In fact, the best ones are those you invent yourself.

A regular story hour is fun for parents, too: There's something enjoyable about snuggling up with a little one and taking him or her (and you too!) into a world of enchantment. A picture book can provide the story or just be a prop: you can point to the pictures and improvise a narrative around them. Remember what you said, though, because your listener will—and will insist that it be told the same way again. Make up stories in which your child is the central figure. And if you're artistic—or even slightly so—you can draw pictures that tell the stories.

The most popular tales among two- and three-year-olds are short on words and long on action. That's why *Mother Goose* has been such a favorite for so many years. Don't just read the stories— act them out. A mommy or daddy who can huff and puff like the Big Bad Wolf or squeal like the Three Little Pigs is the most popu-

Stories take children into the world of words and ideas. Keep them simple, with plenty of action and pictures. Put lots of expression and excitement into your stories.

lar storyteller. Good storytelling for a child also calls for questions, pauses for effect, and reaction from the child. "And what do you think the little pig said then?" brings a delighted, "Not by the hair of my chinny-chin-chin!"

Words to a two-year-old aren't heard just for meaning; they also have rhythm and sound. That's why rhymes are more popular than plain old prose. Read with expression, excitement, and anticipation, and your child will enjoy it most.

AN EAR FOR MUSIC

Between two and three a child begins to like music, too. The child's a little young for Beethoven, Basie, or the Beatles; a simple tune will do. The best ones have a prominent melody and a strong beat. Nursery jingles and marches meet these qualifications—and so, you'll find, do television commercials.

William or Wanda won't yet have perfect pitch. The ability to carry a tune successfully won't develop until about the age of four. But the child will love your singing—however off-key—and probably will plunge in with his or her own little monotone. Children quickly settle on favorites, from lullabies to *She'll Be Comin' Around the Mountain*, and will insist that you provide encore after encore.

If you can play a guitar or a piano—even if you can only pick out a tune with one finger—your child will be enchanted and, being self-reliant, will want to try it alone. A windup music box that plays a simple tune is a favorite toy for many two-year-olds. A stuffed animal with its own built-in music box is a good, soothing bedtime companion.

Although a two- or three-year-old is too young to manipulate a record or tape player, he or she will enjoy listening to recordings. You can buy many inexpensive children's recordings containing simple melodies, the old nursery rhymes, or dramatized storytelling. You'll often find these at secondhand stores or garage sales.

TELEVISION AND CHILDREN

The images and voices of the television screen capture the attention of even a two-year-old. Studies show that three-year-olds can identify television cartoon jingles before nursery rhymes and that many four-year-olds are glued to the set as much as four hours a day.

Most parents have mixed feelings about television and its influences. There seems to be little support for the belief that a heavy diet of television damages children's eyes or otherwise hurts them physically, but its effects on impressionable minds are continually disputed. Most parents despair about the drumfire commercials with their buy-buy-buy message and the heavy dose of violence that still continues, even on children's programs. And no one likes to see a child passively watching a television screen when there are so many more active and exciting things to do. On the other hand, television has its positive side. Children do learn from it, as studies have repeatedly demonstrated; some of the most honored programs are aimed at the preschool set. And, however guilty they may feel about it, almost all parents occasionally find the set to be a convenient baby-sitter. It can be a relief to a tired mother or father to plunk a youngster in front of a television, knowing that he or she will be safe from obvious harm.

One extreme way to handle the problem of television is to throw out the set. A better way is to give children some firm rules about what they can watch and when. And these rules should be taught early, when children first become aware of the television set. Here are guidelines to follow:

• Be aware of your own viewing habits. If television is your chief entertainment, it is naive to expect the child to behave differently.

• Monitor what the child watches. Observe the television fare frequently enough to be satisfied that content is suitable. Even familiar shows should be checked periodically, because some of these programs change approach or story line over the years.

• Retain control of the set. That means the on-off switch. *You* decide what the child can watch and how long he or she can watch it. Call a halt when the time comes.

• Consult television schedules or otherwise familiarize yourself with children's programs so you can influence the child's viewing. Don't automatically assume that a "children's show" is something you'd want your child to watch. Don't unthinkingly assume cartoons are children's fare. Many old and new cartoons are heavily laced with violence.

• Discuss the programs as you would a book. Encourage the child to recall them and tell you about them. Studies show that programs are less frightening or confusing to a child if a parent is present to discuss them. In the same way, commercials have less impact if a child can question an adult about them.

• Don't build the child's life around the television. Schedule other pastimes for weekend mornings or late afternoons. A picnic on Saturday morning is a good substitute for television; late afternoon is a good time for the story hour.

A NEW BED, A NEW CHAIR

When to move your child to a standard bed is strictly a matter for personal preference and pocketbook. Few children physically outgrow the crib until they're four years old or more. A restless sleeper probably ought to remain in an enclosed space until he or she settles down. If you put the child to bed at one end of the crib and always find him or her wedged against the other in the morn-

Though few children physically outgrow a crib until the age of four, many two-year-olds can escape it with ease, even with the rail raised (at left). Think about a "big bed" and, in the meantime, keep the rail lowered.

ing, wait a bit longer to make the transfer. You'll probably also want to wait until the child is consistently dry at night, usually between 2¹/₂ and 3¹/₂ years old.

Most children this age can no longer be kept put by plopping them in the crib. An agile two-year-old quickly learns to scramble over the side and escape, and many evenings will be spent putting him or her into bed—and retrieving him or her again and again. Often, the young fugitive also will flee during the night or rise at the gray light of dawn to toddle into your room and wake you. Some desperate parents try to cover the top of the crib with netting, to prevent escape, but most resign themselves and keep the crib rail in a lower position so the acrobat won't be injured crawling over. Pad the floor with pillows, too, to prevent injury.

When picking a new bed, assume, too, the child will topple from it a few times. Choose a model that is close to the floor. It'll take the child several weeks to become accustomed to the unconfined space. In the meantime, tuck in blankets and linens, and line the floor with pillows. Even though the child is usually dry all night, you'll want to place a waterproof pad between mattress and linens. Toilet accidents will continue intermittently for several years. Pick blankets of synthetic fiber: they can be washed easily, and they reduce the possibility of allergic reaction. Also, the child probably is also ready for a pillow at this time.

The baby also may be ready to eat at the table with you—assuming, of course, you cover the table with a plastic cloth. No doubt your youngster has long since outgrown an infant chair, and even a high chair may be confining. You may wish to substitute a booster added to an adult chair, or you may wish to remove the tray of the high chair for easier access to the adult table.

17

Three to Five Years

HOW THE CHILD GROWS

The average normal four-year-old weighs 37$\frac{1}{2}$ pounds and stands 40$\frac{1}{2}$ inches, an increase of five pounds and 2$\frac{1}{2}$ inches from the year before. The range in size among normal children is 28 to 45 pounds, and 37$\frac{1}{2}$ to 43$\frac{1}{2}$ inches in height. Usually, girls are smaller than boys, although the height and weight of boys and girls fall within the same range.

Here are some things most normal children may learn to do before the fourth birthday.

- dress without assistance, except for difficult buttons;
- identify colors; make comparisons;
- use plurals and prepositions;
- leave parents easily and play out of their sight for long periods;
- draw a figure recognizable as a human;
- hop on one foot, and maybe skip for a few steps.

At five, an average normal child weighs 42 pounds and is 43$\frac{1}{2}$ inches tall. The range of height is 39$\frac{1}{2}$ to 46 inches, and the range in weight, 32 to 50 pounds. Here are some achievements of normal five-year-olds;

- define many words;
- catch a bounced ball;
- put on shoes, perhaps even tie them;
- sing a song with a recognizable tune;
- recognize his or her printed name, and perhaps print it.

THE INFANT ADOLESCENT
Between three and five years of age, your son or daughter goes through a transition so profound that it has been called "the adolescence of the preschool years." As in the teens, the person who emerges from this period is quite different from the one who entered it. The three-year-old is still an infant. Your five-year-old is most clearly a child.

Your role changes, too. The three-year-old is increasingly—even demandingly—self-reliant, but many details of caring for the child still fall to you. The five-year-old can dress, eat, go to the toilet, and even bathe with little help from you; sometimes it seems that mother and dad are only called upon to cut meat and deal with difficult buttons. Even social plans may be made without you: Your five-year-old will scurry off to a friend's house unescorted, play out of your sight for long periods, and come and go with minimum supervision. Your child will want it that way, too, and will want a voice in many family plans.

That doesn't mean a five-year-old is a full-fledged adult, even in miniature. The child still lacks judgment. Your guidance is important—essential—to point the child in the right direction and to make decisions that are beyond childish experience. Conversely, you must not expect too much nor push too fast; though no longer a baby, your offspring isn't grown-up by any means.

And the changes don't unfold at the same rate in all children, or even in the same child. A child may quickly mature physically, develop speech slowly, and change emotionally and socially by fits and starts. Your child at five will be different from your child at three, but in retrospect, it may be difficult for you to pinpoint when the transformation took place.

TALK, TALK, TALK
One of the most marked—and most erratic—areas of development is that of speech. Between three and five years of age, most children gradually master the basics of adult communication, and their speech patterns and cadences come to resemble those of grown-ups. But not all children make it over the hurdle at the same pace. Everyone knows an anecdote about a child who spoke only in monosyllables until age three and a half, then blurted out, "Please pass the butter, mother." Your child, though normal, may not have the urge to communicate as quickly as another equally normal child.

The majority of children, however, become increasingly verbal after passing their third birthday. They learn to say just about anything they want to say, and grunts and gestures fade away as a form of communication. Baby talk and mispronunciations continue, but the intricacies of sentence structure and grammar begin to creep in. Gradually, the child peppers conversation with plurals, pronouns, and prepositions. "Me do it" becomes "I'll do it." and "Mommy do it" gives way to "You do it." A four-year-old knows the proper form is "two kitties" and "three puppies" and understands the difference between "under" and "over," "in" and "on." Nearly all normal four-year-olds can define three or four prepositions, according to the Denver Developmental Screening Test, and can deal with such physically descriptive ideas as "cold," "tired," and "hungry." Almost all can give their first and last names.

At the same time, the mind is stretching in other ways, too. Between three and four, your child learns the concept of number, and by the fourth birthday, he or she may be trying to count. The sequence may come out, "1, 3, 7, 2" or "1, 5, 9, 6" for a year or more yet. If you ask the child his or her age, or the number of puppies in the picture, he or she may be able to hold up three or the appropriate number of fingers. At about the age of four, many children learn to recognize their printed name; a few can even laboriously print it themselves, if the name isn't too long and the letters not too difficult. With a pencil and paper, a four-year-old may be able to draw a creditable imitation of a person.

Recognizing·colors is another area of progress. Seventy-five percent of four-year-olds can identify basic colors, like "red," "blue," and "yellow," and may even select a "favorite color" (although some children progress more slowly in this area than others). Many have even mastered definitions of words and can identify the opposites of "good," "fast," or "right."

The child's mastery of language may become so complete, in fact, that he or she becomes a nonstop chatterbox, driving parents to distraction with a ceaseless babble that begins at breakfast and continues to bedtime and often beyond; even after the light has been turned out, you may hear him or her in earnest conversation with the teddy bear. Most of this monologue is just practice—the child is displaying a fascination with words and sounds. And these endless, one-sided conversations seldom require acknowledgment or reply. But through your conversation, you can help the child develop language skills, sharpen pronunciation, and learn adult cadences. Continue to talk to him or her, pronouncing words the correct way and using simple but grown-up sentences. Don't overcorrect—but don't use baby talk—and the child will learn the lesson.

"BUT WHY, MOMMY?"
One of the favorite sentences your little talking machine will use consists of three letters: "Why?" You'll hear this inquiry from morning to night, and often after you've responded to one "Why?" you'll hear "Why?" again.

Much of the time the child doesn't really want an answer, just some verbal interaction. He or she is playing with words, testing and examining ideas. Your child likes the attention that comes with your response.

"Why?" also represents a new dimension to a child's ever-growing curiosity. Now he or she has learned there are other ways to make discoveries—tapping the accumulated wisdom of a more experienced mommy or daddy. Your child wants to know what you know and looks to you as a fountain of knowledge.

You don't have to be a walking encyclopedia to deal with these questions, and you don't have to answer them elaborately. Keep your answers simple, with a minimum of details; a child who asks about the man in the moon isn't looking for a lesson in astronomy. Nor do you need to consult reference books or authorities. A few facts are enough.

TOILET ACCIDENTS AND BED-WETTING
Even some time after a child has been successfully urine-trained during the day, accidents will periodically occur. They usually happen because the child is excited, absorbed in play, or in an unfamiliar place and doesn't know the location of the bathroom. Accidents are more frequent when the child is outdoors and hasn't time to hurry home.

Treat incidents like these as casually as you possibly can. Usually, the child is already greatly embarrassed by the whole affair—especially if other children witnessed the event—and no lecture is necessary. Just change the child's clothes, and offer a gentle reminder to start for the bathroom sooner in the future.

When a child has been successfully toilet-trained for a while and then reverts to wetting pants, an emotional cause may be suspected. The arrival of a new baby may cause an older child, especially an only child, to return to babyish behavior long since abandoned. So may a move to a new home. Treat the matter casually, and try to deal with the situation that provoked it; reassure him or her of your love despite the newcomer, or point out that the house is new, but mommy and daddy are still here.

Repeated accidents without an obvious emotional explanation may be caused by an infection or irritation of the urinary tract.

Such conditions are more common in girls than in boys; sometimes bubble bath may be the culprit. Consult you pediatrician, who can evaluate the condition and prescribe medication to treat it. A breakdown in toilet training also may be caused by an inborn structural defect in the urinary system. Such conditions can be corrected surgically.

About nine of ten children can remain dry through the night, most of the time, by four years of age. Night training requires much more time than daytime training, however, so don't be surprised if your youngster still has occasional accidents at night until the early school years.

As with daytime toilet accidents, a seemingly spontaneous recurrence of bed-wetting in a child who has been reliably trained to stay dry at night may indicate an emotional or even a physical problem.

THE CHRONIC BED-WETTER

Many people think persistent bed-wetting is rare, but actually it is quite common. One study of 992 Baltimore children showed that between one-fourth and one-third of five-year-olds wet their beds at least once a month; two of three bed-wetters, once a week. Ten percent of seven-year-olds were still not reliably dry, and even one in twenty 12-year-olds wets the bed at least once monthly. Contrary to popular belief, boys and girls were represented in about equal numbers. The problem seemed to run in families.

Why presumably trained children wet their beds on some nights while remaining dry on others annoys parents (and the child, too) and mystifies physicians. The theory that they simply sleep more soundly than the rest of us does not stand up in laboratory tests. A child who suddenly begins to wet the bed after years of being dry may have an emotional problem, but this can be ruled out in the majority of cases. Infection or another physical cause seldom is an explanation, although it should be investigated. And it is not a matter of simply being too lazy to get up and visit the bathroom, as weary parents sometimes allege.

A popular theory today suggests a developmental lag in bladder control. Because the condition runs in families, some physicians suspect an inherited slower maturation of certain nerves. Tests have shown bed-wetters' bladders are of normal size but with a smaller "functional capacity." Even during the day, they visit the bathroom more frequently than other children.

If bed-wetting occurred nightly, it might seem less a problem; constant precautions could be taken. It's the intermittent pattern that causes such friction between child and parent. Repeatedly having to get up in the night to wrestle with wet pajamas and bedsheets leads to the conviction by parents that the child "just isn't trying." It can arouse overwhelming feelings of downright anger, even toward a small child. The first step toward a solution is acknowledging the anger, not trying to make the child feel guilty or ashamed, or calling him or her a "baby," which only complicates things further. Success against bed-wetting can only be achieved by parent and child working together.

Simple measures should be tried first. Place a plastic liner over the mattress and moistureproof sheeting between mattress and linens. Be sure the child visits the bathroom just before retiring. Limiting fluids before bedtime may help, if you don't become so obsessive about it that the child winds up thirsty. Encourage the child to go to the toilet during the night, but it's not necessary to get up with him or her. Install a night-light in the bedroom and bathroom to make night visits easier.

Bladder-training exercises also work for some children, usually those of school age. The child is encouraged to drink large amounts of water during the day, then is urged to wait as long as possible before using the toilet. After a few days, the intervals between visits are said to increase, and within three weeks, according to some reports, children also stay dry at night. Apparently by conditioning the bladder to hold greater volumes during the day, bladder capacity at night is also enlarged.

Your pediatrician may prescribe nightly does of a medication, imipramine, to control bed-wetting. Imipramine's mechanism of action isn't quite certain, but repeated studies have demonstrated significant elimination or decrease of bed-wetting in a majority of children treated. Unfortunately, many children may resume wetting the bed within a few weeks when the drug is discontinued.

Another treatment the pediatrician may suggest is the use of a bladder-conditioning alarm apparatus. A small metal clip is attached to the child's underpants and connected to a small bell or buzzer, usually worn on the shirt or pajama top. Wetting the underpants completes a circuit, sounds the alarm, and wakes the child. After a few nights, the child begins to wake more quickly after urination begins and gets up and goes to the bathroom. After a few weeks, the bladder is mysteriously conditioned so that urination does not occur at all. The method has been reported to "cure" up to 90 percent of bed-wetters in two to ten weeks, with only a few relapses. The method fails most often when the child does not awaken in spite of the alarm—even when other members of the family hear the noise.

Because the biggest problem—and greatest source of annoyance—is cleaning up, the child usually is willing to take responsibility to offset the parents' natural irritation with the daily hassle. A child old enough to dress and undress can be taught to change nightclothing; if the condition persists to an older age, he or she can learn to change bedding as well. A laundry hamper and linen supply in the room will help.

THE CHANGING SLEEP SCHEDULE
Children usually give up daytime naps around the fourth birthday, although many continue to take a short afternoon nap until they reach kindergarten age. If it continues, the nap may be shortened to an hour and a half.

Some children give up naps gradually. They may discontinue sleeping in the afternoon for a few months, then resume again. Oth-

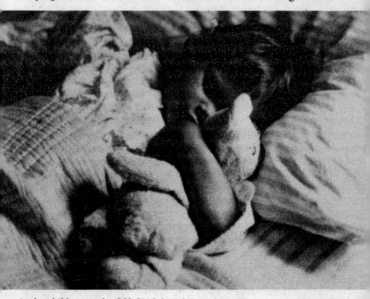

As the child nears the fifth birthday, the number of hours spent sleeping at night usually declines to ten or eleven. Schedules vary from child to child; watch yours to determine the best one.

ers may lie down each day but sleep only on some occasions and not others. In any case, a four-year-old should continue to have a rest period or quiet time in midafternoon, even if he or she does not sleep. Let the child lie down with a book, pencil and paper, or a quiet toy. An afternoon rest is particularly important if the child is attending nursery school and has a full schedule of activities keeping him or her busy throughout the morning. Even after the nap has been eliminated, insist on a rest period when the child seems overtired or keyed up.

The number of hours spent sleeping at night decreases, too, as the child approaches the fifth birthday. The duration is usually about ten to eleven hours, although the need for sleep varies tremendously. There's no best time for a four-year-old's curfew; it can be determined by family style. A common schedule is bedtime at 8 p.m., with the child arising at 6:30 or 7 in the morning, but this does not have to be rigid. Usually, the later a child retires, the later he or she will sleep. If both parents are working outside the home, you may want to enjoy the child more in the evening and allow him or her to sleep later the next day.

HOW TO PICK A NURSERY SCHOOL

There's no set age for a child to start nursery school, assuming you want to send him or her to one. It depends on the child's temperament, personality, and maturity and your own schedule and resources—plus your need for child-care during the day. The usual beginning is sometime between the third and fourth birthday, although some children start earlier. A child usually attends two or three days a week at first and may gradually work up to a full five-day schedule. A nursery school session normally lasts about two and a half to three hours a day. More and more, nursery school is part of all-day child-care.

When you're trying to decide whether your child is ready for nursery school, here are some questions to ask:

• Is he or she toilet-trained during the day? Many schools insist that the child be out of diapers and know how to use the bathroom without adult assistance. The child also should be able to tell an adult when he or she needs to make a trip to the bathroom.

• Is the child able to take care of him- or herself? In other words, can the child tell an adult when he or she is ill or hurt, get help when needed, and be self-reliant enough to play without constant adult supervision? The child should recognize personal possessions and be able to put on jackets and hats with a minimum of help.

Should your son or daughter attend nursery school? One advantage is the chance each child has to adapt to other children. The nursery-schooler with a "me-first" attitude quickly learns cooperation is important.

• Does the child leave you easily? Ease of separation doesn't usually come until after the second birthday, unless the child has become accustomed to a preschool or child-care center. Regardless of age, the child often will cling to you during the first visit, and separation throughout the first month may be difficult.

Should your child attend nursery school? There are three main benefits:

• Nursery schools offer encounters and social interaction with peers in a controlled environment. Your son or daughter learns to adapt and accept the rights and demands of other children and to adjust personal wishes to the requirements of the larger group, a socialization process that helps toward molding them into adults.

• The child benefits from the stimulation of early education.

Nursery schools don't teach the three "R's," but they do stress learning through personal discovery, and they stress the creativity of art and handicrafts.

• It's good for parents. Not only does it allow you more time to yourself, even to resume a career, but it offers an opportunity to meet other parents and exchange child-raising experiences.

Nursery schools, like play groups—and like children themselves—come in all shapes, sizes, and pedagogical philosophies. The Montessori schools, for example, stress a structured learning program leading through the entire preschool years. Children start at two to two and a half and advance through methods of personal discovery based on special teaching materials designed by the founder, Maria Montessori. Open schools stress more freedom, with the child able to follow his or her own dictates around a series of "learning centers." Still other nursery schools emphasize arts, language, or crafts.

The best way to discover the best choice of nursery school for your child is to visit several and observe them. Most schools have such days for parents; a few even have one-way glass viewing areas, so you can watch the children without distracting them. Here are things to look for:

Environment. Is the school structurally safe? Is the play area well enclosed, preventing easy access to the street? Is there adequate adult supervision to forestall accidents? Is the playground equipment appropriate for children of nursery-school age? Is the school satisfactorily clean by your standards? Are toilet facilities adequate for the number of children? Is medical or nursing help available or on call in case of illness or injury?

Most states or municipalities license or regularly inspect nursery schools, but their minimum standards may not be as high as yours.

Personnel. Do staff members regard themselves as teachers or merely custodians? How does the staff interact with children? Are the children watched or left to their own devices? If a child is hurt, does he or she get immediate attention?

Situation. Are children of similar ages and sizes kept together or are three- and five-year-olds mixed indiscriminately? Some group play is fine on the playground, for instance, but each age group or level of development should have its own time. How is the school structured? Your outgoing child may fit in well at a free-wheeling school, but your shy one may belong elsewhere.

What's expected from you? Many schools operate cooperatively to hold down costs, with one or more parents serving as teachers or teachers' assistants each day. Such economy sounds fine, but you must be sure you have the time to contribute—as well as the desire to do so. Will you have some voice in the decisions of the school—and do you want any—as in a public school, or are the structure and operation unyieldingly the same?

Expenses. Tuition for nursery school ranges widely, and there are no guidelines for what is appropriate. Some hidden expenses, however, may include the distance from school—will you need to drive the child there or take part in a car pool? Is there a bus paid for by the school? Is the school atmosphere rough-and-tumble and the equipment primitive, leading to more wear-and-tear on clothes?

Most educators now agree that children require some form of education prior to beginning formal school (about the sixth birthday). But when that starts and under what circumstances is strictly up to you.

THE MARATHON RUNNY NOSE

To many parents, the years from three to five seem like one continuous runny nose. Nursery school, preschool, or any environment filled with children brings one cold after another. You can expect that a preschool child will have seven to eight colds a year, each lasting about two weeks. The rate is even higher in large families, with each child contributing his or her own breed of viruses.

Apart from passing out handkerchiefs and tissues, there's little you (or your pediatrician) can do to combat a cold. Aspirin or acetaminophen in doses appropriate for the child's age may relieve aches and pains; using a vaporizer at night may make the child's breathing easier. Cough medicines, cough drops, or over-the-counter cold preparations are expensive and their value unproved. A cough syrup made of lemon juice and honey is less expensive, but should not be given to children under one year of age because of the risk that the honey may contain spores that cause infant botulism. The pediatrician may prescribe a decongestant to reduce nasal stuffiness. (See Chapter 20, "Common Complaints and Diseases.")

Colds are miserable but not life-threatening. You can't do much to help your child avoid them, and maybe you don't want to. Each exposure helps a child build immunity to that particular strain of virus, thus reducing vulnerability later. That's why a child gets so many colds in the first six years of life, when viruses are first encountered, and why the rate of illnesses caused by viruses declines with age.

Most of the time-honored precautions seem to have little effect in preventing a cold; children whose parents observe them faithfully seem to have just as many colds as those whose parents ignore them altogether. Many people believe that drafts, wet feet, and insufficient clothing "cause" a cold, but there is no evidence for this belief. In addition, keeping a child at home to prevent a cold from spreading is unrealistic. Upper respiratory infections are contagious even before symptoms appear.

Be alert, however, for symptoms not normally associated with a cold. Earache, diminished hearing, or swollen glands may indicate a secondary bacterial infection complicating the original viral illness. These infections can have serious consequences, but if detected early, they may be readily subdued with antibiotics. Consult a pediatrician if any of these symptoms accompany or follow a cold. Medical attention should be sought for recurrent or persistent infections that don't subside within a few weeks.

Some parents believe that removing enlarged tonsils and adenoids will help reduce colds and infections that often follow them, but there is no evidence this is true. Tonsillectomy and adenoidectomy are among the most frequently performed surgical procedures. However, doctors are not even agreed on the value of removing these bits of tissue from the throat and nasal area to relieve the two conditions for which they are most commonly recommended. A tonsillectomy is performed to relieve frequent or chronic infections of the tonsils, usually caused by the streptococcus bacteria; an adenoidectomy to relieve repeated ear infections. Both tissues are known to play a part in the body's defenses against infection, and enlargement of tonsils and adenoids in normal children may indicate these tissues are combating the cold virus, not that they are its victims. As the child grows and the number of infections decreases, the adenoids and tonsils normally shrink in size.

Although enlarged adenoids and tonsils may "squeeze" the eustachian tube connecting ear and throat—thus preventing proper drainage of fluid from the middle ear and increasing chances for infection—additional obstruction may result from slow maturation of the tube itself. If so, it's a problem that cures itself with time. Instead of adenoidectomy, some doctors advocate the insertion of tiny poyethylene tubes in the eardrum, as a means of providing proper drainage from the middle ear.

LYING, STEALING, AND DIRTY WORDS
Not all three- and four-year-olds are angels, and sometimes yours will probably behave in ways you don't approve of.

Falsehoods—you can't really call them lies—are common at this age. Nor can you call them bad—some are so transparent they're funny. A three-year-old still lives in a fantasy world, where impulses and wishes are just as real as facts and deeds. If he or she tells you an elephant ran into the room, upset the milk cup, and raced out again, it's not an attempt to mislead you, nor is it said out of malice. That's what the child wishes were the explanation for the accident. Knowing you may be disappointed or angry, he or she gives you a fabricated account—or more.

Don't engage in a power struggle over an occasional lie. If you accuse the child of lying, his or her instinct is to deny it—and to believe the denial. Show that you disapprove of lying, but use the occasion as an educational experience: "Well, that sounds like a tall story to me," or "I don't care if you broke the cup or Jimmy broke the cup. In this family we don't play with the china." Your answer allows the child to save face, while you get the point across in a fashion that will remembered.

As the child grows older and is better able to distinguish truth from untruth, you can substitute reason. A four-year-old is sensitive to his or her own feelings, as well as those of others, and your talk can be couched in those terms. "I don't like it when you tell fibs to me" lets the child appreciate the consequences of lying in a way he or she can understand.

A five-year-old who lies habitually should cause you to re-examine *your* standards. Children usually tell lies under pressure—when they fear the truth will disappoint you or perhaps cause them to be punished. A five-year-old knows when he or she has failed or fallen short of your expectations. A sustained pattern of lying may indicate that your standards are beyond reach or that you have restricted the child too greatly.

Taking other people's possessions (and, often, lying about it) is another step in growing up. Stealing by a three-year-old is just another manifestation of the child's being dominated by wish and desire. If the child wants something, he or she takes it, because the social limitations adults understand haven't caught up with the child's self-centered impulses. It isn't a serious matter nor is it a precedent. Stealing also may recur at five. At either age, don't ignore the event; just bring it up and deal with it openly and then close the subject.

Don't make a major fuss, and don't directly accuse the child of stealing. If you do, the child may simply deny taking anything at all. "I don't care how it got here. That's Johnny's toy and you take it back" is better than a direct confrontation. "You stole Johnny's toy. I saw you take it" may simply encourage the child to steal more skillfully the next time.

Again, you may wish to examine your own standards. Pre-schoolers seldom steal because they lack personal possessions or because they are deprived. In fact, their thefts may indicate that you have not conveyed the message that other people's property must be respected.

Even a three-year-old quickly picks up blue language and may repeat it, often under embarrassing circumstances. The words sound so odd coming from a tiny mouth that you may laugh in spite of yourself. That may be the worst thing you can do: Knowing such words are good for a laugh, the child may repeat them again later. Don't ignore the words, either. Just bring the matter to the child's attention by saying that words like these aren't used by anyone in your family and that they shouldn't be used again.

Mischief also becomes part of a preschooler's routine—and a bone of contention with parents. Exasperating as it may be when the child pours salt into the sugar bowl, you can usually endure such incidents. Even a pattern of impishness—hiding Daddy's hat, smearing soap on the bathroom mirror—can be written off to harmless devilment. But if the mischief is consistently damaging or destructive, more serious intervention may be needed. A lasting streak of destruction also may indicate the child is troubled and unhappy; an emotional explanation may be looked for.

MONEY, TOYS, ALLOWANCES

Sometime during the preschool years, a child understands that money has value and can be used to obtain possessions. He or she doesn't know much about it and probably can't distinguish between a penny and a dime. By the age of four, most children know that two coins are more desirable than one coin, but they don't understand much beyond that.

Simultaneously—and with the aid of television advertising—children begin to desire toys or other articles that appear on the screen or are seen in stores. Their desires put parents in a bind. You want to buy things for your child, but your resources are limited, and the child doesn't understand either value or limitations.

You'll find yourself saying "No" a great deal during this period—and you may find it answered with a great deal of protest and rage. It's difficult for a child to comprehend why a toy can be bought one day and not another. You'll just have to be firm, distract the child when you can, and endure the outburst when you can't. You can reason more successfully with a four- or five-year-old. By then, most children have learned they can't have everything, although they may continue to want it. You can sometimes tell them when a gift may be bought—"the next time Mommy and Daddy go to the store"—since their sense of time is still vague. Purchases also can be used as rewards.

A child hasn't much use for an allowance until the age of five, when it should be given in small amounts but with the provision that the child can spend it as he or she chooses. This gets across the principle of thrift, as well as the idea of deferred gratification.

Some children respond to a special day when they can receive a reward. Saturday can become Candy Day or Treat Day, for instance, with a small budget earmarked for that day. The amount can be based on the child's age, with money subtracted for each time candy is requested in the interim.

MANNERS AND COURTESY

A three-year-old can learn to repeat the words and phrases most of us use in polite discourse, words like "please" and "thank you." No special lessons are involved in the process. If you as parents are courteous in exchanges with others, and especially with each other, the child will quickly pick up those expressions. If you make a game of "please" and "thank you," their use will be habitual by the time the child is old enough to attend school.

In the same way, your courtesy and thoughtfulness with others will be imitated by the child. As he or she grows older, you can expand the lesson by using words, explaining that people are kind and considerate toward one another because they expect the same treatment in return. Explain simply, yet directly, that all of us are interconnected, and if we offend other people, we will lose their love and support.

Despite these lessons, some children act aggressively toward others: A three-year-old may hit, kick, or bite playmates. You can explain that people have other, better ways to express feelings. Anger is normal, you may say, but telling people you're angry is more acceptable than punching. As with many lessons, you can't expect the child to assimilate this stricture in a single setting. You may have to repeat the lesson several times. But remember not to lecture; keep your message short and direct.

What if other children hit your child? Youngsters quickly learn for themselves to deal with an aggressor. Usually, they just give him or her a wide berth; they will say frankly, "I don't want to play with you." This ostracism is often more effective than striking back. With some children, however, it has just the opposite effect: the aggressive child strikes out even more, hoping to gain more attention by doing so.

In such an event, you'll have to teach your child the limits of tolerance. Most of us discourage children from hitting others or striking back when attacked. But if a child allows him- or herself to be bullied repeatedly, the pattern will continue. In this case, you must make it clear to the child that the whole world isn't reasonable; aggressive people must often be dealt with in an aggressive, physical way when they repeatedly overstep the bounds of tolerance.

OBEDIENCE, REWARD, PUNISHMENT

Obviously, you want your child to do what you say when you want it done. Always give directions with confidence they will be carried out. Don't be tentative; be firm in a way that leaves no room for argument or "Why, Daddy?" But don't expect a three-year-old to obey or perform according to your expectations every time.

As your child grows older, you expect that he or she will distinguish approved behavior from the disapproved variety. Approved behavior brings reward and reinforcement; disapproved behavior brings unpleasant consequences. The relationship between behavior and consequences is the basic lesson of discipline. Those consequences must be appropriate to the act and tolerable to both parent and child.

For gaining approved behavior, reward is the best motivator. Of course, every child needs reward, in the form of positive feedback, completely apart from discipline. But rewarding a child—

Reward is the best answer for good behavior. It needn't be elaborate, so long as the action and reward are linked in the child's mind. Even a simple hug will tell your son or daughter that some ways are better than others.

even with something so basic as a hug—is also a teaching technique. That doesn't mean you should give a bribe to produce proper behavior. It does mean you should link the reward directly to the act. Reward should be bestowed for specific acts of behavior a child can understand and should be produced immediately. Asking a four-year-old to be "good" all afternoon in return for a bicycle next Christmas calls for vague behavior and a distant reward. Tell him or her to pick up toys and praise the child afterward—deed and reward are then readily and unmistakably linked.

With older children, reward need not be immediate, but steps toward an eventual reward should be taken at once. Employing a system of delayed reward, you can give the child a penny (or a gold star) for each night he or she remembers to brush their teeth.

For disapproved behavior, you want an act that communicates your displeasure. Just showing by expression or attitude your unhappiness may be enough. "Time out" is another. That means physically separating the child from you and from the scene—banishing him or her to the bedroom, bathroom, or corner. Using a clock with an alarm helps to make the point. Ignoring the child's behavior, surprisingly, also may be effective. When a child persists in an annoying act, even punishment may reinforce the behavior by giving it attention; when mother screams, at least the child is being noticed.

Almost all parents resort to physical punishment occasionally. Spanking works best when directly connected to the misdeed and administered immediately. Children can understand a swat delivered in anger better than being deliberately "turned over the knee" for their own good or being punished "after Daddy comes home." By school age, physical punishment is outdated. Being whacked is degrading to a five-year-old.

The least effective motivator is the unfulfilled threat. If you repeatedly tell a child, "Don't do that or I'll spank you," you must be prepared to carry out the punishment if the disapproved behavior continues. Otherwise, the only lesson the child learns is that Mother or Dad talks a lot but doesn't do much.

BUT WILL HE OR SHE OUTGROW IT?

Some behavior that seems attractively cute at three should be worrisome if it still persists at five. A toddler who walks unsteadily is merely amusing, but a hesitant five-year-old may legitimately concern the parents. A three-year-old who calls his sister Barbara "Babawa" gets a laugh; a five-year-old with a lisp may be the target of other children's taunts. Parents may be told (or may tell themselves), "He'll outgrow it." "She'll come around soon." But will he? Will she? When should you be concerned about your child's development?

Physical and behavioral progress covers a wide range, as this book has tried to show. Some problems that worry parents are actually well within the spectrum of normal growth; the child is simply marching to a different drummer, adhering to a personal inner rhythm. Yet early detection of a problem is important. The sooner it's discovered, the more readily it can be corrected.

Obviously, warning signals to parents may differ according to the area of development. But here are general guidelines for intervening in developmental problems that worry you.

• Follow your own instincts. Parents see the child most—and under the greatest variety of circumstances. Don't be swayed by your mother-in-law's diagnosis, "That child walks funny," or, conversely, by a neighbor's judgment, "My sister walked like that, too, and she grew up just fine." (On the other hand, respect the judgment of a trained outsider, a teacher or child-care specialist, for instance, who can professionally compare your child with many others.) If it looks wrong to you, by all means seek help. But don't be goaded just because it seems a child's contemporaries are ahead of him or her.

• Consult your pediatrician, but if you are not satisfied with the verdict, ask for a consultation or seek a second opinion. If you're still concerned, try to identify the leading authority on the problem in your area, and seek his or her advice. But don't shop for doctors, which is expensive and counterproductive, and don't be put off by a doctor's "He'll outgrow it." If you're still worried, ask for any examinations or tests that may clear up the matter once and for all.

• Once the verdict is in, be prepared to deal with it. If examinations show normal bone structure, you can be sure a child will eventually overcome a "funny walk." An exam that shows no structural defect in a lisping child's vocal organs can be similarly reassuring. Be patient in helping the child grow out of the condition. Don't call a stammer or lisp to his or her attention or urge him or her to try to walk differently. Pointing out the problem may only ingrain it more deeply and make it more difficult to overcome.

• Be alert for possible behavioral problems, as well as those of physical development, and seek help if concerned. Most preschoolers lie sometimes, but a chronic liar may require help. Youngsters play with matches, but one who consistently sets fire needs professional assistance.

• Don't worry about minor habits or mannerisms. Preschoolers often develop such habits as nail-biting, face-twitching, stuttering, or stammering. A few may suck their thumbs again after having given up such consolation. The less you say about these conditions the better. Unless such habits are part of a persistent pattern of emotional tension, most of them disappear within a short time.

Ninety-nine out of 100 children outgrow the problems that concern their parents. But if your child does need help, get it as soon as possible.

18

Five to Six Years

HOW THE CHILD GROWS

Between the fifth and sixth birthdays, the average normal child gains five pounds and grows 2½ to three inches. Average weight is 47 pounds; average height, 45½ inches. The range of normal weight is 35 to 55 pounds; the range of height, 43 to 49 inches.

Between five and six years of age, most children can do the following:

- put on and take off most clothing and probably tie shoes;
- print their first name, if it isn't too long or difficult, and recognize it;
- know both first and last names and be able to tell them to an adult;
- count from one to five in proper sequence and perhaps from one to ten;
- make a recognizable drawing of a person, including arms and legs;
- take care of toilet needs with only very rare accidents;
- wash face and hands and brush teeth with supervision;
- identify most colors;
- understand that a nickel or dime is a more valuable coin than a penny.

A CHANGE IN THE MENU

After several years of picking at food and acting as if eating it were somehow foreign to the laws of human nature, your five-year-old's appetite may suddenly begin to increase—the result of a new upturn in the growth rate.

Over the next three years, the average normal child gains 15 to 20 pounds. The change won't be an abrupt one, however, and you may not immediately notice that your child is eating more until his or her clothes begin to look too small!

Mealtime is now a family occasion, and no special diet is necessary for the growing child. The proper nutritional balance in the food you serve the rest of the family is fine for a five-year-old. He or she will still probably prefer simple food and may reject strongly flavored or heavily seasoned dishes. Most children at this age are still leery of cooked vegetables but will eat raw carrots, celery, cucumbers, and even cauliflower. Fresh fruits provide important nutrients, and most children have several favorites. Fruit juices are popular, too.

By now, your child may have a well-developed taste for sweets and junk foods, and you may want to restrict their consumption.

Milk remains a useful ingredient in a child's diet but need not be consumed in the quantities of the early bone-building years. One or two glasses a day is plenty. Any more only fills up the child and quenches the appetite for other equally useful or even more important nutrients. Skim or fat-free milk is adequate.

You don't have to give your child vitamin tablets if he or she is receiving a balanced diet, although you may wish to continue them. If the local water supply is not fluoridated, fluoride tablets may be continued as well.

A five-year-old's busy social schedule may interfere with regularly scheduled mealtimes; he or she will want to gobble on the run to resume romping with friends. You may feel you almost have to tie the child to the chair to get a decent meal eaten. Later, when everything is put away, the child may return, sniffing for snacks. Maintain your rules of regular mealtimes, but you can allow the child to leave the table as soon as he or she is finished.

THE SCHOOL BELL RINGS

Until now, home and family have been the dominant influences in your child's life. Now you'll share that responsibility with the school. A five-year-old probably will spend half a day in school five days a week.

Traditionally, a child begins kindergarten at five, first grade at six. But those starting dates aren't rigid. The spectrum of development among children is very wide, and some five-year-olds are more prepared for the social and educational experiences of kindergarten than others are. Many teachers strive to give children individual attention to bridge these differences, but this can be a demanding task. In any case, "five years old" is a nebulous term. A child who has just celebrated a fifth birthday is probably quite different from the five-year-old who is a month short of being six.

Most kindergartens now stress preparation for academic work, usually in the form of recognizing letters and preparing for reading. An astute teacher recognizes the children who will respond to such work. Unfortunately, children themselves often feel pressured to keep up with their faster-moving classmates. Despite the teacher's best effort, they may feel they're lagging behind and therefore are failures.

Many educators and psychologists recommend that some children wait a year before starting kindergarten or first grade. They may be urged to spend an additional year in nursery school. Boys, in particular, may be less ready than girls in those skills that are needed for school, and some boys are not ready for kindergarten until the age of six.

When the calendar shows your child is scheduled for school, you may wish to ask yourself these questions:

• Is the child socially mature? Can he or she take care of personal needs? Does your child mix well with other children? Does he or she accept separation from you easily?

• What are the child's strengths and weaknesses? Will he or she flourish best in a structured environment or in a more easy-going one?

• How developed is the child's ability with language? Does he or she talk well and understand most words?

Remember the kindergarten year isn't just an academic period. It's a time of transition, as the child moves from a life in the home to one spent increasingly outside it. You want to make that transition as smooth as possible.

THE PRE-SCHOOL PHYSICAL
Although your child has probably been visiting a pediatrician or well-baby clinic regularly, he or she needs a thorough pediatric examination before starting kindergarten. (Indeed, many school districts require some sort of pre-school physical before the child can begin classes.) Schedule it well before school starts, so any problems can be handled easily.

Because the senses are at the heart of learning, the eyes and ears, in particular, should be tested. Sometimes a slight impairment in vision or hearing isn't noticed by the parents and doesn't make itself evident until the child begins to struggle with classroom work. The pre-school physical examination should be more exten-

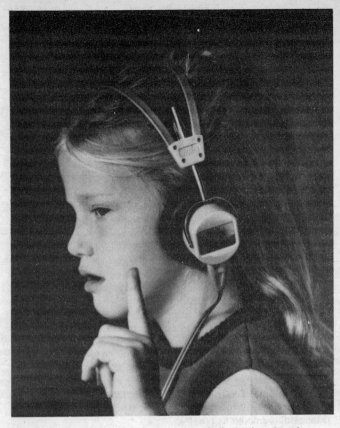

Because sight and sound are at the center of effective learning, the pre-school physical is crucial. Vision must be checked thoroughly. An audiogram (below), which measures hearing ability, also should be part of the examination.

sive than just measuring the child's ability to read the eye chart posted on the doctor's wall. The doctor should, in addition, check the ability of the child's eyes to focus and, at the same time, look into the possibility of eye infections.

The hearing test should include an audiogram, which measures sensitivity to tones and frequencies as well as loudness. The doctor also should look for accumulated fluid in the middle ear, which can cause mild to moderate hearing loss.

Most doctors want to hear the child speak, too. In case of a "cute" speech pattern, the doctor may recommend the child visit a clinic or speech pathologist, because a speech impairment can hinder proper pronunciation and stand in the way of learning.

At this point, you'll also want to check the child's shots. DPT and polio boosters are due between the fourth and sixth birthdays. In many states, beginning students must produce a complete record of immunizations showing they've received all the recommended shots before they can be admitted to school.

SAFETY ALONG THE WAY

Safety should be the first lesson of kindergarten. If your child walks to school, be sure to cover the route with him or her beforehand. You want a five-year-old to be familiar with the route before trying it alone. If possible, escort your son or daughter to school the first few days and meet him or her for the trip home. If an older child in the neighborhood also attends the school, ask if they can walk together.

Teach the child to observe all the basic rules of pedestrian safety; stop at intersections, look both ways before crossing, and always walk within crosswalks. Teach your child always to stay on sidewalks and to follow the directions given by crossing guards or police who may be on the scene. Also, every child should be taught to walk through an intersection and not run across the street.

A child who rides a bus to school should learn the correct way to enter and leave the vehicle. Even if the driver escorts the child across the street after disembarking, he or she should learn to look both directions before crossing. Go with the child to the bus stop the first few days, and meet him or her on the return trip, especially if the walk home covers several blocks.

School bus drivers usually control children's behavior on the bus. But tell your child to take a seat quietly, to remain in the seat throughout the ride, and not to engage in horseplay while the bus is moving.

Before joining a car pool to transport children to school, make sure that all the parents involved agree on safety regulations. Each car in the pool should have a seat belt or restraining harness for every child; belts or harnesses should not be shared. There should be no more passengers than can be seated comfortably. Children should always enter and leave the vehicle from the curb side, never the street side, and the driver or another adult should help them from the car. At the school, load cars off the street or when a teacher or other school employee is present.

A FEELING OF SECURITY

A five-year-old usually knows his or her first and last name and can recite each of them plainly enough for an adult to understand. The child can usually also print at least his or her first name and probably can recognize his or her name if printed in block letters on paper or on the inside of clothing or boots. Before the first day at kindergarten, help your son or daughter to memorize the family phone number and your street address (or be able to describe the home), so that he or she can tell another adult when lost.

Especially in these days when many parents work or are busy with other duties during the day, schools usually require that you list the name of a friend, neighbor, or relative to be contacted in the event of an emergency when you cannot be reached. The name of the family physician or the child's pediatrician and the work telephone number of one or both parents usually also must be kept on file. However, the child also should be instructed whom to call in an emergency when you are not at home. He or she should know the phone number and address of that person (a neighbor or close relative, perhaps) and how to reach the person's home.

Always instruct the child beforehand in case the routine varies. If he or she is to go to a different home after school, make sure the plan is clear to the child before the school day begins. Many schools require that you file a written note in case of change of plans or, at least, call the child's teacher. If you're not going to be there when the child usually comes home and another person will be waiting, make sure the child expects that. Never let a five-year-old come home to an empty house—it's a scary feeling.

Mark all of the child's belongings, including jackets, hats, and overshoes, so he or she can recognize and find them easily. Try to choose garments that can easily be distinguished, even by a child who is not yet able to read a printed name. Color-code shoes and boots with green (right) and red (left) markers, so he or she can easily match the right piece of footwear to the appropriate foot. You can use a similar color key on gloves and mittens.

THE PARENTS' ROLE

You have a part to play in the child's schooling, too. Even a kindergartener brings home a blizzard of papers and handicrafts for you to inspect and admire. It might be difficult for a busy parent to review every last scrap of paper that arrives, but as often as possible, you should look at the child's work and examine it.

Always find something to praise in the child's work, however difficult it may be to decipher. The leading statement, "Tell me

Schooltime! Safety on the way should be the first lesson. If your son or daughter will walk to school, make sure he or she knows the way. If possible, accompany the child there and back for the first few days.

about your picture," is more encouraging to a fledgling artist than an incredulous, "What is that?" Avoid criticism, even constructive criticism, and try not to show amusement at the child's efforts. Laughing at him or her only makes a child feel foolish. Don't overdo the praise, though; even a child recognizes that you can say only so much about a page of printed "b's" and "d's." Try to be specific in your praise. "That's a nice tree" tells the child you really are paying attention.

Like adults, children don't always want to talk about the day's events. Don't pressure with "What did you learn today?" Just show interest and let them volunteer their recital of kindergarten happenings.

Remember that education isn't something that goes on only within school walls. Review lessons as asked by the teacher, but also help the child to review and practice what is being learned. Supply pencils and paper for printing and drawing, for example, and keep a well-stocked library of books that will help him or her reinforce reading techniques. Experiences, visits, and travel also stimulate the child's curiosity and help with informal learning.

Whether or not you join a parents' group at the child's school is strictly up to you; don't be stampeded into membership if you don't feel you have time to devote to it. But visit the classroom when possible, and discuss the child's progress with the teacher. And if you are not satisfied with the teacher or with the school program, make your opinions known.

A SENSIBLE SCHEDULE

Beginning kindergarten may dominate a child's life but shouldn't be allowed to disrupt it. A five-year-old still needs adequate rest, regular mealtimes, and a schedule that keeps activities in perspective.

The need for sleep is gradually lessening, but for most children it remains at about ten hours a night. Because school hours are consistent, bedtime should come at a fairly regular hour, too. Usually, a five-year-old should be in bed by 8:30 p.m. and awaken about 7 a.m. A kindergartener on an afternoon schedule might sleep later. The morning timetable should allow enough time for the child to eat a good breakfast before school begins.

For afternoon kindergarteners, call the child in from play sufficiently ahead of time to allow a brief rest period before school. When the child returns from school, he or she should have another period to rest and unwind, much the way an adult wants to unwind after a day at work.

Entry into kindergarten often is the signal for a flurry of other activities outside the home. Many five-year-olds are enrolled in crafts classes, gymnastics, music lessons, or swimming. These activities stimulate a child and expand his or her horizons but shouldn't be allowed to overwhelm the day. Two regular activities outside the home in addition to school are probably plenty for most children in kindergarten.

BACK TO BABYHOOD

In the first days of school, you may be dismayed to find the child returning to habits that had been given up a long time ago. A five-year-old who has long since stopped thumb-sucking may suddenly pop the thumb back into the mouth; another child may dig out the disreputable "blanky" that provided solace in infancy. Whining and crankiness are common. Some children begin to have toilet accidents or wet the bed after years of being dry and toilet-trained.

These reversals are natural, temporary, and seldom related to specific events at school. Although kindergarten is usually a low-key environment, it's a new and often demanding experience for a five-year-old and quite a step up from nursery school. Youngsters themselves seem to recognize they are moving into an adult world. Although they respond to this challenge, often with eagerness, they also feel pressure that makes them—just as adults do sometimes—long for easier days.

Most children adjust to the new way of life within a few weeks. Because the change in temperament may partially be related to fatigue, you may wish to suggest that the child resume a short afternoon nap for a while. A brief quiet time after the child returns from school also may help. Of course, if the behavior persists or seems to be part of a broader pattern of emotional upset, you should seek assistance.

BACK TO WORK FOR MOTHER?

The majority of women who have worked before pregnancy return to their jobs within six months after birth, according to surveys. But many women prefer to wait until the youngest child enters school before resuming the careers or education that has been placed on hold. If this is your choice, it calls for some shifting of responsibilities for the child who has previously been cared for exclusively by mother at home.

The change isn't always easy for either parents or youngsters. Many children are unhappy to learn that mother will no longer welcome them after school. "How come you have to go to work?" may be a difficult question to answer. Try to explain that although mother likes being at home, she also likes her career or schooling, just as children love their homes but have interests elsewhere. Financial reasons may persuade older children. They can understand that mother's job may enable the entire family live more comfortably.

Any new arrangement should become a family project. Most fathers today share in child-care responsibilities, but with mother's return to work, fathers may have to take on additional duties. (Some may even choose to become full-time homemakers themselves.) Even young children can take a role. A five-year-old can help to keep his or her own room neat and perform regular chores such as sweeping porches, helping with yardwork, and caring for pets. Older ones can have greater responsibilities.

It's better to establish a regular child-care arrangement outside the home than set up a makeshift one or allow the child to arrive at an empty house to wait. Often, you'll find other parents in the same boat, and a cooperative child-care arrangement can be established.

Other possibilities to be explored include a child-care arrangement at your place of employment, now offered by an increasing number of employers. Sometimes municipalities or schools offer after-school care programs or playground activities that continue until parents finish work. You may be able to find a friend who will supervise the child during the after-school hours.

Whatever course you choose, always be sure school authorities have a phone number of a friend or relative and a telephone number where you can be reached. Discuss with your employer beforehand how you'll handle an emergency.

THE CHILD IS INDEPENDENT

More and more your child is becoming a little adult. Usually able to dial the telephone and self-reliant enough to walk to a friend's home, your son or daughter will make his or her own social plans that must be fitted into those of the rest of the family. In fact, sometimes you'll have that "empty-nest" feeling, as the child spends less time with you and more with peers. It won't be quite so easy to engage in a spontaneous family outing; the child's plans may conflict with yours.

You'll also find that even a five-year-old wants some voice in his or her life. You can't just pick out clothing for the day and expect the child to wear it docilely. Children begin to show tastes of their own—which may clash with yours—and to be adamant about them. Peer pressure and television commercials also shape their ideas.

You don't have to cater to a child's every whim, but you'll have to be prepared to take them into account. You can allow latitude in picking (or buying) clothes by narrowing the selection of shirts, for example, to three and allowing the child to make the final choice of which to wear or buy. The child can follow his or her own social schedule when it doesn't conflict with the family's plans; his or her ideas should be considered but not allowed to sway the family's decision.

You're entering a stage where you'll have to be prepared to say "No" and be unpopular. Although your child is entering a new phase of maturity, supervision still lies with you.

SECTION
4

Advice for Every Day

Bringing up children has
rough places as well as smooth.
From bloody noses to sudden
illnesses to embarrassing
questions, difficult moments
can test your strengths and skills
as a parent. You can't foresee
everything. But the following
sections can help you understand
your child better and be ready
for some of the future needs.

19

Difficult Questions

The omnipresent "Why?" may be the easiest of an inquisitive child's questions to answer. More difficult are questions parents find embarrassing or confusing—or questions that have no simple answers. Many of these have to do with the facts of life, but others relate to style of life—your own or others—and to human differences in a changing and pluralistic society.

Although these questions deal with adult topics, children often ask them before the age of six—so you should be prepared for them. You'll see that some arise out of your child's life, but others seem to come out of a clear sky.

Children ask questions for information and for reassurance. Before answering, there are certain things to know and remember and certain rules to observe. Here are the most important:

• Children usually don't want too much information. A few basic facts simply expressed are enough. Explaining the origins of life to a five-year-old doesn't require a biology text.

• Children usually have some information (often inaccurate) before they ask, as well as their own feelings about the subject. Ask your own questions before you answer, then tailor your response to the child's knowledge. Make the conversation a dialogue, not a lecture.

• Never avoid questions, postpone them ("Go ask your father"), or make jokes. Children are entitled to immediate and direct answers on subjects important to them.

• Make it easy for your child to obtain additional information.

For children who can read, simple books are available dealing with such topics as sex, death, divorce, and adoption; for those who don't yet read you can buy phonograph records. Don't push such materials on a child, but offer the book or record, and leave them where they can be found and used.

• Answer a child's questions in a relevant way. Make it clear that the answer for your family may not apply to other families.

• Listen for the unspoken questions as well as the spoken ones. The child who asks about a relative's death is probably also asking, "Will I die?" and "If *you* die, who will take care of me?"

• Be concerned about the child who repeatedly asks the same question and seems never satisfied with the answer, indicating an unusual interest in the topic.

Here are just a few of the questions you may have to deal with—and possible ways you might answer, along with information to help shape your replies:

Q. Jason's dad isn't going to live with them anymore. His dad and mom are getting a divorce. Why are they doing that?

A. Sometimes grown-ups just aren't happy together. They decide that everyone in the family would be better off if they didn't live together anymore. It doesn't have anything to do with the children. Both of them still love Jason and will still take care of him.

Q. Are you and Daddy happy?

A. Yes, right now we're really happy. Oh, we have quarrels sometimes, but that's like you and Jennifer. You two are happy with each other again after your quarrels.

Q. But Grandma says you were married and divorced from someone before.

A. I wasn't happy then. My husband and I tried to be happy, but we had so many problems between us we just couldn't seem to solve, no matter how hard we tried. Now that I'm married to your father, we're all happy, and we're taking care of any differences very well.

The second thought may be unspoken, but it usually motivates the child's inquiry. To children, divorce is a kind of death—the end of a relationship as they know it. Divorce and death cause some of the same questions to pop into the child's mind: What will happen to me? Where will I live? Who will feed me? And—perhaps most important: Is it my fault? Your answers to questions about divorce must reassure the child that he or she is still loved and cared for, even though the family is separated. You should stress that adults, not children, cause the separation.

Q. Why did Grandma die?

A. She was very old and sick, and she wasn't strong enough to go on living.

Q. Will I die, too?

A. Everyone dies at some time. It's one of those things that's bound to happen, just like we know the sun will come up in the morning. But if we are careful and take care of ourselves, it won't happen for a long time.

Q. What will happen to me if you die?

A. Daddy (or Mommy) will still be with you. There will always be people to take care of you.

Questions about death frequently arise around the age of five when a child recognizes that parents are human and fallible and that the world is not permanent. This realization frightens a child, who feels that he or she may be abandoned as a result of a parent's death. First soothe the child's worries about his or her own future before discussing the biological facts.

Another question often is, "What will happen to *me* after I die?" The answer to this question depends on family beliefs about an afterlife.

Questions about religion, church, and God are among the most difficult for contemporary parents to deal with. If the parent has a certain grasp of his or her own beliefs, explaining them to a child may not be too hard, especially if the family subscribes to an organized faith with a central body of belief. Many churches have their own printed materials, books, and even records that help parents formulate answers to children's religious questions.

Many parents, however, have only a vague notion what they believe about God and religion and aren't regular churchgoers. The child's questions make them examine their own beliefs. As always, the best course is to answer in terms of your personal ideas, not a creed that others subscribe to or that you have been taught but no longer accept.

Especially with a young child, begin by determining what the child already knows or has heard. Your task may be less to answer questions than to clear up confusion resulting from what Johnny told him or her. Then try to deal with only a few simple ideas. A three-year-old with no real concept of time isn't ready for a lecture on the afterlife. Better to suggest that God represents all that is good in the world, that he is everywhere, in all things and persons including children (an idea that fascinates the young), and is watching over the world.

Some people think you shouldn't tell a young child that God is a person or that heaven is a literal place in the sky. It probably does no harm; it helps children grasp the idea, and if you don't personally happen to hold such beliefs, you can help the child modify them later. Probably the important message is that God is responsible for the good in the world, and he is somebody to look up to.

Q. Why does Gregory have black skin and mine is white?

A. All people are different. I have brown hair, but your mommy's hair is black. Your eyes are blue but Rachel's are brown. Skins are different, too. There are a lot of different kinds of people, but they're all people and they act and feel just like you do.

Behind racial questions is often concern about difference: Why am I different? Why are they different from me? Young children like to resemble others; they want to be part of the crowd, yet seek a distinctiveness and individuality. Such questions often reflect a child's need to know that, despite the differences, he or she is still worthwhile.

Q. Why do you and Daddy both have to work? Linda's mommy doesn't work.

A. Linda's family is different from our family. In our family, it's better for all of us when your dad and I both work. We like being with you, and we like what we do when we work. You have things you like to do—play with your friends, go to school—but that doesn't change the way you feel about your home. That's the way it is with grown-ups, too.

It's nice to earn more money, too. That helps all of us do things and buy things we all enjoy.

When children raise a question about both parents working, their fears really have to do with separation and change. Your answer to the question should be framed in terms of assuring the child that you will still spend time with him or her and that your basic relationship won't change.

If working outside the home is essential to the family's financial welfare, you should tell the child so. Otherwise, the cash benefits of a paid job should be played down. If you tell an anxious child that you're working so the family can have a new car, he or she may feel you're placing material things ahead of time spent with him or her. You may even be told, "I don't want a new car. I'd rather have you home."

In either case, the child should understand that the decision to work or not to work is for adults to make, although the child's feelings will be respected.

Q. You know Dave, the man who lives in Brian's house? He's not Brian's dad. Brian's mom and Dave aren't even married.

A. That may be fine for them. People all have their own ways of doing things. Your mom and I wanted to be married, but some people don't feel the same way. The important thing is that Dave and Brian's mother are happy with each other and happy with Brian, just like we're happy with each other and with you.

Q. Sally told me that her parents adopted her. What does that mean?

A. Children come into families in different ways. You and Adam came out of my body. But some mothers can't have babies that way, even though they want them very much. So Sally's parents let some people know that they wanted a baby very much, and these people found Sally, whose other mother couldn't take care of her. Parents love children who are adopted just as much as we love you.

Q. Why do you and Mommy argue? Sometimes you don't seem to like each other very well.

A. Remember the other day when you were really angry at me? But now you're not angry, and we like each other. Or after school yesterday you were angry at Ed, but today he's your friend again. Grown-ups are like that, too. They don't agree about things, and sometimes they get angry at each other, but that doesn't mean they don't love each other.

Q. Where did Mrs. Shepard's new baby come from?

A. It grew inside of her, in a special place mothers have for babies to grow in.

Q. Did I grow in you like that?

A. You certainly did! That's where all babies live and grow until they're ready to be born.

Q. But how does the baby get in there?

A. That baby doesn't start as a baby. There's a little seed inside the mother waiting for the father to come along and start the seed growing. Then it takes almost a year for the baby to grow and come out into the world.

Q. What does the father do?

A. The most important thing he does is put the father cell inside the mother to start the baby growing. But he helps with the birth, too.

Q. How does the baby get out?

A. A mother has a special passageway made just to bring the baby out into the world. It's down between her legs. The baby grows in the mother until he or she is big enough and strong enough to live outside. Then little by little the baby comes out the passageway. The mother helps and so does the doctor.

Q. Does it hurt?

A. Only a little, and only for a while. The baby is very small, about as big as a doll. He or she is just a little bundle. The mother's muscles stretch for the baby to come out.

When discussing the facts of life, keep your information simple and straightforward. During the preschool years, avoid highly technical terms for fertilization, pregnancy, and parts of the anatomy. Choose your own words and style, but try always to get across the message that babies grow inside their mothers after a cell has been planted by the father.

Children see their parents or other children without clothes, and as they grow older, they recognize the distinctions between male and female anatomy. These distinctions should be discussed directly, without embarrassment. Don't make a point of explaining the differences. Treat them casually and gradually, as they come up:

Q. What is that on Dougie?

A. That's called a penis. Little boys are made differently from little girls. Dougie's penis shows that he's a boy. A little girl has a vulva that shows she's a little girl.

Later, this knowledge will help an older child to understand in more detail how babies get started: "The father's penis fits into the inner passageway of the mother, the one the baby comes down. The father's cells are called sperm, and they pass up into the mother. When a father's cell joins with a mother's cell, or egg cell, a baby begins to grow."

Throughout childhood, you can expect your son or daughter to explore and show interest in his or her own or other human bodies. This should not be a cause for embarrassment or correction. A young child touches genitals in the same way he fondles fingers or toes; at age three or four, two children may examine each other's bodies with no motive other than curiosity. If you discover them, don't make a scene. Such explorations are harmless and—as with many other topics that embarrass adults—the more matter-of-fact the treatment, the better the result.

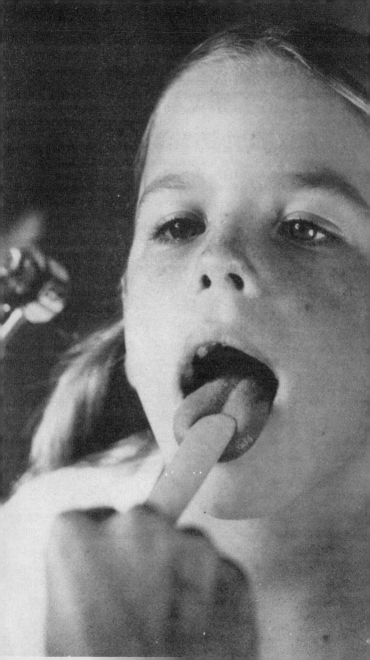

20

Common Complaints and Diseases

Most children—including your baby—usually are happy and healthy, but every normal child has occasional bouts of illness that are alarming to parents. Fortunately, these spells of sickness are seldom serious or long-lived. As parents, your first task is to recognize and treat the symptoms as quickly as possible, help the child feel better, and know when to seek medical help or advice.

Some of the more common problems of infancy and childhood already have been discussed to some extent in the earlier chapters of this book. The symptoms and treatments are described in more detail below, along with those of less frequent illnesses. Chapter 8 tells when—and, equally important, how—to call your pediatrician in the event of a child's illness.

COMMON SYMPTOMS

Abdominal pain. It is difficult to predict the consequence of sharp or dull abdominal pain. Do not give laxatives or other medications, and do not offer solid food until the pain subsides or has been evaluated.

Recurrent mild pain without apparent cause should be discussed with your physician, as should sudden, sharp pains, especially in a very young child. Appendicitis is uncommon under the age of five but should be suspected in any child who has pain or tenderness in the abdomen, especially if the abdominal pain is accompanied by nausea and vomiting.

Abdominal cramps sometimes are caused by food that is difficult to digest—the "green apple" syndrome. Your suspicions may be confirmed sooner if you simply recall the child's most recent meals. Although painful for a time, such cramps usually disappear rapidly.

Colds. (See also Chapters 8 and 17.) There's no need to dwell on the symptoms of the common cold—the familiar pattern of runny nose, rattly cough, and noisy breathing. The watery discharge from the nose gradually thickens and becomes yellow, then green, before the cough subsides. The normal course in a child, treated or untreated, is one to two weeks.

You can't shorten a cold. But you can relieve an infant's strained and noisy breathing by using a bulb aspirator to suck mucus from the nostrils. An aspirator with a rubber tip, or an ear syringe, is best for an infant's delicate membranes. If the mucus is too high in the nose to be removed successfully by suction, it may be loosened by injecting two or three drops of salt water (mix a level teaspoon of salt in a pint of lukewarm water). Dried and crusted mucus in the nasal passages may be loosened by using a vaporizer at night (see Chapter 9).

Nonprescription decongestants to relieve stuffiness are never recommended for a child under one year and should be given to an older child only on the advice of a physician. Avoid commercial cold preparations, too, unless a physician advises you to use them. The value of these medications for children is still disputed. They may cause side effects, such as drowsiness and irritability.

The value of chest rubs and other traditional home treatments has not been proved scientifically, but some parents praise them. Do not use medicated nose drops without a physician's advice.

Constipation. Constipation, even in adults, is difficult to define. An infant may have a bowel movement only every two or three days and not be considered constipated as long as the movements are of normal consistency. Bowel movements are considered to be a problem only if they are hard enough to seem painful. Remember, however, that most infants normally strain, grunt, and turn red during a movement.

If a baby does seem constipated, increase the amount of liquids, especially juices. A child who is eating solid food may be given more fruit, especially prunes or prune juice, if he or she will accept it. Constipation in toddlers or older children may be relieved by bran cereal, or by mixing bran with other foods.

Enemas, or laxatives such as castor oil or milk of magnesia, should not be given. Your physician may prescribe a stool softener.

Cough. A cough generally accompanies any cold, as mucus drains into the throat and the child tries to clear it. Like other cold symptoms, the cough gradually subsides. Over-the-counter cough medicines should not be given, because they are expensive, probably don't help much, and can cause side effects in young children. Make your own cough medicine by mixing equal parts of lemon juice and honey (but do not give honey to children under one year of age).

A persistent cough in the absence of a cold should be reported to the physician.

Croup. Although a potentially terrifying experience for both parents and child, croup isn't necessarily a serious situation. The name comes from the deep, crowing sound a child makes while struggling for breath, the result of a narrowed larynx and trachea. It begins suddenly, usually at night when the child awakes abruptly, unable to breathe normally. The child has ordinarily had a runny nose or cough for a day or two but seemed well otherwise.

Croup is most often caused by a viral infection, which inflames the larynx and upper trachea and causes spasm of the muscles of the larynx. Cold or warm mist seems to end the spasm and often brings dramatic relief. The quickest way to provide it is to place the child in a closed bathroom with a hot shower running. There are, however, other causes of breathing difficulty, so a physician should always be consulted when an episode occurs.

Diarrhea. Like constipation, diarrhea defies definition. During the first weeks of life, bottle-fed and breast-fed infants may have six to nine liquid bowel movements daily. Thereafter, they usually decrease to three or four a day within the first year. A child normally has a consistent pattern, but it is not unusual for a child who usually has one or two movements a day suddenly to have three or four without apparent cause. Movements may also change considerably in consistency or color without a change of diet. Frequent loose stools in an infant seldom are significant unless other symptoms are present, like fever, irritability, or failure to gain weight.

Sudden diarrhea in a child over six months of age usually signals an internal viral infection. Typically, vomiting comes first, followed by diarrhea as the vomiting subsides. Both can dehydrate a child, damaging the tissues by quickly withdrawing large amounts of liquid from them. Make sure the baby continues to drink liquids during an episode of diarrhea.

If a child vomits more than once in an hour, stop all solid foods and substitute clear liquids, a tablespoonful every half hour at first, gradually increasing the amount. Water or apple juice may be given, along with carbonated beverages, to replace lost carbo-

hydrates, potassium, and salt. When vomiting diminishes and
diarrhea begins, continue the clear liquids but in larger amounts
and less frequently. As the diarrhea subsides, give bland foods,
such as cereal, bananas, and applesauce or—as our grandmothers
knew—chicken broth.

Earache. Two-thirds of children under two have had at least one
middle-ear infection; half of those have suffered two or more. By
the age of six, one in five children has had at least six episodes. The
common condition, agonizing to parents as well as children because of the difficulty of relieving the pain, usually strikes during
the course of a cold and results from otitis media, an infection of the
middle-ear cavity behind the tympanic membrane, or eardrum.
Cold-caused stuffiness in the eustachian tube connecting ear and
throat prevents proper drainage of the middle ear, allowing bacteria
to proliferate. Accumulated pus and fluid press on the eardrum and
cause it to bulge outward, sometimes causing excruciating pain.
The pain may be accompanied by fever, vomiting, or diarrhea.

An early clue to ear infection in an infant may be refusal to
take formula, accompanied by irritability or fussiness. A few infants will pull or scratch at the affected ear, as if to relieve the pain.
Fever is sometimes present. If the child is recovering from a cold,
you usually can suspect the cause of the discomfort. Older children
can report the pain, thus simplifying diagnosis and treatment (although children may have ear pain without infection).

The condition should be reported to a physician, because bacterial infection requires treatment with antibiotics. Aspirin or acetaminophen (an aspirin substitute) may relieve pain; a heating pad
applied to the ear may comfort the child. But don't try to clear the
ear by poking anything into it, and don't give decongestants, ear
drops, or nose drops without consulting a physician.

Some babies are more prone than others to ear infection. The
eustachian tubes in these children may be constructed in such a way
as to become blocked or clogged more easily. Children usually
grow out of ear infections by the age of eight as the configuration of
the tube changes. Recurrent ear infections may require special
treatment, including control of chronic nasal congestion caused by
allergies, removal of adenoids, surgical insertion of tubes through
the eardrum (see Chapter 17), or daily antibiotic therapy.

Febrile seizures (convulsions). About 3 percent of normal children at some time have a convulsion, or generalized seizure, when
fever is present. These attacks don't seem to be related to the height

of the fever but may be associated with the speed with which it rises. Seizures are brief, usually subsiding within ten minutes, although they seem an eternity to terrified parents. They occur most frequently between one and two years and seldom occur before six months or after the age of five.

When a seizure begins, parents can do little except to wait it out. Remove anything in the child's mouth. The child may be held or placed on his or her back to prevent falls or collisions with furniture. See the doctor as soon as possible.

Usually, febrile seizures aren't damaging and do not mean the child will be seizure-prone as an adult. However, one of three children who has experienced one seizure will have a second during another episode of fever. You may wish to discuss anticonvulsive medication with the doctor.

Fever. The rectal technique for measuring an infant's temperature is described in Chapter 8. After the age of four, children are old enough to have temperatures measured by the oral (mouth) or axillary (armpit) method. Keep the thermometer in place at least two minutes (measured by the clock) for an accurate reading.

In infants of two months or less, any rise in temperature above normal should be reported to the pediatrician for evaluation. Even a low-grade fever may indicate infection in a newborn.

Otherwise, a high fever by itself often doesn't require consulting a doctor. Even a reading of 103 or 104 degrees may have little significance if the child seems healthy in other respects and is in good spirits. The fever itself causes no damage. In fact, certain more serious conditions are marked by a slight, rather than substantial, rise in temperature. Most fevers accompany a cold or other viral infection. Fever persisting in the absence of other symptoms should be reported to a physician.

If fever makes the child uncomfortable, aspirin or acetaminophen will help. Acetaminophen, which is available in liquid form, is considered safer for infants under one year. Aspirin is not recommended for treatment of fever during chickenpox or influenza infections because of a possible association with a rare, serious disease called Reye's syndrome. The usual dose of either medication is about five milligrams per pound of body weight, or by age as follows: two 80-mg tablets for 2- to 3-year-olds; three tablets for 4- to 5-year-olds; four tablets for 6- to 8-year-olds; and five tablets for 9- to 10-year-olds. The dosage may be repeated every four hours.

You also can lower temperature by removing as much of the

child's clothing as possible. A diaper without an undershirt is enough for a feverish infant. A bath in lukewarm (not cold) water also helps to bring down fever.

Sore throat. Soreness in the throat with or without fever or other symptoms may represent a streptococcal ("strep") infection, particularly in a child of school age. The throat should be examined by a doctor who can obtain a throat culture and determine the need for antibiotic treatment. Rheumatic fever, which can cause damage to heart valves, is a possible consequence of untreated strep throat but now is much less common in most areas of the country. In some communities it is extremely rare.

Swollen glands. Lymph nodes in the neck and at the angle of the jaw are part of the body's defense system. They enlarge during respiratory and other infections and may remain swollen weeks or even months after other symptoms have disappeared. Occasionally, the swelling may be accompanied by a sore throat.

If the glands are enlarged to a diameter of an inch or more, it could indicate a bacterial infection. Consult your pediatrician.

CHILDHOOD DISEASES
Chickenpox. No vaccine is yet in use for chickenpox, which now is the most prevalent of the so-called childhood diseases, particularly among the nursery-school set. Highly transmissible from child to child, chickenpox usually begins with a mild fever and loss of energy; it varies in severity, and some children have no other symptoms. Most commonly, a single blister appears, often on the face. Blisters then appear on other parts of the body, sometimes including the scalp and gums. The blisters are often preceded by small red spots or bumps. After a few hours, these develop into clear blisters with yellow centers (pustules) and become crusted (scabs). Typically, pustules, scabs, and red spots may be seen in the same area of the body. Fever and headache usually disappear within three days of their appearance.

The most troublesome symptom is the intense itching. Because scratching may cause infection, cut the child's fingernails and give regular baths in cool water. A soothing lotion also may help. Acetaminophen may relieve itching as well as reduce fever, but aspirin is not recommended because of the possible increased risk of the rare but serious Reye's syndrome. The pediatrician may prescribe antihistamines to reduce itching in severe cases. The child is most infectious before the rash appears; one case in a nursery school or kindergarten can quickly sweep the entire school. Contagion is no longer a problem after all the blisters have developed into scabs. The chickenpox rash usually subsides within ten days.

Conjunctivitis. So-called pinkeye is an inflammation of the thin membrane lining the inner eyelid and eye. It may be caused by infection (mildly contagious), allergy, or irritation caused by smog or chemicals. The eyes become sore, red, and itchy; tears flow, along with a yellow discharge. Itching and drainage can be relieved by washing the area around the eye with cotton moistened in warm water or by placing a warm, damp washcloth on the eyes. A pediatrician may prescribe eye drops or ointment.

Measles (rubeola). Measles is preventable with a single immunization given at the age of 15 months. This potentially serious communicable viral infection begins with fever, cough, and runny nose; the eyes become red and watery. On the third or fourth day, fine white spots, circled in red, sometimes appear inside the cheeks. On the fourth day, a fine rash breaks out on the face, becomes blotchy, and spreads down the neck and trunk. The fever may continue and even rise after the rash develops. The rash may last five days. The child may want to remain in bed and avoid bright light. A liquid diet is best, along with aspirin or acetaminophen to lower the fever and make the child more comfortable. A cool-mist vaporizer may relieve the cough.

Mumps. This viral infection of the salivary glands can be prevented, along with measles and rubella, with a single immunizing shot given at the age of 15 months. Transmitted by direct contact with a mumps victim, the illness usually begins with an earache and fever. About a day later, swelling begins in the angle of the jaw directly below the ear; it may spread to behind the jaw and under the chin, with one or both sides involved. The amount of swelling varies widely but it usually disappears in about a week. Aspirin or acetaminophen lowers the fever and makes the patient more comfortable. Alternately applying cold and warm compresses to the swelling also may help.

Roseola. A mild viral infection with rash, roseola should not be mistaken for measles. It is mainly confined to babies and children under three. The illness begins with a sudden high fever of 104 to 105 degrees, fussiness, and a sharp drop in appetite. Otherwise, the child may not seem ill at all and may be playful. The fever subsides after three to four days, and a blotchy red rash appears on the face and body. A liquid diet and aspirin or acetaminophen may be used to make the child more comfortable.

Rubella (German measles). German measles can be prevented by proper immunization. A mild viral infection, rubella is spread from person to person via infected droplets from the respiratory tract. The illness begins as a cold does, with mild fever, headache, runny nose, and enlarged lymph nodes. Small red spots appear first on the face, then spread to neck and trunk and frequently to the arms and legs. The rash usually lasts about three days. There is little specific treatment, beyond aspirin or acetaminophen to reduce fever. The infection's chief danger is to women in the first three months of pregnancy, since an unborn child may be affected.

Scarlet fever. This once-frightening disease is now known to be strep throat with a rash, and is no more severe than strep throat without a rash, which can be checked with antibiotics. It usually begins with sore throat, chills, fever, headache, and possibly vomiting. A rash consisting of fine bumps—described as "goose flesh on a sunburn"—appears on the chest one to three days after the child becomes ill and spreads down the body; the child's face may become flushed but remain pale around the mouth. Aspirin or acetaminophen may be given.

Whooping cough (pertussis). This once-common disease can readily be prevented by a series of inoculations beginning at two months. The name whooping cough graphically describes this bacterial infection's most prominent symptom. The disease is spread via droplets from the respiratory tract of an infected person and begins with a mild cough that gradually increases in severity and is more frequent at night. After about two weeks, coughing spells become so severe the child chokes, reddens, and may vomit. Each cough ends with the characteristic whoop; the spells last four to six weeks. The rare victims today usually are hospitalized.

SKIN CONDITIONS
Canker sores. This irritating viral infection of the mouth causes small painful ulcers on the gums and the inside of the cheeks, usually in the area where the two meet. The sores usually last about a week. Mouthwash or a salt-water rinse may relieve irritation and ease the soreness.

Eczema. This condition may be a reaction to irritating substances that contact the skin or, rarely, a symptom of food allergy. Eczema is most prominent during the first two years of life and begins with patches of light red or tannish pink, rough scaly skin often on the face, in the folds of the arms, or on the backs of the knees. The scales may flake off in a fine powder. Even mild outbreaks can be extremely itchy. Eczema can be treated effectively by avoiding common skin irritants and applying topical medication.

Fever blisters. Commonly called cold sores, fever blisters are caused by the reactivation of an earlier infection by the herpes simplex virus, to which most children are exposed. The initial infection may cause sores in the mouth or gums, fever, and malaise, or no symptoms may be apparent; afterward, the virus remains in many tissues of the body. Exposure to another virus, to sunlight, or even to emotional stress may "revive" it. The usual cold sore begins with a painful, itchy area of swelling on the lip, followed by an outbreak of oozing tiny blisters, which form a scab. The sore usually lasts about a week.

Hives. These raised, itchy welts may erupt anywhere on the body. Most often the cause is unknown, but in some children, hives may result from sensitivity to medicines, certain foods, or other substances. The eyelids, lips, and, in extreme cases, the inside of the throat may swell. Consult your physician immediately. Usually, hives disappear in a few hours or, at most, a few days; with a sensitive child, they may recur often. Bathing in lukewarm water may relieve itching, or your pediatrician may prescribe antihistamines.

Impetigo. A common bacterial infection that is mildly contagious in children, impetigo usually starts as a small, red bump, with an oozing of thin, yellow liquid from the center. The discharge usually dries to form a light, honey-colored crust. If not treated, the blisters will spread to other parts of the body. The pediatrician may prescribe soaks in warm water and an antibiotic ointment or may give oral antibiotics. The child should have a personal washcloth and towel to prevent spread of the infection to others in the family.

Lice. These small insects infest the head and body and are more common among nursery-schoolers and kindergarteners than most parents realize. Unfortunately, lice are easily spread from child to child. The first symptom is itching in the scalp. Your pediatrician can prescribe medication that will kill lice and their eggs.

Pinworms. These are the most common intestinal worms in children and are spread by ingesting the eggs or touching infected objects and then putting the fingers into the mouth. The first symptom usually is itching around the area of the rectum, especially at night. Girls may complain of pain during urination. Sometimes the tiny, white, threadlike worms can be seen in and around the rectum, on bedclothes, or on a child's underwear. Medication is more than 90 percent effective. Usually, the entire household will be treated; it may also be necessary to sterilize bedding and clothing.

Prickly heat. Too many layers of clothes in hot weather cause this skin rash, which is most prominent in infants. The rash appears as raised, pinhead-size bumps with yellow centers on face, neck, and truck and doesn't seem to cause itching or discomfort. Dress the child more lightly, so the rash has time to heal.

Ringworm. No worms are involved in this contagious and common fungus infection, which usually is seen on the scalp but may occur anywhere on the body. The infection may spread from child to child. Ringworm is named for the characteristic circular, itchy patches that are slightly raised around the outside. Your pediatrician may prescribe a topical medication, which clears most cases quickly.

Scabies. A skin condition caused when an itch mite buries itself under the skin and lays its eggs, scabies is characterized by inflamed areas that itch intensely and may even become infected and start to drain. The itching seems to be most severe at night and may disturb the child's sleep. Scabies is most common around the wrists and armpits and between the fingers and toes but may be found anywhere on the body. Scabies may last several weeks. Your pediatrician may prescribe medication to kill mites and reduce itching and may also give antibiotics in case of infection. In most cases scabies is contracted by contact with another child who is suffering from the condition.

Thrush. This stubborn yeast infection is most common in the mouth but may also appear in the diaper area. (See "Diaper Rash," page 165.) Thrush usually occurs (and may recur) during the first year. The first symptom of the oral variety may be a refusal to feed because of the soreness, although some babies show no discomfort. Inside the baby's mouth, you may see patchy white spots on lips, tongue, gums, palate, and cheeks that look like milk but can't be removed by wiping or scraping. The physician may prescribe an oral medication.

RESPIRATORY PROBLEMS

Bronchiolitis. A viral infection of the bronchial area, bronchiolitis is marked by rapid, labored breathing and wheezing. The area below the ribs pulls in sharply during inhalation. Bronchiolitis is most common in infants and young children, especially in winter, and seems to occur in epidemics. Consult your pediatrician promptly.

Bronchitis. Another viral infection of the bronchial tubes in the lower respiratory tract, bronchitis is sometimes diagnosed as a common cold and may follow one. The dry, hacking cough usually predominates, and nasal congestion is mild or absent. There may be low-grade fever. The cough often lasts three to four weeks and is worst at night. Otherwise, the child may not act ill. There is no effective medication but a cough suppressant may allow the child to sleep easier. The condition is most common during the first three years.

Pneumonia. An inflammation of one or both lungs usually is caused by either bacteria or virus. The illness frequently develops in the aftermath of a cold, and symptoms may come on suddenly. Fever may rise sharply, accompanied by a deep, harsh cough and rapid, grunting breathing. Sometimes the child's chest hurts. The cough may be so severe that it causes the child to vomit. Call the pediatrician immediately when the disease is suspected; hospitalization is still sometimes necessary. Antibiotics, however, usually bring rapid improvement. Bed rest is necessary, along with a bland diet. Viral pneumonia is not helped by antibiotics. Pneumonia vaccines are under development, but are not ready for general use.

Tonsillitis. An infection of the tonsils caused either by bacteria or virus, tonsillitis may strike some young children repeatedly. Although there are usually sore throat and enlarged lymph nodes in the neck, other symptoms vary. There may be high fever and difficulty in swallowing; sometimes the child complains of a headache. The symptoms may begin abruptly or gradually. Bacterial tonsillitis can be quelled with antibiotics, but there is no effective treatment for viral infections. Salt-water gargles or sprays may relieve some of the soreness. In recurrent cases, the pediatrician may recommend that the tonsils be removed by a surgeon. Tonsillectomies are less commonly performed now than they were in previous years.

BABY RECORDS

How could you ever forget your baby's very first step? Or the excitement of that moment when your son or daughter unmistakably called you "Mama" or "Dada"? Alas, memories fade, as new firsts succeed the old. A few months from now—but especially a year or two hence—you may be unable to completely retrieve an important landmark that was once frozen in time.

The record section provided on the following pages will help jog such memories later. For the future, mark down each shining moment in your child's present. Record each step on the child's ladder toward maturity and each achievement you will wish to cherish in years to come.

The areas of child development are arranged here according to when the majority of normal children pass each landmark. But, again, a word of caution: your child may attain these milestones sooner—or later—than other children. Exact dates mean nothing, except sentimentally. Of 20 children born on any given date, one will be walking well in seven months. But another year may pass before the other 19 are fully ambulatory. Years in the future, it will be impossible for anyone to distinguish those children who walked "early" and those children who walked "late."

As for height and weight, your child's dimensions are determined more by his or her heritage and nationality than by any given schedule of projected growth.

A "baby record" does have practical uses, of course. Charting the child's pattern of growth or development can help predict when the next hurdle may be cleared—and to show when you're expecting too much. And it may help a doctor or teacher in dealing with the child in later years.

But a baby book is primarily meant for memories and anticipation. Start now to record the highlights of your child's early years, for enjoyment both today and tomorrow.

Baby's name in full _____

Born _____
(Year, month, day, hour, and minute)

At _____ Hospital _____
(City)   (State)

Father _____
(First name   middle name   last name)

Mother _____
(First name   middle name   last name)

Address _____
(At time of baby's birth)

Subsequent addresses: _____

_____

_____

1 TO 4 MONTHS

GROWTH

	Pounds/Ounces	
At one month	_____	_____
At two months	_____	_____
At three months	_____	_____
At four months	_____	_____

DEVELOPMENT

Weeks

Six weeks: Hold head up at a 45-degree angle when lying on stomach _____

Follow an object with eyes for a short distance _____

Keep head erect when held in a sitting position _____

Months

Three months: Sit with head steady. Follow an object moved from one side of head to the other _____

Bring hands together in front _____

Laugh, squeal, and coo _____

Listen to voices and recognize yours _____

Smile, socialize, and respond to people _____

Four months: Turn head in all directions and support self on arms _____

Roll over _____

Grasp and hold an object _____

Babble in word-like syllables; coo, gurgle, chortle, squeal _____

Look at self in a mirror and smile _____

Recognize mother and siblings _____

Bear some weight on legs when held in a standing position _____

Be pulled to sitting position _____

5 TO 8 MONTHS

GROWTH

	Pounds/Ounces	
At five months	_____	_____
At six months	_____	_____
At seven months	_____	_____
At eight months	_____	_____

DEVELOPMENT

Months

Five months: Sit up for 30 minutes with back supported _____

Bring feet to mouth and suck on toes _____

Reach for objects and often grasp them _____

Shift objects from hand to hand; drop one to pick up another _____

React to name _____

Anticipate a whole object by seeing a part _____

Show emotions; may pro-test—loudly—when something is taken away _____

Six months: Sit well with support. Get a toy that is out of reach _____

Pull back on a toy when you pull _____

Turn toward a voice _____

Attempt to recover an object that falls _____

Recognize a familiar face _____

Eight months: Grasp objects with thumb and finger _____

Play peekaboo _____

Say "dada" and "mama" _____

Sit without support; get self into a sitting position _____

Stand well while holding your hands _____

Creep on stomach _____

9 TO 12 MONTHS

1 TO 2 YEARS

GROWTH

	Pounds/Ounces	
At nine months	_____	_____
At ten months	_____	_____
At 11 months	_____	_____
At 12 months	_____	_____

DEVELOPMENT

	Months
Ten months: Play patty-cake	_____
Identify "mama" and "dada" and call them by name	_____
Pull to stand	_____
Walk or sidestep, holding onto furniture	_____
Wave bye-bye	_____
One year: Indicate want without crying	_____
Drink from a cup, spilling only a little	_____
Take a few steps	_____
Stand alone, stoop, and return to stand	_____
Understand many words	_____

GROWTH

	Pounds/Ounces	
At 18 months	_____	_____
At two years	_____	_____

DEVELOPMENT

	Months
15 months: Use a spoon and spill only a little	_____
Imitate a parent doing housework	_____
Scribble with a crayon	_____
18 months: Remove some or all of clothes	_____
Build a four-cube tower	_____
Walk up steps, holding rail	_____
Point to a baby's picture in a book	_____
Use name for him- or herself	_____
Two years: Combine words to make simple statements	_____
Identify one or more parts of the body	_____
Follow simple directions—if only a single step is involved	_____
Wash and dry hands, with parental supervision	_____

2 TO 3
YEARS

GROWTH

	Pound/Ounces	
At 2½ years	_____	_____
At three years	_____	_____

DEVELOPMENT

	Months
Identify pictures of animals by name	_____
Pedal a tricycle; propel a kiddie car with feet	_____
Dress with supervision and button some buttons	_____
Play interactive games, tag, for instance	_____
Tell first and last names	_____
Use plurals, pronouns, and prepositions in speech	_____
Copy a circle with a crayon	_____
Understand such words as "cold," "tired," "hungry"	_____
Know where things belong and help to put them there	_____
Follow simple, one-step directions	_____
Feed him- or herself almost completely	_____
Be toilet-trained during the day and remain dry all night some of the time	_____
Recognize and identify some colors	_____

GROWTH

	Pounds/Ounces	
At 3½ years	_____	_____
At four years	_____	_____

DEVELOPMENT

	Months
Dress without assistance, except for difficult buttons	_____
Identify colors; make comparisons	_____
Use plurals and prepositions	_____
Leave parents easily and play out of their sight for long periods	_____
Draw a figure recognizable as a human	_____
Hop on one foot, and maybe skip for a few steps	_____

GROWTH

	Height/Weight	
At 4½ years	_____	_____
At five years	_____	_____

DEVELOPMENT

	Months
Define many words	_____
Catch a bounced ball	_____
Put on shoes, perhaps even tie them	_____
Sing a song with a recognizable tune	_____
Recognize his or her printed name, and perhaps print it	_____
Balance on one foot for ten seconds at a time	_____
Walk with a motion from heel to toe	_____

5 TO 6 YEARS

GROWTH

	Height/Weight
At 5½ years	_____ _____
At six years	_____ _____

DEVELOPMENT

Months

Put on and take off most clothing and probably tie shoes _____

Print first name, if it isn't too long or difficult, and recognize it _____

Know both first and last names and be able to tell them to an adult _____

Count from one to five in proper sequence and perhaps from one to ten _____

Make a recognizable drawing of a person, including arms and legs _____

Take care of toilet needs with only very rare accidents _____

Wash face and hands and brush teeth with supervision _____

Identify most colors _____

Understand that a nickel or dime is more valuable than a penny _____

6 TO 7 YEARS

GROWTH

	Height/Weight
At 6½ years	_____ _____
At seven years	_____ _____

DEVELOPMENT

Months

Take care of nearly all personal needs, including bathing, dressing, and going to bed _____

Define many simple words and explain simple concepts _____

Recognize most letters of the alphabet, perhaps recite them in sequence, and recognize some simple words _____

MEDICAL RECORDS

In our mobile society, it's important for you, as well as your physician, to keep family health records. If you move to another town, change doctors, or transfer to a different school, these records you keep can be important references and can be used for consultation.

The examples below will give you an idea of the records you may want to keep. Use them to devise your own, and, when possible, have your physician make the entries personally. If this cannot be done, enter the necessary information yourself immediately after the illness or health event.

This information can then be shown on request to another doctor or to authorities at your child's school. Such information should always be kept up-to-date. You may also wish to file copies of birth certificates, records of inoculation, or other important documents in this part of the book. If you did not receive this information at the time, you should obtain it now to keep your records complete and current.

FAMILY MEDICAL HISTORY

	Birth date	Illnesses
Father	_____	_____
Mother	_____	_____
Brothers	_____	_____
	_____	_____
	_____	_____
Sisters	_____	_____
	_____	_____
	_____	_____

Family illnesses, allergies, or
chronic conditions _____
_____
_____
_____
_____
_____
_____
_____

ILLNESS & INJURY RECORD

Illnesses:

Nature	Date	Physician
_____	_____	_____
_____	_____	_____
_____	_____	_____
_____	_____	_____
_____	_____	_____
_____	_____	_____
_____	_____	_____
_____	_____	_____
_____	_____	_____
_____	_____	_____

Injuries:

_____	_____	_____
_____	_____	_____
_____	_____	_____
_____	_____	_____

BIRTH RECORD

Date of birth _____

Duration of pregnancy _____

Mother's health during pregnancy:

Illnesses _____

Drugs/medications used _____

Problems _____

Delivery:

Normal _____ Cesarean section _____

Medications during labor _____

Monitoring _____

Problems _____

_____

Birth measurements:

Weight _____

Length _____

Conditions at birth:

_____

Type of feeding:

Breast _____ Bottle _____

Duration of hospital stay (days) _____

Blood type and Rh _____

Other information _____

_____

HOSPITALIZATION RECORD

Nature	Date	Physician
_____	_____	_____
_____	_____	_____
_____	_____	_____
_____	_____	_____
_____	_____	_____
_____	_____	_____
_____	_____	_____

Allergies:

_____	_____	_____
_____	_____	_____
_____	_____	_____
_____	_____	_____

Other Information:

_____

_____

_____

_____

IMMUNIZATION RECORD

Immunization	Date	Dose	Physician
DPT.........	___	___	___
	___	___	___
	___	___	___
	___	___	___
DT booster ...	___	___	___
Tetanus booster ...	___	___	___
Polio	___	___	___
	___	___	___
	___	___	___
	___	___	___
Measles.....	___	___	___
Rubella	___	___	___
Mumps	___	___	___
Tuberculin test.....	___	___	___
Others	___	___	___
	___	___	___

DENTAL RECORD

Upper Teeth

1 central incisor
2 lateral incisor
3 cuspid
4 first molar
5 second molar

5 4 3 2 1 1 2 3 4 5

Lower Teeth

1 central incisor
2 lateral incisor
3 cuspid
4 first molar
5 second molar

5 4 3 2 1 1 2 3 4 5

Age Teeth Appeared

Upper Teeth		Lower Teeth	
Right	Left	Right	Left
1 ___	___	1 ___	___
2 ___	___	2 ___	___
3 ___	___	3 ___	___
4 ___	___	4 ___	___
5 ___	___	5 ___	___

	Age
Thumb-sucking	___
Pacifier......................	___
First brushed teeth	___
Brushed teeth unassisted.................	___
First flossed teeth	___
First visit to dentist.........	___
Preventive care	___
Orthodontic procedure	___
X-rays......................	___

NEWBORN GLOSSARY

Acrocyanosis
Dusky bluish color to the hands and feet of newborns present soon after birth that persists for a few days. The circulation through the skin capillaries is not fully developed.

Birthmarks *(Hemangiomas)*
- Capillary Hemangioma *(Storkbites)*
Superficial blood vessels on the back of the neck, forehead, upper eyelids, nose, and upper lip. Many fade or disappear. Some, like those on the back of the neck, may remain.
- Cavernous Hemangioma
Involve both skin and the underlying tissues. They are soft, compressible, and bluish. Overlying the cavernous hemangioma may be a capillary or strawberry hemangioma. Most will resolve spontaneously after getting larger during the first six to nine months of life. They should be watched for at least a year before attempting treatment.
- Strawberry Hemangioma
Bright red, spongy collection of elevated blood vessels. Rarely present at birth, they often appear during the first week of life. They may increase in size for the first six to nine months before disappearing completely.

Bohn's Nodules *(Epstein's Pearls)*
Small pearl-white bodies toward the back of the palate of newborns that disappear in a few weeks without treatment.

Breast Engorgement
Engorgement of the breasts is noticeable a few days after birth and is due to maternal hormones that cross the placenta into the baby. Milk may be secreted (witches' milk). The engorgement lasts about six to eight weeks.

Caput Succedaneum

The head is misshapen and lopsided at birth, with swelling over the part of the head presented first. Small skin hemorrhages are frequent. Common among the firstborn and when the head is large. The swelling disappears within a few days.

Cephalohematoma

Localized swelling along the side (or both sides) of the head, usually to the back. Due to bleeding under the scalp, it appears a few days after birth and disappears in a few weeks. In some, calcium is deposited, and the swelling may persist for several months.

Craniotabes

The sides of the head can be indented with the finger, like a table tennis ball, but quickly spring back into place.

Erythema Toxicum *(Newborn Hives, Flea Bites)*

Benign skin condition seen frequently in newborn infants and lasting only a few days. Splotchy red areas on the trunk and extremities. Some contain a raised yellow blister in the center. Their cause is unknown.

Fontanel *(Soft Spot)*

The anterior fontanel is located at the top of the head, to the front. It is a diamond-shaped opening covered by a tough, thick membrane that closes completely with bone within 12 to 18 months. The posterior fontanel also can be felt in the newborn, at the top and to the back of the head. It closes by the age of two months.

Funnel Chest *(Pectus Excavatum)*

Hollowlike depression at the lower end of the chest bone (sternum). The mild ones require no treatment. The occasional severe cases may require surgical correction at a later age.

Harlequin Color Change

With the infant lying on a side, one side of the body may appear reddened and one side pale. The change in color occurs at the midline of the body. When the infant is placed on his or her back, the color changes disappear quickly.

Hydrocele

Swelling in the scrotum due to the collection of fluid surrounding the testicles. Fairly common in newborn males. Disappears within a few months. Treatment is not necessary.

Jaundice
Yellow discoloration of the skin, eyes, and membranes of the mouth seen in over 50 percent of full-term and 80 percent of premature infants. Due to the products released from the destruction of red cells in the newborn period and to immaturity of the liver. It appears about the second or third day of life and begins to disappear before the fifth day. It is usually gone by the third week. No treatment is necessary for the condition.

Lanugo
A fine downy growth of hair prominent over the back, shoulders, forehead, and face. It is more noticeable in premature babies. It disappears in the first few weeks.

Laryngeal Stridor
Infant makes crowing noise when drawing breath. This common condition disappears within the first few months of life. It seems to be related to obstruction or narrowing of air passages.

Milia
Obstructed sweat and oil glands appearing as pinhead-size white spots on the nose, cheeks, and chin of newborns and disappearing within a few weeks.

Mongolian Spots
Areas of bluish-gray color found over the lower back, particularly in babies with dark skin. They may be more widespread and found elsewhere on the body but tend to disappear within one to two years.

Molding
A temporarily misshapen head caused by an overlapping of the skull bones to allow the infant to pass down the birth canal. The bones soon assume their proper position.

Nipples, Supernumerary
An accessory nipple present just below the regular breast, it may occur on one or both sides. No breast tissue develops nor does it function.

Periodic Respiration
Irregular, rapid, often shallow respiration for several seconds, followed by a few seconds when there is no breathing. Common in premature babies but may be seen in some full-term infants.

Pilonidal Dimple
An indentation of the skin covering the lower end of the spine. In later life, these impressions may become infected.

Pseudostrabismus
The eyes give the impression of crossing. The epicanthus, a fold of skin at the inner angle of the eye, may be prominent, causing the band of white in one eye to appear narrower than in the other eye, and producing an illusion of crossed eyes.

Pseudoptosis
The eyelids in the newborn may operate independently. One eye may be open and the other partially or completely closed. This lasts only a short time.

Reflexes
• Grasp Reflex

Touching the palm of either of the infant's hands with a finger results in his or her grasping the finger vigorously.

• Moro Reflex *(Startle Reflex)*

In response to loud noises or sudden changes in position, both upper extremities are extended outward simultaneously. With the infant on his or her back on a flat surface, raising the baby a short distance and suddenly releasing him or her elicits the startle reflex.

• Rooting Reflex

When the cheek is stroked, the baby's head turns toward that side of the face, with mouth open for sucking.

• Sucking Reflex

Vigorous sucking movements when lips are lightly touched.

• Tonic Neck Reflex *(Fencing position)*

On the back, the head is turned to one side, causing the baby to extend the arm and leg on the side the head is turned to and flex the opposite upper and lower extremities.

Stools
• Meconium

The newborn's bowel movements during the first few days of life. Appear greenish-black and slimy. About 70 percent of infants will have their first bowel movement within 12 hours; 95 percent, within 24 hours.

• Transitional

Thin, loose, yellowish-green bowel movements seen from the third to fifth day of life. They contain mucus, curds of milk, and remnants of meconium.

Subconjunctival Hemorrhage
Small red spot of blood noticed in the white part of the eye due to rupture of a blood capillary during birth. It resolves quickly.

Sucking Callus
A small blister visible in the center of the upper lip of sucking infants. Condition lasts only a short time.

Tongue-tie
A condition in which the attachment from the tongue to the floor of the mouth (frenum) is located closer to the tip of the tongue than normal. In almost all cases, the frenum stretches as the infant gets older. Surgery rarely is necessary.

Umbilical Cord Vessels
After it's cut, the end of the umbilical cord is carefully examined to determine the number of blood vessels. The normal number is three—two arteries and a vein. The presence of a single umbilical artery should make the physician suspicious of some congenital abnormalities, particularly abnormalities of the kidney.

Umbilical Hernia
A bulge covered by skin at the navel that is most prominent with crying or straining. It often occurs around the time of birth. This is caused by a small opening in the muscles of the abdomen and contains a loop of bowel. The opening usually closes by itself during the first four to five years of life. The condition is more prominent among blacks than whites.

Undescended Testes *(Cryptorchidism)*
Both testes are found in the scrotum in a full-term male newborn. Cryptorchidism is the failure of one or both to descend normally. No treatment is necessary because the testes may descend later.

Vaginal Discharge
A white discharge from the vagina common in female newborns, it lasts a few weeks. Vaginal bleeding also may occur. This is related to maternal hormones that cross the placental barrier into the baby.

Vernix Caseosa
Cheeselike material that covers the skin of newborns and is thought to protect the infant against superficial infections during the birth process.

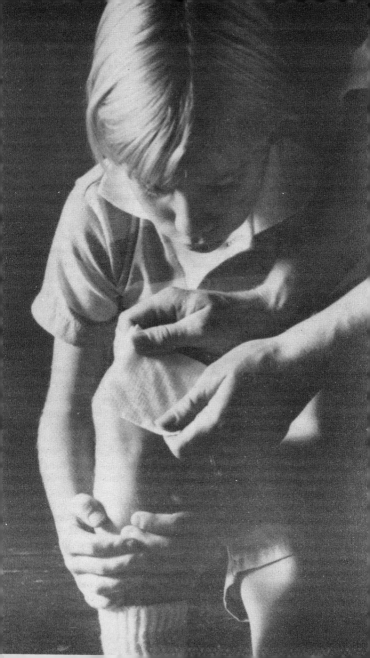

FIRST AID FOR CHILDREN

Accidents happen to young children. Fortunately, serious ones are rare. Yet each year, nearly 5,000 American boys and girls under five years of age die in mishaps—more than succumb to the seven leading fatal diseases combined. The most common causes of accidental death, in order, are automobile accidents, drowning, fires, swallowed objects, falls, poisoning, gunshot wounds, and inhalation of gas or fumes.

Earlier chapters have described safety precautions that should be taken by every household to protect young children. They include using seat belts and other restraining devices while riding in an automobile; fencing of swimming pools and close supervision in the bathtub; and "babyproofing" the house by removing from the child's reach all dangerous substances, objects small enough to be swallowed, poisons and medicines, and weapons. Close vigilance is necessary throughout infancy.

Teaching also is an important part of preventing accidents. If you do have a backyard pool or even a wading pool, make sure your child learns how to swim at the earliest possible age. With firm but loving commands, make it clear that matches, fires, hot stoves and utensils, and cigarettes are no-nos and that dangerous play in high places where falls might occur is strictly taboo. Because you cannot watch every single minute, these lessons must be continued with a growing child. As he or she approaches school age, you'll want to teach your child how to ride a bicycle or tricycle safely and how to travel as a pedestrian.

No education will forestall all accidents. So be prepared. Most mishaps are minor; scrapes, bruises, bumps, and cuts are an inevitable part of growing up. Your role is to provide comfort and a

THE FAMILY FIRST-AID KIT

You can buy a fairly complete first-aid kit at a pharmacy or department store, but a prepared kit isn't necessary. Your own medicine cabinet already may be amply stocked. Always keep first-aid supplies together, so you won't have to hunt for them in an emergency. Check regularly to see if supplies need to be replenished. First-aid supplies for the car are necessary, too.

The list below comes from recommendations made by the American Medical Association and others concerning first-aid supplies you should have on hand. Store these supplies in a moisture-proof container; they may be transported on family outings. A safe method is to keep them in a metal box with a combination lock with the combination printed on the lid.

Quantity	Item
20	Paper cups, for giving fluids.
1	Flashlight.
1	Blanket.
	Newspapers (to place under the person on cold or wet ground).
10 of each	Individual adhesive bandages in ½-inch, ¾-inch, 1-inch, and "round" spot sizes.
Box of 12	2x2-inch sterile first-aid dressings, individually packaged, for open wounds or burns.
Box of 12	4x4-inch sterile first-aid dressings.
1 roll	Roller gauze bandage, 1 inch by 5 yards.
1 roll	Roller gauze bandage, 2 inches by 5 yards.
1 roll each	Adhesive tape, 1- and 2-inch widths.
2	Triangular bandages, 36x36 inches, folded diagonally, for use as a sling or to hold dressings.
6	Safety pins, 1½-inch size.
1 bar	Mild, white soap, for cleaning wounds, scratches, etc.
1 pair	Scissors with blunt tips, for cutting bandages and tape.
1 pair	Tweezers, for removing splinters.
1	Tourniquet—wide strip of cloth, at least 3 to 4 inches by 20 inches, for use when bleeding can be controlled in no other way.
1 container	Syrup of ipecac, for use in suspected poisoning.
1 3- to 4-ounce bottle	Rubbing alcohol.
1 pair	Nail clippers.
1 container	Aspirin or aspirin substitute (acetaminophen), adult strength.
1 container	Aspirin or aspirin substitute (acetaminophen), children's strength.
1 bottle	Calamine lotion, for insect bites.

little basic first aid. More serious emergencies call for medical intervention or trained help. However, you must be ready to take interim measures until the community rescue squad or paramedic unit arrives or the injured child can be brought to a hospital or physician.

Plan what you'll do if your child or a playmate is injured seriously. Post emergency numbers near the telephone. The list should include the common 911 number, if your community uses it, plus numbers for police, fire department, rescue squad, poison control center, and physician. Write down the numbers, and try each of them in advance to be sure they have been listed correctly. Test them periodically to be sure they haven't changed. Minutes count in an emergency, and it's no time to page through a telephone book with nervous fingers.

Know the most direct route to the doctor's office or emergency room; be able to direct someone along that route, so you can comfort the child rather than drive the car yourself. Always ask your doctor whether you should bring the child to the office or whether the doctor will meet you at a hospital.

A basic first-aid course is helpful. The local chapter of the American Red Cross or a nearby hospital, college, or YMCA may teach such courses; at the least, someone there can tell you where one is taught. Keep this book or another simple first-aid manual in a place where you can find it quickly. Some pharmacies distribute a first-aid guide that can be posted on the family bulletin board or inside the bathroom medicine cabinet.

RULES TO REMEMBER

Regardless of the nature of an accident or injury, certain rules for treatment and care apply. Here are the most important:

1. **Don't get hurt yourself.** You'll be valueless to the victim if you're injured in a foolhardy attempt to help. If you cannot reach the victim without risking injury, wait for assistance.

2. If the child is in danger of further injury and you can safely move him or her, do so, but always try to keep movement to a minimum.

3. If there appears to be an injury to the head or neck, do not move the child unless absolutely necessary; then try to move the head and neck as a unit. Cushion head and neck with pillows when moving.

4. If the child is unconscious, be sure the head is turned to the side, or tilt back the head to make sure the airway is open.

5. Cover the child with a light blanket.

6. Give fluids by mouth only if the child is awake. A good rule is to allow the child to drink only if he or she can hold a glass. If in doubt, don't, because the child may require an anesthetic or surgery later.

7. Avoid stimulants and pain killers. Minor medications, such as aspirin or an aspirin substitute (acetaminophen), may be given in dosages appropriate for size and weight; they're usually listed on the container.

8. Remain with the child; send others for help. If you are alone and must go for help, make sure an unconscious child is breathing and that the airway is open.

FIRST-AID TREATMENTS

Here are basic procedures for handling common childhood injuries and emergencies:

Abscess. If a tender, inflamed, and throbbing area develops around a finger- or toenail or at the site of a cut (signs of an infection), apply a warm, wet compress to relieve pain. A thick sterile bandage, clean towel, or sanitary napkin soaked in warm water will do. Change the compress as it cools. The moisture will soften the skin, allowing it to break and release the pus. An abscess is seldom an emergency but should be examined by a physician. Watch for a fever, a swelling surrounding the abscess, or red streaks that travel up the involved limb.

Animal bites. Wash the wound thoroughly with soap and water to remove saliva; hold the wounded area under running water to rinse it well. Dry with clean gauze. The wound should be examined by a physician; a tetanus shot may be recommended. Although rabies is rare among urban pets, the animal should be identified and observed for a period of ten days to see if it develops symptoms of the disease. If the bite is the result of an unprovoked attack by a wild animal, such as a skunk, bat, squirrel, or chipmunk, an attempt should be made to capture the animal; if it cannot be caught, anti-rabies shots may be necessary. In some communities, you're required to report all animal bites to health authorities. Your own domestic pets should be inoculated against rabies, and the inoculations should be kept current.

Human bites. If the skin is not broken, wash the area with mild soap and water, and dry with clean gauze. An antiseptic or dressing is not necessary. Ask your physician about any human bite that breaks the skin, because such bites frequently become infected.

Bee, wasp, and hornet stings. A cold compress or calamine lotion will relieve itching; diluted household ammonia or rubbing alcohol applied to the sting and surrounding area also may help. If the stinger—seen as a small dark object in the center of the wound—remains in place, scrape or flick it out with a fingernail; do not attempt to remove it with tweezers. The movement may inject more venom into the wound.

For intense itching or multiple stings, give the child a cool bath to break the itching cycle, and apply a soothing bath lotion. Oral antihistamines also may be given. In severe cases, a physician may prescribe an ointment to be applied to the sting.

Some children have a severe reaction to only a single sting. If the child's throat or the interior of the mouth swells, if breathing becomes difficult, or if the child becomes drowsy or unconscious, immediate medical attention is called for. Phone your physician and take the child to the emergency room of a hospital. Discuss with the doctor what to do in the event of a repeat sting.

Broken bones. Don't attempt to move a child who may have a broken bone. Speed seldom is important in the treatment of broken bones. Keep the child covered and lying down while waiting for the emergency squad or ambulance. Give nothing by mouth in case the child requires an anesthetic or surgery later.

Do not attempt to set broken bones. If the child must be moved from an exposed or dangerous place, apply an emergency splint fashioned from any rigid material, including boards, sticks, rolled newspapers, or even a folded pillow. The splint should be on both sides of the affected limb and should extend above or below the adjacent joints. To immobilize the area of the break, tie the splint with bandages above and below it. If the spine may be fractured, do not attempt to move the child under any circumstances. Wait for emergency help.

Bruises. Most require no treatment. For major bumps, apply ice or cold cloths immediately to keep down swelling. Elevating the bruised limb also will lessen swelling. If the skin is broken, treat the bruise as an open wound.

Burns. If the area is small, immerse the burned part in water or hold directly under an open faucet, to relieve pain and reduce local

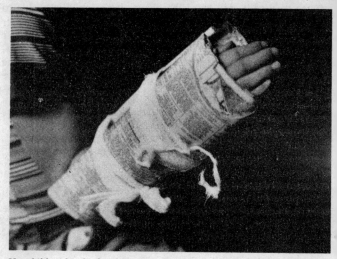

If a child with a broken bone must be moved, apply a splint made from any rigid material. Place on both sides of limb, extend above and below adjacent joints, and tie with bandages above and below break.

reaction to the burn. Wash with a mild soap. Burn ointment or butter is not necessary for minor burns. A dry, sterile dressing will keep out air and provide relief from pain.

Do not attempt to treat major burns, especially those in which the skin is broken. Never deliberately break blisters. Cover the child immediately with a clean sheet, and take him or her to a hospital or summon an ambulance.

Chemical burns. When the burn is caused by lye, caustic soda, or any other corrosive substance, you must flood the burned area immediately with cold water; strip off all clothing that may have come in contact with the chemical, and quickly place the child under a shower. Acid burns also should be flooded, then rinsed with a neutralizing solution of baking soda. After washing the area, you should phone a physician or the local rescue squad. Chemical burns always should be examined by medical personnel, especially if the corrosive substance has dried.

Choking. When a child chokes on a piece of food or other object, coughing usually will expel the object. If the child is unable to cough, or coughing produces no results, turn a small child over your arm or knee and give four sharp blows between the shoulder blades with the heel of the hand. If the airway remains obstructed, turn the child on his or her back and give four sharp thrusts on the breastbone as if giving cardiopulmonary resuscitation (CPR). (See page 385.) Do not apply pressure to a child's abdomen.

Eye injuries. If the eye is cut, torn, or damaged, do not attempt treatment. Take the child immediately to a physician or a hospital's emergency room. Bruises to the eye that cause internal bleeding also should receive immediate medical attention. If you can see bloody discoloration when looking at the child's pupil, take the victim to a hospital.

Specks in the eye. Keep the child from rubbing the eye, because the object may scratch the membrane covering the eyeball. A time-honored treatment is to draw the upper eyelid down and away from the eye, holding it by the lashes. Tears may wash out the object.

If this method fails, flush the eye with clear water or an eyewash. You also may place the child's head directly under a moderate stream of water, so the water splashes directly on the eye.

If chemicals—including cosmetics, toothpaste, or aerosols, as well as lime, plaster, and other caustics—enter the eye, flood with water, then call a physician or emergency department for immediate treatment.

Fainting. Rare in children, fainting is caused by a temporary deficiency in the blood supply to the brain. The child usually is pale and may crumple to the ground. Keep the victim lying down until he or she recovers consciousness, lowering the head or elevating the feet to hasten the return of blood to the brain. Make the child more comfortable by loosening tight clothing. Sprinkling water on the face to revive the victim isn't necessary.

Falls. In any fall from a high place or when the child is unconscious or seems to have suffered a severe impact, take him or her immediately for emergency treatment. Or phone the physician and report the symptoms. For infants, immediate evaluation is very important.

Even if the fall seems slight, a physician should be consulted if the child appears drowsy, acts dazed, turns pale, has memory lapses, or vomits after the accident.

Frostbite. If a child who has been outdoors in cold weather has tissue that appears blue or black and becomes painful indoors, suspect frostbite. Cover the affected area with your own hand to raise temperature and restore circulation gradually, or cover with warm—not hot—towels or blankets. Soak the affected part in lukewarm water. Do not rub the frozen area with snow or apply intense direct heat in an attempt to raise the temperature quickly.

Hiccups. These usually clear up spontaneously without treatment, but everyone has a favorite remedy for bothersome cases. Two suggestions are: 1. Give the child a teaspoon of granulated sugar, to be swallowed dry; 2. Use a tongue depressor or a small spoon to tickle the back of the child's throat, causing him or her to gag. Other remedies include simply ignoring hiccups, having the child drink a glass of water as slowly as possible (some persons add a pinch of baking soda), having the child hold the breath as long as he or she can, or pulling out the tongue as far as possible to trigger the gag reflex. Persistent or recurrent hiccups lasting for several hours should be reported to a physician.

Infected wounds. Signs of infection around a cut or scrape are redness and swelling, often accompanied by a feeling of heat and throbbing pain. If possible, immerse the infected area in warm water. Repeat three or four times daily. If the area is not easily immersed, apply a bulky bandage made from a small towel or sanitary napkin, and pour the solution over it, repeating the treatment until the inflammation has disappeared. Consult a physician if the area is large or seems to be spreading.

Mouth-to-mouth resuscitation. Any time a child has stopped breathing, artificial ventilation may be necessary. Some incidents that may stop breathing include immersion in water, lack of oxygen, electric shock, poisoning, or inhalation of gas. Whatever the cause, move the child to safety and begin mouth-to-mouth breathing at once; if breathing is stopped for more than four to six minutes, irreversible brain damage or death may result. If more than one adult is present, one should phone for a paramedic ambulance while the other begins treatment. If you are alone, drag the child to the phone, take the phone off the hook, dial Operator or the 911 emergency number, and give address and key information between breaths.

To start resuscitation, place the child on his or her back, and clean visible foreign matter from the mouth with your fingers. Tilt

For mouth-to-mouth resuscitation, tilt the head back, with chin pointed toward ceiling. Use both hands to lift the lower jaw from behind. It should jut out, preventing the tongue from falling back.

Place your mouth over the child's nose and mouth to make a leakproof seal. Breathe into the child's nose and mouth with shallow puffs of air—about 20 per minute. See text for more details.

the head back with one hand and lift the neck or chin with the other. This should provide a clear airway and in some cases may result in the spontaneous resumption of breathing. Place your face near the mouth of the child, listen, and feel for breathing and watch for chest rise. If the child still is not breathing, maintain the open airway position and place your mouth over the child's mouth and nose to make a leakproof seal. Breathe into the child's mouth and nose with shallow puffs of air at a rate of about 20 breaths a minute, or one breath every three seconds.

Your breath should cause the child's chest to rise and fall. If it does not and breath doesn't seem to be entering the child's body, check the position of the head and jaw to be sure the airway is clear. Turn the child's head to the side briefly to allow any substances to clear from the throat. If the airway still seems blocked, you should assume that the airway is blocked by a foreign body. (See choking, page 382.)

At times both breathing and circulation may have ceased. After artificial ventilation has been begun, stop to check for a pulse. Place two fingers on the inside of the child's arm between the armpit and the elbow. If no pulse is felt after ten seconds, cardiopulmonary resuscitation (CPR) should be started. Repeated rhythmic compression of the chest over the breastbone causes the blood to circulate even if the heart has stopped.

A rapid compression rate of about 80–120 per minute simulates the rapid heart rate of a child. Compression should be applied directly over the breastbone at the level of the nipples, at a depth of about ½ to 1½ inches, depending on the size of the child. For an infant, use only two fingers; use the heel of the hand for larger children. Breaths should be interposed between compressions at a rate of one breath for every five compressions. Treatment should continue until help arrives.

CPR cannot be learned from a book under emergency circumstances. Take a CPR course beforehand. The American Red Cross, American Heart Association, the YMCA, or other agencies provide such instruction in many communities. At the least, a parent should become familiar with the technique by reading this book or other instructional material beforehand.

Nosebleed. Pinch both nostrils closed between thumb and forefinger. Pressure should be applied just below the nasal bone. Keep the child in an upright position, so blood does not trickle back into the throat. Maintain the pressure with your fingers for at least two minutes, then check to see if the bleeding has stopped. Another method is to place a small wedge of cotton inside the nostril, holding it there with pressure outside the nostril for five minutes. If the nosebleed recurs or persists, seek medical help.

Poisoning. Drugs, medicines, cleaning fluids, and other such substances are the most common causes of childhood poisoning. If you see evidence that a child has swallowed any of these, act fast. Telephone the poison control center in your community, if one exists, or your physician or hospital, and be prepared to give immediate first-aid treatment.

First, try to determine what was swallowed, because treatment differs according to the substance. But don't waste time looking for the container or for an antidote; information on bottles and cans may be out of date.

For many poisons, the doctor or poison control center may recommend syrup of ipecac to induce vomiting. Have some available—it can be purchased without prescription. The usual dose is one tablespoon of syrup of ipecac for one-year-olds and above; two teaspoons for children under one year. If vomiting has not occurred within 20 minutes, the dose may be repeated. Do not give ipecac unless instructed.

When the child vomits, hold him or her face downward in your lap so the vomited material clears the throat and is not swallowed. If vomiting does not occur within 20 to 30 minutes, the doctor may suggest a second dose of ipecac. The dose should be repeated only once.

Ipecac should *not* be used and vomiting should *not* be induced when the offending substance is a corrosive such as lye, cleanser, disinfectant, ammonia, or drain or toilet-bowl cleaner, because substances that burn on the way down also may burn on the way up; nor should ipecac be used for kerosene, gasoline, or turpentine. In these cases, the physician or poison control center may administer medication to offset the effects and speed transit through the system.

If ipecac is not available, vomiting sometimes may be induced by feeding the child warm water or milk and then tickling the back of the throat with a tongue depressor or spoon.

Unless you're told otherwise, do not wait for vomiting to occur before getting medical help. If possible retrieve the poisonous substance and take it with you.

Poison ivy, poison oak, and other skin poisonings. Thoroughly wash the affected area with soap and water to remove the irritating plant oils. Then repeat the lathering five or six times. Strip off all clothing that may have come into contact with the plant, and launder it immediately. Wash the area again—this time with rubbing alcohol—rinse with clear water, and dry.

Small, local patches of rash may be relieved by applying a topical drying agent (calamine lotion, for example). In extensive cases or when the outbreak oozes, appears infected, or continues to spread, consult a physician.

Shock. Shock may accompany any serious injury. It results from an injury-caused disturbance of the supply of oxygen to the tissues and inadequate blood pressure. Signs of shock are: rapid but weak pulse; pale face; cold, clammy skin; nausea; shallow breathing; and thirst. Keep in mind that not all of these symptoms will be present in every case.

Keep the patient lying flat, head level or lower than the rest of the body or with legs elevated 12 to 18 inches. Cover with a light blanket or coat to lessen the loss of body heat.

If the child is thirsty, small amounts of water may be given. Other fluids should not be given because of the possibility that the child may later require an anesthetic or surgery.

Snakebite. A surprisingly large proportion of poisonous snakebite victims are small children, who are likely to be playing in suburban woodpiles or gardens where snakes may be found. But in most cases, the bite does not penetrate the skin; even when the skin is broken, rarely is the wound injected with the snake's poison. Very few children are endangered by poisonous snakebite and require antivenin, horse-serum treatment.

Indications of venomous snakebite are severe swelling and pain at the site of the bite. Usually, two puncture wounds from the fangs can be seen. To be effective, treatment must begin immediately. Summon a physician or paramedic ambulance, or set out for an emergency center, notifying personnel that you are en route. Begin first-aid measures in the meantime. Remove the child from the danger area; make no attempt to capture the snake to determine if it is poisonous. Carry the child; do not allow the child to walk or move about. Tie a tourniquet (see page 392) above the joint above the bite, tightly enough to restrict the blood flow but not to cut it off completely. *Do not pack the wound in ice or give the child alcohol.*

You may attempt to remove the venom from the wound by suction. Make incisions one-eighth inch long at each fang mark, and apply suction by mouth or suction cup. This must be done within 30 minutes. Suction is particularly important if the wound is on the body, neck, or head.

Because many people fear snakes and snakebite, reassurance is very important. Remain with the child, and try to reduce anxiety.

Splinters. Foreign bodies that protrude from the flesh may be removed with tweezers or the fingers. If the entire splinter has been removed, wash the area with mild soap and water, then apply antiseptic. If the splinter is completely embedded in the tissue, wash the area first. Then sterilize a needle or knife point by passing it through a flame. Remove the splinter by probing it with the sterilized point, being careful not to touch the point with your fingers. Use an antiseptic afterward.

If the object is buried deeply or is too large to be removed easily without damaging the surrounding flesh, seek emergency help, or visit your physician. A tetanus booster may be necessary is none has been given within five years. Check your immunization record.

Sprains. Injuries to a wrist, ankle, or knee may be either fractures
of a bone or sprains (a stretching of the ligaments surrounding the
joint). Both cause pain, swelling, and limited use of the joint. It is
not always possible to determine the difference without an X ray. A
physician or emergency personnel should see all such injuries.

Swelling may be kept down by soaking the joint in cold water
or by applying cloths soaked in ice or cold water. An ice pack also
may be used. Keep the limb elevated. If movement causes marked
pain, immobilize the joint with a "pillow" splint. Place the limb on
the pillow, fold around the affected area, and tie with a cord. Also
use a pillow splint to transport the patient.

Sunburn. Babies and children have tender skin that burns easily.
Sunbathing should be limited to the early morning and late afternoon when the sun is low. As with adults, exposure should be gradual. Five minutes is enough time to spend in the sun the first day.

If a child is to be in the sun for an extended period, cover
exposed areas with a sunscreen ointment containing PABA—
paraminobenzoic acid. Sunscreens are numbered by the amount of
ultraviolet rays they block. Number 15 gives total blockage.

When serious sunburn does occur, notify your physician. For
mild cases, ease discomfort by placing cold, wet compresses on the
affected areas or by applying cold cream or a baby lotion.

Swallowed objects. Most small objects swallowed by a child will
pass through the system harmlessly. This is especially true of buttons and other round items, but even open safety pins, tacks, and
similar sharp objects usually do not harm the stomach or bowel.

Do not give the child a laxative, and do not induce vomiting.
Notify a physician, who may follow the object's progress by X ray.
If the physician considers the object dangerous—and particularly if
it has been ingested into the lungs—it may be extracted by inserting
a flexible instrument down the windpipe. (See choking, page 382.)

Tick bites. Ticks are small insects that burrow into the skin; several
varieties transmit serious diseases. They are common in damp
grass and wooded areas during the spring and may attach themselves to small children, especially in the scalp, and to domestic
animals.

During tick season, routinely inspect small children who have
been playing outdoors. If a tick is found, do not pull it off by the
portion of the body protruding from the site; that may leave the
head imbedded in the flesh. Instead, cover the tick with petroleum

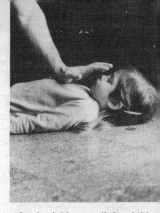

When a child chokes on food or another object, kneel on the floor and drape the child across your thighs, head lower than the trunk. Deliver four sharp blows between shoulder blades.

After back blows, roll the child over and apply four chest thrusts with the heel of the hand. Alternate back blows and chest thrusts until the object is dislodged from the airway.

Straddle a choking infant over your arm, supporting head with hand under jaw and chest. Deliver four back blows. Turn the baby over, and deliver chest thrusts, using two or three fingers.

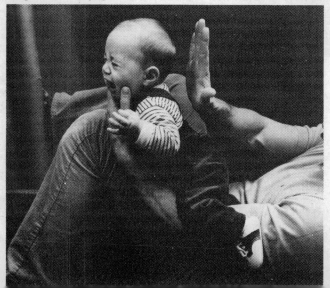

jelly, facial cream, or other thick substance. After a few minutes, remove the tick carefully with tweezers. Treat the wound with antiseptic.

Toothache. A child's aching tooth should be seen by a dentist as soon as possible. In the event a toothache strikes at night or when a dentist is not available, give the child aspirin or aspirin substitute (acetaminophen), appropriate for age and size; do not use stronger pain killers. If a cavity can be seen, clean it out with a toothpick tipped with cotton, then plug it with cotton dipped in oil of cloves. A heating pad, hot-water bottle, or ice pack also may relieve discomfort.

Unconsciousness. Serious accidents, such as a severe injury or burn, poisoning, gas inhalation, or electric shock, may cause unconsciousness. Sunstroke or heat exhaustion also may cause unconsciousness, but rarely in children.

If breathing has stopped, begin mouth-to-mouth resuscitation at once. (See page 384.) If the child is unconscious from a fall, avoid turning the head and neck. If breathing appears adequate, keep the patient lying on the back, with head turned to the side to keep the airway open. Remove constricting clothing, and cover lightly. Summon emergency help; don't wait for the child to revive. Take care in moving an unconscious child because of the possibility of head injury.

Don't give water or other substances by mouth to an unconscious child, and don't shake him or her in an attempt at revival.

Wounds with minor bleeding. Clean the wound gently with a soft washcloth, using mild soap and water. Begin at the edge of the wound and wash away from it, not toward it. Most bits of dirt or other contaminating substances that remain in the wound can be removed by washing; if not, pick them out with sterilized tweezers. Afterward, flush the wound with clean water.

Wounds with severe bleeding. Don't bother to clean the wound; stop the bleeding first. Place a sterile gauze pad, clean handkerchief, or sanitary napkin over the wound, and apply firm, steady pressure with the heel of your hand. Maintain the pressure until the bleeding stops, usually within five minutes. If bleeding is in one of the limbs, keep the limb elevated. Consult a physician about gaping wounds; sutures may be needed to promote healing.

If the bleeding does not stop, a tourniquet may be tried—but only as a last resort. Tourniquets—tight bands of cloth or rope wound around the limb above the wound to shut off the blood supply—are dangerous because tissues die if deprived of circulation for too long. If you resort to a tourniquet, write down, or tell someone, the exact time at which it was applied. Loosen it regularly to restore circulation.

Wounds by puncture. Any wound caused by a sharp object that might have carried germs deep into the flesh should be seen by a physician. This is true even if the object appears to be clean. Wash the wound with mild soap and water, rinse with cold running water, run a stream of water into puncture to wash out germs, cover with a bandage, and seek medical help. If shots are not current, a tetanus booster may be necessary.

INDEX

A

Abdominal pain, 349
Abscess, 380
Accidents, first aid for, 377–92
Accidents, toilet, 288–89, 310–11
   bed-wetting, 310–13
Acetaminophen for fever, 353
Acrocyanosis, 371
Activity level, baby's, 185
Adaptability, baby's, 185
Adenoidectomy, 318
"Adolescence of preschool years,"
   308
Adoption, child's questions about,
   345
Afterbirth, 100
Aggressive behavior, 280–81, 322
Airings for babies, 176
Air travel
   with baby, 196
   during pregnancy, 28
Alcohol use during pregnancy, 29
Allergies
   breast-feeding as protection,
     126
   to milk, 217
Allowances, 320–21
Alternative birth centers, 68
Ammonia-related diaper rash,
   165–66
Amniocentesis, 82–83
Amniotic fluid, 9, 11–13
Analgesics and anesthetics in
   childbirth, 76–79

Animal and human bites, 380–81
Apgar score, 114–15
Appetite, declining
   for milk, 229, 250
   in second year, 263–64, 284
Arguments, parents', child's
   questions about, 345
Artificial ventilation, 384–86
Aspirin for fever, 353
Attention span, baby's, 186–87
Axillary method of taking
   temperature, 177

B

Baby food. *See* Feeding
Baby-sitters, 197–99
   baby's anxiety about, 241, 262–
     63
Baby talk, use of, 214
Backache during pregnancy, 54
Backpacks and baby totes, 193
Bag of waters, 9, 11–13
   breaking of, 101, 106
Bassinets, 86–87
Bathing
   baby, 167–68, 169–73
     necessities for, 91, 92
   during pregnancy, 30
Bed, child's, 303–5
   for newborn, 86–89
Bedding, 88–89
Bedtime. *See* Sleeping
Bed-wetting, 310–13
Bee stings, 381